FROM ECONOMIC THEORY
TO POLICY

By

E. RONALD WALKER, Ph.D.

*Professor of Economics in the University of Tasmania. Economic
Adviser to the Tasmanian Government. Formerly Economic
Adviser to the New South Wales Treasury*

THE UNIVERSITY OF CHICAGO PRESS
CHICAGO · ILLINOIS

THE UNIVERSITY OF CHICAGO PRESS · CHICAGO

Agent: THE CAMBRIDGE UNIVERSITY PRESS · LONDON

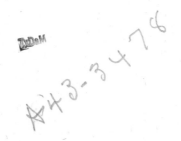

To R. C. MILLS

Teacher, Colleague, Friend

PREFACE

THIS book, which began to take form some years ago as a study by an academic economist engaged chiefly in teaching and research at Sydney University, developed into a destroyer of leisure for a person increasingly immersed in the practical affairs of Australian state and Commonwealth governments. It was originally intended that it should contain, in addition to a discussion of the problems involved in the application of economic theory to policy and of the changes which are required in the economist's equipment, some illustrative essays in the application of economic theory of the type sketched in these pages. The discussion of theory, however, assumed larger proportions than I expected, and any further analysis of concrete problems would have made the book unduly long. It is my hope that I may be able to undertake a portion of the revision of economic theory which is here represented as necessary, if theory is to make the greatest contribution to policy; and I had intended that this work should be followed by one on international trade—a field in which the points developed here might receive considerable elaboration. For the present, however, it would seem that any further considerable work in economic theory must be classed, as far as I am concerned, among the things one hopes for as part of post-war reconstruction.

I have had useful comments on particular points from Messrs. R. J. Heyward, S. J. Butlin, R. G. Osborne, and John Burton; and from my brother, K. F. Walker. The Index was prepared by Mr. J. S. G. Wilson, and the typescript by Miss Una Shaw. To all these I extend my sincere thanks.

The work would never have reached its present stage if it had not been for the encouragement of two others. Mr. Hartley Grattan urged me to have my book published in the United States and by his continued interest impelled me to make the final effort to bring it to completion, shortly before I was called to my present position at the end of 1941. My wife has heartened me when I have despaired of finishing it and supported, with the utmost patience and good humor, the sacrifices which my preoccupation has imposed on her. Beyond this she has assisted me to see the problem of objectives more clearly than would have been possible without her help.

Publication has been delayed by the outbreak of war in the Pacific and might have been postponed indefinitely but for the good offices of Professor J. B. Condliffe, of the University of California. I am very grateful to him for finding me an American publisher, and to the University of Chicago Press for its interest in the work of a distant scholar.

The book is dedicated to Professor R. C. Mills, head of the Department of Economics of Sydney University and chairman of the Commonwealth Grants Commission, who, as my first teacher and colleague, has taught me much more than economics. I would like to think this book worthy to be offered in tribute to one who always inspires his students and colleagues to give of their best; and, whatever his judgment of it as a work on economics, it carries my admiration and affection.

E. RONALD WALKER

DEPARTMENT OF WAR ORGANIZATION OF INDUSTRY
MELBOURNE
November 1942

TABLE OF CONTENTS

CHAPTER I

THE GULF BETWEEN THEORY AND POLICY

As the range of governmental action is extended ever more widely, the problems of policy formulation and administration grow ever more complex. In the selection of objectives and methods alike, the statesman needs all the help he can get; and, as so many governmental problems lie in the field of economics, the economist is increasingly prominent among the specialists whose aid is sought. The depression gave a great impetus to the employment of economists in advisory and other positions and the economic reorganization which war necessitates—even in nonbelligerent countries—has further augmented the demand for the services of those whose teaching and writing have established a claim to the understanding of these matters.

This is a great source of satisfaction to the economist; he has long felt that the community did not appreciate the use which might be made of his specialized knowledge; and this recognition of its practical utility, though tardy, is a welcome support to his professional self-respect, for the principal incentive to economic studies, and the justification of specialization in this field, have always been found in the hope that they will contribute to the solution of concrete problems. Pure theory, like any other intellectual pursuit, holds a fascination for the initiated; and scientific curiosity may impel the economist to explore problems which have no obvious bearing upon current practice. But the value of economics in the eyes of the public and of most students derives from the belief that its main body of doctrine is relevant to policy. Even the skeptic does not question the relevance of economic studies to problems of policy, though the quality of the economist's perfomance and the accuracy or adequacy of his findings are often the subject of bitter criticism.

The persistence of this skepticism must be faced; it is encountered not only among "practical men" and the devotees of other sciences but also in the ranks of the economists themselves. Indeed, the position of the economist in relation to policy is somewhat anomalous. His advice is sought because "practical men" are at a loss, confronted as they are with problems which reach beyond their own experience.

But this advice is still to some extent suspect, as being too theoretical or academic, too lacking in "practical judgment." The economist himself, while eager to prove the value of his professional skill, is, or should be, acutely conscious of its limitations—of the gulf between the economic theory of all academic schools and the process of policy-making. Not all economists recognize the width of this gulf. Some, on the other hand, regard it as unbridgeable—a moat round their ivory tower. Others, intent upon making a contribution to public policy, do their best to fill in the gulf for themselves, by acquiring a wide personal knowledge of practical affairs. The success of such individual efforts, however, can hardly restore the economists' professional *amour propre*. If, as one may be tempted to conclude, the principal qualification of an economic adviser is to be a man of the world rather than a good economist, enthusiasm for scholarship will be increasingly confined to the cloistered academic; and the compliment which the practical man pays to economic science by asking the economist's advice becomes an empty one.

Such a conclusion, however, cannot be accepted without further examination. If problems of economic theory can be solved by the application of scientific method, cannot the problems of applied economics be dealt with in the same way? Why is there a gulf between theory and policy? And what are its dimensions? Are there no principles of bridgebuilding as reliable as those which enabled the economist to construct his ivory tower of theory? Metaphor aside, these are fundamental questions for the economist who believes in the utility of his science. The limitations of economic theory in relation to policy must be surveyed. If there is any hope of reconstructing theory in a more useful form, the attempt must be made. If its application to concrete problems requires collaboration with other sciences, the points of liaison must be established. These questions are of interest for the philosophy of science or methodology. But they are also of practical importance, because the practical man is confronted with policy problems beyond the competence of his unaided common sense. Our discussion of the relations between theory and policy and our essays in the further development of economic theory will be dominated by the latter consideration rather than by an academic interest in systems.

THE SELF-IMPOSED LIMITATIONS OF ECONOMIC THEORY

The gulf between economic theory and policy is partly due to the appalling complexity of the practical problems with which policy is concerned and the prevalence of obstacles to the use of scientific method. Every branch of science has its own external limitations of this sort. But there are also the limitations which economists, conscious of the independent status of their science, have imposed upon themselves by their definitions of the scope and method of economics. In the last hundred years the tendency has been to draw these self-imposed boundaries closer and closer, in the attempt to delimit a field within which the findings of economics would be as incontestable as the proved theories of other recognized sciences.

The "political economy" of the eighteenth and early nineteenth centuries mixed abstract reasoning with description of existing conditions, speculation about the future, and discussion of ethical principles and political expediency. In an attempt to attain objectivity and certainty—in short, to win for economics a place among the "sciences"—later writers have shed much of the ethical, technological, and sociological content of the older political economy and have made much of the distinction between the explanation of things as they are and the prescription of how they should be. Taking the former task as their province, most modern economists deny the competence of their science to formulate ends or objectives. The positive findings of economics, within its own restricted field, are presumed to constitute instrumental knowledge which may guide the choice of means to achieve a given objective, once that has been independently established as desirable. Only in this way, it is argued, can economics contribute to the success of policy.

As typical of the modern view we may quote a recent work on economic policy:

In any consideration of problems of public policy the question of what is "sound" inevitably arises. Those who are looking for definitive answers or solutions of that sort will not find them in this book. Solutions and definite recommendations of public policy are necessarily based as much on subjective evaluation as on scientific observation. A judgment of what is sound is as much a matter of the objectives desired as of the probable consequences of a given line of action or inaction. It is, of course, desirable, when feasible, to indicate what consequences will presumably follow alternative lines of action. The bases of choice can thus be made more clear.[1]

It might be added that, if the consequences of alternative lines of action are made sufficiently clear by economic analysis, this is sometimes tantamount to a definite recommendation.

However, a survey of the literature of modern economics reveals

[1] L. S. Lyon, M. W. Watkins, and Victor Abramson, *Government and Economic Life*, I (Washington, 1939), ix.

that this exclusion of the normative viewpoint is by no means complete. The textbooks are full of discussions of the "advantages" of large-scale production, the "disadvantages" of barter, the "gain" from international trade, the "dangers" of state intervention, the "equity" of progressive taxation, and similar points with an ethical flavor. In the so-called "welfare economics" of Marshall, Pigou, and Cannan, ethical questions are frankly raised and solutions proposed. A Swedish professor has found material for a whole book on the contrast between the British economists' lip service to scientific objectivity and the political or ethical flavor of their writings.[2] Few economists would contest the view, however, that the attempt to establish a *wertfrei* economic science has been, if not completely successful, nevertheless worth while, permitting a greater concentration upon the mere description and explanation of the operations of the market place and a corresponding advance in understanding of cause and effect. After all, it may be said that there has been no scarcity of ethical teaching of a general nature but there have been countless false ideas as to how the economic system actually works.

The shedding of technology and sociology, along with ethics, as political economy has evolved into modern economic theory, has been less wholehearted and less generally approved, because the abstraction of economic aspects of behavior from the rest of social life is a comparatively new achievement of the human intellect and its value is not self-evident. If university courses and modern textbooks be taken as a guide to the subject matter of any science, it must be admitted that the study of legal institutions and technical processes still has a place in economics, although the status of these subjects in the body of doctrine varies from school to school. At one extreme the abstract theorists, whose position has been defined and defended by Professor Lionel Robbins,[3] maintain that economics is in no way connected with the explanation of technique or institutions but takes these, along with the wants and the physical and moral resources of members of the community, as the *data* of economic theory. For these economists the economic problem is, given all the data, to allocate the available resources between various uses according to some definite principle; and economic analysis attempts to discover this principle and to exhibit the transactions by which it is made effective. The

---

[2] G. Myrdal, *Das politische Element in der nationaloekonomischen Doktrinbildung* (Berlin, 1932).

[3] *Essay on the Nature and Significance of Economic Science* (2d ed.; London, 1937).

principle is often referred to as the "principle of maximization," although the abstract theorists find some difficulty in agreeing as to what is to be maximized without introducing ethics or sociology. At the other extreme the institutionalists, attempting to obtain and to convey a picture of "economic behavior" as a whole, give to technics and social institutions at least the same status as they give to theory. Indeed, their discussion of theory, such as the theory of supply and demand, bears all the marks of a foreign body. Between these extremes the eclectics, who make up the majority of economists, find it impossible to avoid mixing some description of wants, technique, and institutions with formal argument and abstract theory. After all, much of what is called "monetary theory" is, in fact, a description of the technique of banking and foreign exchange and of social habits and conventions. On the other hand, in describing "industrial organization" many an academic economist deals, not with conditions as they exist in the world outside the cloisters, but with conditions implied by an armchair theory of costs.

Nevertheless, the attempt is made to distinguish between the pure theory of the market and the description of practice. Generous surveys of wants, technique, and institutions are more and more the exception in economics textbooks. These matters are increasingly relegated to "allied subjects," to be studied and, if possible, explained by the appropriate specialists, while the economic theorist follows up his own specialty. No doubt this specialization has facilitated progress in the exploration of the problems of market equilibrium under various assumed conditions; but the resulting body of economic doctrine is inevitably more remote from practical affairs than were the writings of Adam Smith or even of Alfred Marshall. To this extent the gulf between theory and policy is of the economists' own making. If it was necessary for the growth of theory to make this gulf, to cross it is equally necessary for the application of theory to policy.

When the old-fashioned economists attempted to define the scope of economics, their purpose was to mark out that portion of the field of policy which they had been led to study, from the other problems in respect of which they felt they had no special competence. How far the economist should go into the technical details of industrial processes or into the causes of particular human attitudes and institutions was generally regarded as a matter of convenience rather than principle. The abstract theorists, however, have sought to define economic theory anew, in such a way as to exclude the study of technique and institutions. All these are "grouped among the *given* factors influencing the relative scarcity of different economic goods,"[4] while economic theory studies only the principles by which these scarce goods are allocated between alternative uses. Now what is *given* cannot be at the same time the subject of study. The adoption of this definition imposes a limitation upon the economist's range of inquiries and discourages any effort on his part to study scientifically the way in which these *given* factors develop.[5] Since changes in wants, technique, and institutions are dominant causes of that complexity in economic problems which drives the practical man to seek the aid of the economist, such a restricted definition tends to widen the gap between economic theory and policy.[6]

EXTERNAL LIMITATIONS UPON ECONOMIC INVESTIGATIONS

To some extent the self-imposed limitations of economic theory reflect the difficulty of doing scientific work in any wider field. The pure theorist can work in his study; he needs neither laboratory nor field work, as long as he confines himself to working out the logical implications of a *given* set of conditions relating to the scarcity of various goods. But, if the economist takes wants, technology, and social institutions as part of his subject matter, his material is scattered throughout the world. Some of it may reach him in the shape of statistics and descriptive literature and may therefore be available for examination within four walls. But there will always be enormous gaps and imperfections in the material available to the academic worker, and even to the economist in government service. Many of the facts which are necessary for a complete picture are not recorded at all; others are recorded but secretly.

Of those that are not recorded, some could be, through special investigations; and the amount of new factual material made available in the United States in recent years is considerable.[7] But cost is a limiting factor to such research. It is true that a physicist may be prevented from pursuing certain experiments because he cannot afford

4 *Ibid.*, p. 33.

5 Professor Robbins' own essays in sociology are the exception that proves the rule.

6 At this stage it might be asked: What definition should be adopted? The answer is: "None that can be compressed into a single phrase." Subsequent chapters define present-day theory by showing what it consists of and, by indicating the lines along which a realistic theory must be developed, present the case for a broader definition.

7 E.g., the monographs of the Temporary National Economic Committee and reports of other Congress committees.

the necessary equipment. But the economists' freedom of factual inquiry is much more restricted by this type of limitation, especially in countries where funds for social research and trained field investigators are less abundant than in America.

The obstacle of privacy, however, stands in the way of many attempts to record hitherto unobserved facts, as well as denying access to material which particular persons or individuals have already prepared for their own purposes. Here the economic scientist is at a still greater disadvantage as compared with the physical scientist. Nature rarely burns the evidence. The physicist is not dependent upon police power or somebody's willingness to co-operate. In some fields the government economist may be able to arrange for the veil to be torn aside or lifted discreetly; and in others the privilege of an inside view may be more readily accorded to an investigator who has nothing to do with the government. But in neither case is the economist free to follow his scientific curiosity wherever it leads. The directions in which factual investigations can be pushed depend largely upon the play of social forces. In the case of pure theory, however, no such limitation exists. If social forces are to control the course of theoretical speculation, it is by sanctions against the *publication* of particular theories; free inquiry is restricted only in so far as it may be discouraged by the censorship of what the investigator discovers and wishes to make public.

Apart from the denial of access to facts the publication of which might affect particular interests, there is always the danger that personal or class bias will limit the economist's interest in certain facts and thereby discourage their investigation. This danger has been commented on so frequently that, if mere discussion and condemnation could exorcise it, bias would no longer exist.[8] But it will always constitute a limitation upon the factual material which is accessible to the most disinterested economist.

The economist who is reluctant to abandon the study of actual processes for the realms of pure theory is faced, therefore, with the difficulty that the available descriptive material, while overwhelming to any single brain, is at the same time inadequate. Fortunately, he need no longer rely chiefly upon books written by men whose knowledge of the real world was obtained from other books; but in many countries the academic economist has less information at his disposal about business practices and conditions in his own country than about those of the United States.

[8] Cf. J. A. Hobson, *Free Thought in the Social Sciences* (London, 1926).

There is, however, a further external limitation upon the economist's knowledge of the facts at any particular time, namely, the tendency of material to be out of date as soon as it has been recorded. This
has been stressed, above all, in relation to quantitative studies.

> Even if the constants which economists wish to determine were less numerous, and
> the method of experiment more accessible, we should still be faced with the fact that
> the constants themslves are different at different times. . . . . This malleability in the
> actual substance with which economics deals means that the goal sought is itself per-
> petually shifting, so that, even if it were possible by experiments exactly to determine
> the values of the economic constants to-day, we could not say with confidence that
> this determination would hold good also of to-morrow. Hence the inevitable short
> comings of our science.[9]

In this impermanence of the material, Professor Robbins finds support
for "bigger and better realistic studies":

> If we are really convinced that we have, as it were, continuously to rediscover the
> magnitude of some of our constants, then how much more urgent, how much more
> obligatory are the claims of continuous investigation. The chemist or the physicist
> may indeed hope that within finite time, he, or at least his descendants, may have dis-
> covered *all* the necessary empirical information—applications thenceforward to be a
> matter of tables and formulae. But for the economist if he wishes—as we all wish—
> to go beyond mere qualitative generalisation, there can be no such hope. Day by day,
> in Sisyphus-like activity, he must discover his co-efficients anew.[10]

The difficulty does not arise only in quantitative studies such as the
estimation of the elasticity of demand. Technique, trade practices,
consumers' tastes, the institutional framework—all are subject to frequent changes of varying magnitude. When the practical difficulties
of factual studies are borne in mind, the Sisyphus analogy seems so
apt that it can hardly serve as a source of inspiration.

A survey of recently observed facts is not enough. All realistic
studies which are not frankly historical, contain a large element of
prediction regarding the continued relevance of certain facts which have
been observed in the past or speculation as to how conditions may
have changed since the facts were examined. There must therefore
be a gulf between any theory relating to *given* conditions and a policy
which must take account of changing conditions. The London *Economist*, while praising Professor J. R. Hicks's recent contribution to pure
theory,[11] doubts "whether it meets the challenge presented to economists to-day as much by workers in other fields of science as by the

---

[9] A. C. Pigou, *Economics of Welfare* (3d ed.; London, 1929), p. 10.

[10] L. Robbins, "Live and Dead Issues in the Methodology of Economics," *Economics*,
August, 1938, p. 351.

[11] *Value and Capital* (London, 1939).

public—namely—how are the results of changes in economic factors worked out for a world in which 'other things' never remain the same."[12]

All the limitations outlined above restrict the practical utility of the economist's knowledge, even if political and administrative conditions are favorable to the best use of it.[13] The next question is whether or not these limitations must be accepted as immutable and, if not, which lines of work offer the greatest promise as a method of bridging the gulf between theory and policy.

A mere multiplication of statistical and descriptive studies is no solution of the problem. Even if the difficulties noted above can be gradually reduced, "the facts by themselves are silent."[14] The economist believes that economic theory, despite its inadequate contact with current conditions, does confer an insight into cause and effect which cannot be gained by the mere assembly of observations and statistics. A concrete problem cannot be approached at all, unless the necessary factual material is at hand; but skill in interpreting the facts and predicting their consequences is not to be had by compiling tables of statistics on all manner of subjects or stuffing one's head with all the descriptive information to which access can be gained. If the necessary skill could best be obtained in this way, there would be no place for the economist, as such, among the practical man's advisers. "Economic advice" could be better obtained from statisticians, engineers, lawyers, advertising experts, accountants, historians, and, if their science is any more realistic than that of the economists, sociologists. There is perhaps some significance in the fact that some of these specialists do tender advice on economic matters and are sometimes listened to when they are expounding, not their professional subject, but their own private economic theories.

But, since economists have attempted to shed technology and sociology in order to concentrate on a narrower range of problems, may not the solution be through a synthesis of specialties? The economist has been tilling his field; have not technicians and sociologists been tilling theirs? Cannot these specialists each contribute his quota?[15] But there

[12] *Economist*, September 23, 1939, p. 566.

[13] Special difficulties arising from the latter side will be considered in chap. ii.

[14] A. C. Pigou (ed.), *Memorials of Alfred Marshall* (London, 1925), p. 166.

[15] Cf. E. F. M. Durbin, "Methods of Research—a Plea for Co-operation in the Social Sciences," *Economic Journal*, June, 1938, p. 183.

still remains the problem of synthesis. It would be futile for all the specialists, including the economic theorist, to present their several advices on various aspects of a problem to the practial man, leaving it to him to effect a synthesis. The practical man who would be capable of doing so is extremely rare—almost as much an abstraction as the "economic man" of the textbooks. In real life he would push aside the specialists and look for somebody who was willing to tell him *what to do*. No, where economic problems are concerned, it is the economist who must provide the synthesis, if he desires that policy should be guided by economic knowledge.

The student of applied economics must, without abandoning his modernity, follow the path of the classical political economist in this respect; he must take the most reliable information (or estimates) relating to wants, technique, and institutions and, with the aid of his pure theory, work out a scheme of cause and effect in realistic terms. If he is not satisfied with the factual material provided by others, because it is unreliable or incomplete, he must go after the information himself. In particular, he must have some estimate of the changes that are likely to take place in wants, technique, and institutions in the period under consideration. If other sciences have not addressed themselves to this particular problem, the economist must undertake it himself. If he finds it continually necessary to explore certain territory to obtain information that is essential to his purpose, the question arises as to whether he should regard every such investigation as an *ad hoc* expedition or work over the whole field in a systematic way, with a view to establishing a time-saving technique. A disregard for the conventional boundaries of economic theory may pay handsome dividends, not only in the form of greater certainty on specific issues, but also in the enlargement of the economist's general competence.

ECONOMIC SOCIOLOGY OR COMMON SENSE?

But does not all this take the economist into the realms of sociology? Or, at least, must he not draw heavily on the work of sociologists? Might it not be better to allow the sociologist to effect the necessary synthesis of economic theory and other elements, even if this means that governments need sociological advisers rather than economic advisers, with the possible exception of economists to advise the sociologists.

This possibility has often been considered by economists. It is more than fifty years since Alfred Marshall, in his inaugural lecture at Cambridge, dismissed the contention that sociology might complete economic theory: "It does not exist; it shows no signs of coming into existence. There is no use in waiting idly for it; we must do the best we can with our present resources. The only resources we have for dealing with social problems as a whole lie in the judgment of common sense."[16] This dictum still sets the tone of much comment on sociology by English economists. Professor J. R. Hicks, in a symposium on collaboration among the social sciences, states that the economist, after "running away" with a problem involving extra-economic elements, "always wants to hand the problem in the end to some sociologist or other—if there is a sociologist waiting for him. Very often there isn't."[17] Again, Mr. R. F. Harrod, in his presidential address before the British Association in 1938, said that "the notion that investigations in other branches of study should be asked to help forward their lame brother economist and guide him on his proper path must, in the interest of intellectual honesty, be set down as fatuous and derisory."[18]

In the symposium referred to above, Mr. G. S. Shove, while pleading for breadth of social studies, says that "nothing could be worse than to substitute a smattering of ill-digested technical information for plain horse sense." But, he agrees, "the other social sciences can help" the economist "by enlarging his knowledge of human institutions and informing his judgment in the same way as direct observations and actual experience do this; not by providing cut and dried answers to set questions." This assistance from the other social studies cannot best be given "by diverting the natural current of their development so as to make them bear more directly on the economist's problems. What we economists most want from the experts in neighboring subjects is an exposition of their results, of the evidence on which these are based, and of the leading trends in their speculations and controversies, accurate enough to satisfy their scientific conscience, but not too bulky or too full of technical apparatus to be assimilated by those who are obliged to occupy most of their time with other matters."[19] Certainly this will be necessary before economists can accept Dr. Löwe's claim that "sociology offers the specific data which adapt

[16] Pigou (ed.), *Memorials of Alfred Marshall*, p. 164.

[17] *The Social Sciences* (London, 1936), p. 135.

[18] "Scope and Method of Economics," *Economic Journal*, September, 1938, p. 411.

[19] *The Social Sciences*, pp. 153, 160–63.

the generalizations of economic theory to the particular conditions of space and time."[20]

Meanwhile, the economist, although he must fill out his theory with specific data, seeks the latter by observation and the exercise of common sense. Professor Parsons, who looks forward to greater collaboration between economics and sociology as the latter develops a "logically comparable theoretical system," has praised the "middle ground" which Taussig adopted between abstract theory and mere fact-finding.

> In the range of alternatives which have been open to the passing generation, an open mind and a judicious appraisal of the importance of things not readily amenable to economic analysis, combined with a steady insistence on the fundamentals of the traditional analytical scheme itself, has been the only way in which a just balance between the empirical and theoretical interests of the field could be upheld.[21]

This raises the question of whether or not the time has yet come for a further advance, by the development of a theoretical scheme in which "things not readily amenable to economic analysis" shall be given full weight. For the economist's reliance upon common sense is sometimes a source of embarrassment. When dealing with a concrete problem the economist must go beyond pure theory of the hypothetical type, namely, "If A, then B." Instead, he must be prepared to say: "Since A, therefore B." If his studies yield no scientific basis for the affirmation of the first premise, he must stress that he is offering only his personal opinion regarding the trend of future developments, even though the technique of economic analysis has assisted the formulation of his opinion. The question then arises as to what check the statesman or businessman can impose upon the economist's personal opinion. If the only check is the personal opinion of other individuals who also claim no scientific basis for their views, the contest is not between the economist's advice and that of other advisers but between their personal reputations for hard-headedness and a grasp of practical affairs. And how much confidence can the economist have in his own personal opinion? "An open mind and a judicious appraisal" of the noneconomic factors are all very well; but the necessary qualities are possessed in varying degree; and there is no guaranty that two equally open minds, after an equally judicious appraisal of things not readily amenable to economic analysis, will come to the same conclusion.

---

[20] A. Löwe, *Economics and Sociology* (London, 1935), p. 134.

[21] T. Parsons, "On Certain Sociological Elements in Professor Taussig's Thought," in *Explorations in Economics: Notes and Essays in Honour of F. W. Taussig* (New York, 1936), p. 363.

Differences of opinion among economists, on practical policy, are for this reason common enough. It is still more disconcerting, however, when the economist's opinions are indorsed by his colleagues but contradicted by the march of events. Individual errors of judgment, on insufficient data, do not always cancel one another out.

The economist who advises on policy, however confident of his own common sense and however wide his factual knowledge, still needs all the help he can get in ordering the many factors which have to be taken into account when dealing with a practical problem. The conceptual scheme of economic theory is believed, at least by economists, to be an indispensable guide; it therefore seems strange that he should willingly launch out upon the sea of "things not readily amenable to economic analysis" without some similar conceptual scheme to guide him. "To anyone acquainted with the history of science it seems almost obvious that scientific understanding has, beyond a quite elementary stage, advanced in proportion to the possibility of bringing facts into relation with a systematic theoretical scheme,"[22] and Professor Parsons has been working toward a general sociological theory of motivation "in which the economic elements will have a highly important place but will of course not stand alone."[23] This implies looking to sociology, not for the specific data to convert pure theory into realistic economics, but for a more comprehensive theory to assist the economist's interpretation of such facts as can be observed. But a sociological theory of this type, adequate for the economist's purpose, is still a promise, not yet an actual achievement.

Nevertheless, the need for a wider theoretical scheme is apparent, not only from the viewpoint of the sociologist, but also from that of the economic practitioner, who is forced to make up his mind on matters not readily amenable to analysis of the usual type—and on which his opinion is, for the correctness of his judgment, just as crucial as the soundness of his economic theory. An attempt is made in later chapters to develop a theoretical scheme considerably wider than that of present economic theory and to show how it may be applied to the study of concrete problems. It is treated as an extension of economic theory rather than as a separate social theory, for reasons which will

[22] *Ibid.*, p. 372.

[23] *Ibid.*, p. 378. The theoretical scheme Professor Parsons has in mind has not been published in its complete form. Hints may be obtained from *The Structure of Social Action* (New York, 1937) and "The Motivation of Economic Activities," *Canadian Journal of Economics and Political Science*, May, 1940, p. 187. Although my own theoretical scheme is rather different in conception, my debt to Professor Parsons' writings will be apparent in chap. iv.

be elaborated as the discussion proceeds and need only be indicated at this stage. Not only is it designed for the use of the economist, but it builds out from present-day economic theory; moreover, it is not a general theory of society but is restricted to features normally designated as "economic." Although practical convenience suggests that what is attempted can best be described as an enlargement of economic theory, it matters little if others prefer to regard it as a contribution to economic sociology. Far more important is the question as to whether it helps to bridge the gulf between theory and policy; and it is on this that it should be judged, along with the other suggestions contained in the book.

PLAN OF THE WORK

The general problem having been introduced, it is convenient to set out briefly what is attempted in the following chapters. Our first step will be to gain a somewhat fuller picture of the demands which are made upon economists by governments and of the political and other conditions under which an economic adviser is required to work. While these conditions must be experienced to be fully realized, it is important that academic workers who are seeking to improve economic science should have some account of the practical difficulties and opportunities of bringing it to bear upon policy formulation. Admittedly, these conditions vary somewhat from country to country and from time to time, so that generalization has its dangers. Nevertheless, it is worth checking the published impressions and proposals of others who have aspired to advise on practical matters against the view gained from one's own activities in this field.

With our understanding of the practical problems of the economic adviser, it is to be hoped, enriched, we shall undertake a closer examination of economic theory and its present limitations. In particular, the relation of theoretical analysis to factual studies will be discussed, with a view to determining just how economic theory can be "applied" to concrete problems. This will lead to a consideration of some of the outstanding deficiencies of present-day theory from this viewpoint and of the requirements of a more realistic body of theory. On the one hand, we shall consider in the chapters on "Theoretic Blight" and "The Problem of Behavior," certain flagrantly unrealistic tendencies in the development of economic theory which widen the gulf between theory and policy. Positive suggestions to improve the position will be made. On the other hand, we shall investigate the possibility of extending economic theory in such directions as will facilitate the study of those aspects of concrete problems, which, although usually described as "economic," are not adequately covered by the usual theoretic scheme. Two separate but related contributions will be offered for consideration; first, a theory to cover certain nonmarket activities which are vital to economic policy and may easily upset predictions based on a theory which covers only the operations of the market and, second, a theory of economic development to guide the factual study of changes in those conditions which present economic theory takes as given and does not investigate.

Even at this stage a disclaimer may be necessary. The theory of economic development here advanced is not a philosophy of history or a "formal outline of probable developments";[24] and the chapter on "Beyond the Market" contains nothing like a complete theory of social action. The economist is not advised to take all knowledge for his province. Practical problems require the exploration of territory beyond the confines of present-day economic theory, but only of *neighboring* territory. What is offered here is some additional intellectual equipment which may help the economist to make fewer mistakes when dealing with matters hitherto considered "not readily amenable to analysis."

All this is concerned with improving the economist's performance in the explanation and prediction of events, by the development of a more realistic theory. But there remains the question of objectives. "Without an adequate ethics and sociology in the broad sense," writes Professor Knight, "economics has little to say about policy."[25] Although economics has attempted to shed ethics in order to obtain greater objectivity, the question still remains as to whether economics can throw any light upon what ought to be done, as distinct from what is done. This question can be considered either in terms of economics in the sense of an abstract theory or in terms of a realistic account of how the economic system works at a particular time and place. It will be argued that the economist cannot in practice divest himself of all responsibility for the choice of objectives and that the choice of ends is often influenced by beliefs about the way the economic system works. We shall undertake an examination of some of the objectives which have been explicitly or implicitly indorsed by economists, including abstract equilibrium theorists as well as "welfare economists."

[24] Robbins, *Nature and Significance of Economic Science*, p. 132.
[25] F. H. Knight, "Ethics and Economic Reform," *Economica*, November, 1939, p. 422.

In considering how far the choice of particular objectives may be influenced by the findings of positive economics, we shall take account of the extensions of economic theory which are proposed in other sections of the book. Anybody who prefers to describe those theoretical schemes as economic sociology rather than as new branches of economic theory may therefore object that portions of this discussion of objectives relate to the role of sociology, not economics, in the selection of ends to be pursued. Here, again, terminology is relatively unimportant; the substantial question is whether studies of this type can assist in the formulation of objectives as well as in the choice of instruments of policy.

CHAPTER II

ECONOMIC ADVISING IN PRACTICE

ACCORDING to a recent count there may be as many as five thousand "economists" in the federal service of the United States;[1] in the District of Columbia alone there were, in 1937, over two thousand classified positions described as "economics, statistics, and political and social science."[2] Even if "we cannot say today with any certainty who is an economist,"[3] these figures suggest that the competence of economic science to assist the process of government was well established in the United States, even before the advent of economic mobilization for defense. In no other country is the position of the economist in governmental machinery so well defined. In Great Britain one finds men in the civil service with an advanced economic education, but they are rarely designated as "economists" or "economic advisers." The latter term, in fact, is just as likely to be applied to officers without academic training in economics. Although academic economists were absorbed into various departments in the war of 1914–18, they do not appear to have generally been accorded a special status.

In 1928 the Liberal Industrial Inquiry urged the need for a "general economic staff" to advise the cabinet. Two years later the MacDonald government established an Economic Advisory Council, consisting of several ministers and a number of outside experts and assisted by a staff that included academic economists. There were two standing committees, one on scientific research and one on economic information, which met fairly regularly. But in 1935, for instance, the council itself did not meet at all. Dr. Jennings concludes that, "while it cannot be said that the experiment has failed, it cannot yet be said that it has succeeded."[4] Following the outbreak of war in 1939, a Committee of Economic Survey was appointed under the late Lord Stamp, which included academic and official economists and

[1] M. A. Copeland, "Economic Research in the Government," *American Economic Review*, September, 1941, p. 533.

[2] National Resources Committee, *Research a National Resource* (December, 1938), p. 49.

[3] Copeland, *op. cit.*, p. 533.

[4] W. I. Jennings, *Cabinet Government* (London, 1937), pp. 247–49.

investigated problems for the Economic Policy Committee of the cabinet. This organization subsequently developed into the Survey of Economic and Financial Plans and finally into the Economic and Statistical Secretariat to a new Cabinet Co-ordinating Committee on Economic and Financial Policy. According to one observer, this secretariat "is quite an effective organ of thought, stimulation, admonitory comment and initiative."[5] Positions have been found for academic economists, too, in various departments of the United Kingdom government since the outbreak of war.

It is, however, impossible for an outsider, particularly in another country, to assess the extent to which the economists in the government service, in peace or war, influence practical policy. Accordingly, our discussion will be based primarily on Australian conditions and on the testimony of one or two American economists who have broken silence regarding the conditions under which they have worked.

RESEARCH BUREAU OR CONFIDENTIAL ADVISER?

In academic and other nonpolitical circles there is general agreement that governments should institute economic advisory services on a generous scale. This agreement is based on the belief "that many of the mistakes and blunders made by Governments are due, not to illwill or prejudice, but to sheer unpreparedness and ignorance."[6] But very different conceptions are current as to how these advisory services should work. At one extreme is the dream of an independent research bureau, financed out of public funds, with complete freedom to investigate economic problems and to appraise the policies of the government, whether the politician likes it or not. The reports of such a bureau, it is hoped, not only would show the government what it ought to do but would also provide public opinion with the necessary ammunition to force the government to do the right thing. At the other extreme is the role of the executive's confidant and personal adviser on economic matters, who helps the politician or administrator to make up his mind on various problems as they arise. All statesmen have their intimate advisers, and it is argued that the place for the economist who desires to influence policy is within this inner circle rather than in an independent institute. (Of course, this type of adviser may himself feel the need for a research bureau to help him decide what

[5] H. Finer, "The British Cabinet, the House of Commons and the War," *Political Science Quarterly*, September, 1941, p. 342.

[6] Liberal Industrial Inquiry, *Britain's Industrial Future* (London, 1928), p. 117.

advice to give, but not to supply material to the public for a campaign to press a particular policy upon the person he is advising.)

The Liberal Industrial Inquiry's proposal was for "a thinking Department within the Administration, at the elbow of the inner ring of the Cabinet." The proposed duties of the Economic General Staff were set out in the following general terms:

i) To engage in continuous study of current economic problems affecting national policy and the development of industry
ii) To co-ordinate and, where necessary, to complete statistical and other information required by the Government and by Parliament
iii) To act on its own initiative in calling the attention of the Cabinet to important tendencies and changes at home and abroad
iv) To suggest to the Government plans for solving fundamental economic difficulties, such, for instance, as measures for stabilising trade conditions, avoiding unemployment, and developing national resources.[7]

The personnel, it was suggested, should consist of the chief and deputy chief of the Economic General Staff, the permanent secretary of the Treasury and the permanent heads of the other economic departments. Apparently, the chief-of-staff was to be in the position of a confidential adviser to the prime minister—"a position of such power and importance that he can take up the handling of any question he chooses with the assurance that the Prime Minister and the Cabinet will, whether or not they do what he asks, at least listen seriously to what he says."[8] The authors of the proposal reveal a full appreciation of the practical pitfalls: "An advisory department is always in danger of being frozen out, and being handed all the problems to the examination of which it is politic to give some measure of lip service but which do not really matter. . . . ." It may easily become "an academic body drafting endless memoranda, probably excellent memoranda, which nobody reads." Consequently, "a body of this kind will be useless unless it is clothed with great prestige and placed at the centre of the administration."

The Liberal Industrial Inquiry did not make a specific plea for the use of academically trained economists in this connection. Apart from the possibility of having a recognized economist as chief or assistant chief of the staff, the place for economists is presumably in the secretariat of the general staff. "The higher personnel of the Secretariat should be very few in number, the best experts available, and well remunerated on Civil Service standards."[9] But the emphasis is on spe-

[7] *Ibid.*, p. 117.
[8] *Ibid.*, p. 118.　　　　　[9] *Ibid.*, p. 119.

cialized study of economic problems rather than on the contribution which can be made by the economic theorist.

It was also suggested that the Economic General Staff might initiate and organize much of the work traditionally done by royal commissions and departmental committees and that the general staff, with the assent of the prime minister, might set up *ad hoc* committees, including outside experts "to report, sometimes for publication and sometimes for the private information of the Government, on particular problems and projects."[10] The reference to publication may suggest a desire to have the best of both worlds; but it was apparently not considered that the advice of the chief of the staff would be publicized.

The British Economic Mission to Australia (1928–29) indorsed the proposal for an economic advisory service under the federal government. "This new service must necessarily deal with problems which directly affect the political life of the country, and it must accordingly be placed and regarded as entirely outside the sphere of political influence and its recommendations considered as scientific and unbiassed."[11] It was not clear whether this economic service, like the existing Council for Scientific and Industrial Research, should publish its findings on its own initiative. This has been strongly urged, however, by some Australian advocates of the economic general staff idea. Sir Herbert Gepp writes:

> With the institution of an economic council, members of parliament would be inclined to fear that, if the findings and recommendations of the council were published, the work of parliament would be overshadowed by the importance of the work and advice of the new body. Yet it is essential that the reports of the council be published if they are to be of maximum value. If it were not the rule that reports should be regularly and immediately published, governments might be tempted to delay, or refrain from, publication; because the findings and recommendations could not be used to support election promises or party shibboleths.

There is also "the need of educating the community to a sound outlook upon the national economy." If compromise is necessary, "it may be wiser to publish the facts found, without publishing the actual recommendations made to Cabinet."[12]

---

[10] *Ibid.*, p. 120.

[11] *Report of the British Economic Mission* (1929), p. 34.

[12] Sir Herbert Gepp, "The Place of an Economic Research and Advisory Council in the Modern State," in *Democracy's Danger* (Sydney, 1939), p. 175. Sir Herbert Gepp was formerly chairman of the Australian Development and Migration Commission and has been a member of numerous royal commissions.

Somewhat similar functions for an economic research bureau are envisaged by Professor Bland. He says:

I am satisfied that the Cabinet needs a special economic division similar to that created for industry in the Council for Scientific and Industrial Research. It will not be political, but a specialist bureau which collects and analyses data. Its most appropriate location would be at the University, financed by and yet detached from the Government. Alternatively, it might be associated with the Government Statistical Office, where machinery already exists for the collection of other essential data. It would comprise a small number of permanent men, expert in different fields, and its personnel could always be increased by drawing temporarily upon University staffs, or other scientific bodies. . . . . The bureau would undertake research either at the request of the Cabinet, or Parliament, or on its own initiative. Its material would, like that of the Statistical Bureau, be available to the Government, the public or Parliament. Indeed, it could be hoped that Parliamentary Standing Committees would make ample use of the bureau, when discussing economic and social measures presented to Parliament by the Cabinet. I am not concerned that this course would have the effect of slowing down the work of government. Speed may be exhilarating, but it is very exacting, and in the matter of legislation it is still good advice to hasten slowly. The investigations of such a bureau would also be of incalculable value in educating public opinion to the significance of cause and effect. It is an indispensable part of the machinery for enabling a control to be exercised on behalf of the people.[13]

Here the emphasis is on public information as a method of influencing the behavior of governments, as well as on providing the government with adequate knowledge for its own guidance.

There are several reasons why an independent research bureau of this type is likely to have only limited influence on policy, at least under Australian conditions. In the first place, the economist has not the scientific prestige of the physical or biological scientist; indeed, at the present stage of development he cannot honestly claim the same degree of scientific certainty regarding practical problems as can the soil chemist or the entomologist. The findings of an economic research bureau will not be accepted by the politician as a mandate on economic policy, unless he is independently convinced that the course recommended is, in all the circumstances, the most appropriate. Second, the proposals of a research bureau must be integrated within the administrative framework, as well as the exigencies of the political situation. It is questionable whether an independent institute can possess the necessary intimate and up-to-date knowledge of these aspects of the problem. Frequent exchange of personnel between the research bureau and administrative services has been suggested as the obvious solution to this difficulty; but this may in practice reduce the

[13] F. A. Bland, "Overhauling the Machinery of Government," in W. G. K. Duncan (ed.), *Trends in Australian Politics* (Sydney, 1935), p. 166.

former's independence. Third, there is the problem of communication. Publication of reports is no guaranty that they will be read, either by the official or by the public. The best channel to the mind of a minister or executive is by direct personal approach or through his personal advisers; and, if these do not include an economist, the findings of the economic research bureau may suffer considerable distortion in transmission, even with the best will in the world. If the less direct approach, via the public, is desired, somebody must break down the reports of the bureau into a more popular form; publication must be replaced by propaganda, and the independence of the bureau will soon be called in question, since the reports will receive much public attention only if the subject is highly controversial at the moment of publication. Finally, it may be noted that the politician, while obliged to court public opinion, must take the ultimate responsibility of decision and will, in any case, be unwilling to appear as a mere implementer of the findings of a research bureau. It may be part of his duty to secure the best available advice but not to abdicate in favor of an independent group of social scientists.

It has been said that when an American wishes to attack a government department, he writes to Washington for the ammunition. Perhaps in the course of time this disinterested attitude will become still more widespread. But it is significant that Professor Copeland, discussing research in the United States government, should record his opinion that, "with a fair amount of ingenuity in form of expression, the research worker can find a way to say almost anything without violating the canons of governmental propriety."[14] To influence policy, however, the findings must be translated into practical terms by somebody, and this becomes a form of political activity.

This view does not contest the desirability of independent research into problems of economic policy or discount the need for the wide dissemination and public discussion of the findings of research workers who have no political ax to grind. Indeed, it is to be regretted that private benefactors have not made provision in Australia for social research on any considerable scale. In view of this deficiency of private generosity, it is natural to look to governments instead. But in view of the fact that information is a political weapon it requires an infrequent degree of noble-mindedness to subsidize research and public education on matters which promise to be a source of embarrassment to the

---

[14] *Op. cit.*, p. 532.

government. It is very doubtful whether this difficulty can be overcome by linking such proposals with the government's own need for expert advice.

The above conclusion is not based on a priori speculation but on the experience which has been gained as the result of actual developments in the organization of economic research and advisory services in Australia. On several occasions governments have demonstrated their aversion to financing independent research bodies, as distinct from *ad hoc* commissions of inquiry. On the other hand, increasing use has been made of economists as confidential advisers, as research officers within the departments, and as members of commissions of inquiry.

Following the report of the British Economic Mission, mentioned above, the Commonwealth government, in 1929, passed legislation to enable the appointment of a director of economic research, with a research bureau under his control. This legislation has never been repealed; but the bureau has not been established. The government was defeated at the polls before appointing the director of economic research, and no succeeding government has considered it necessary to carry out the intentions of the act. In the ensuing years of depression the advice of economists was sought on several occasions. The questions at issue were of intense political interest; and the public advocacy of various measures by practically all the economists of any standing made it extremely difficult to find an economist with the requisite prestige and knowledge of Australian conditions who would not be regarded as partisan. It is possible, however, that mere revulsion against its predecessor's policy is sufficient explanation of the Labor government's failure to proceed with the idea and that the gradual development of other internal advisory services has satisfied later governments.

In the state of Queensland, a Bureau of Economics and Statistics was established, by a special act, in 1930. The bureau was under the control of a director, appointed by the government, but, like the auditor-general, responsible to parliament and not to any particular minister (although the act was to be administered by the minister for Labor and Industry). The director was to be permitted great freedom in the choice of subjects for investigation and in publishing, as well as being required to report on, any matter referred to him by the government. The bureau was also to report on any economic matters which might be of assistance to the State Industrial Arbitration Court and "to promote effective measures to combat unemployment, and to encourage improved relations between employers and employees." The first director was Mr. J. B. Brigden, who had already left the chair of economics in the University of Tasmania to accept an advisory position in the shipping business.[15]

Although the bureau undertook a wide range of investigations, including the preparation of an index of business conditions and statistics of interstate trade,[16] its duties in relation to the Arbitration Court brought it under fire from the trade-unions and the parliamentary (Labor) Opposition. The director had recommended wage reductions in 1930 and 1931; and, although by mid-1932 he advocated no further reduction, "the unions, disregarding all the other work of the Bureau, had come to regard it as existing for the purpose of persuading the Industrial Court to reduce wages."[17] During the 1932 elections the leader of the Opposition promised to abolish the bureau if returned to power. In effect, however, the new Labor government reconstituted it as the Bureau of Industry, with functions similar to those of the Bureau of Economics, with the exception of that of regularly advising the Arbitration Court. There was no restriction upon the bureau's power to give the Arbitration Court information if asked to do so. But part of the bureau's energies was to be diverted to the investigation of proposals for loan expenditure and assistance to industries. In this way the government retained an economic advisory service, while clipping its wings. The same director was reappointed, but the new bureau was made responsible directly to the treasurer and financially dependent upon the government. (The former bureau had £5,000 per annum reserved by law). Nevertheless, the bureau has not been starved and has continued to publish statistical material, having taken over the state statistical bureau from the registrar-general.[18]

The Queensland experiment suggests that an economic advisory service, once established, will not be lightly sacrificed for the sake of

[15] Subsequently chairman of the National Insurance Commission, now secretary to the Department of Munitions.

[16] See *Economic News*, issued by the bureau, June, 1932.

[17] B. H. Molesworth, "The Bureau of Industry in Queensland," *Economic Record*, June, 1933, p. 105; see also the same author's "Establishment of a Bureau of Economics and Statistics in Queensland," *ibid.*, May, 1931, p. 115.

[18] The present director is Mr. Colin Clark, who has freedom to publish independently in his own special field of national-income studies.

political fireworks. At the same time it illustrates the practical difficulties which arise if an economic bureau, supported by the government, publicizes recommendations on contentious matters of policy.

During the depression, Australian economists undoubtedly played
a considerable part in the formulation of policy. Previously, their
chief channel to the official mind had been through newspaper articles and reports. Occasionally an individual economist sat as a member of a royal commission, and several had appeared as witnesses before such inquiries. When an academic economist offered evidence
before the Tariff Board in 1927, he was not well received;[19] but in the
same year the prime minister invited a group of economists "to undertake an independent inquiry into the economic effects of the Australian
tariff."[20] The publication of this report undoubtedly enhanced the
prestige of the profession in relation to practical problems, but not
sufficiently for economists to be called in to advise at the first signs of
depression in 1929. It was interesting to the Australian people to find
that the Bank of England should send a university professor as adviser
to Sir Otto Niemeyer, who visited Australia in 1929 and warned the
government of the economic difficulties that lay ahead. The largest
Australian commercial bank then took a professor (E. O. G. Shann)
as economic adviser; and another professor (D. B. Copland) gave evidence before the Commonwealth Arbitration Court in support of the
proposal to reduce the basic wage in 1930. But most of the advice
given by economists at that time was in the form of lectures, articles,
and manifestoes. It was not until January, 1931, that three professors
were asked by the Australian Loan Council (Commonwealth and
states) to consult with Treasury officials who were preparing a report
on the financial situation—a report which was not adopted. But in
May, 1931, a similar committee was empowered to "co-opt the services of economists," and, with the aid of four professors, it drafted the
report which became the basis of the Premiers' Plan. Professor Cop-.
land wrote:

It was only the Premiers' Plan, because it had to be adopted by Premiers. The
plan was, in fact, a composite product of the Australian economists, and Shann's part
in its enunciation was all important. He greatly assisted in bringing the economists
together, and in giving them a focal point through which they could influence banking and financial policy. He went about among bankers, under-treasurers, premiers,
and politicians, persuading them that drastic situations required drastic remedies.[21]

[19] Cf. F. C. Benham, *The Prosperity of Australia* (London, 1928), p. 266.
[20] See J. B. Brigden and Others, *The Australian Tariff* (Melbourne, 1929).
[21] D. B. Copland, "Edward Shann," *Economic Journal*, September, 1935, p. 600.

In 1932, too, a committee of four economists and two businessmen was asked to make a survey of the economic position.

Reviewing the work of the Australian economists in the depression, an American observer comments that

the economists were used only in a haphazard fashion. That is to say, they were called on only on special tasks and with a particular problem to report on. And if they tried to broaden the bases of their inquiries in order to make their work more effective, governments not infrequently were resentful. Economists never had an opportunity to make a report on an entire economic programme.[22]

And it is true that they continued issuing an occasional manifesto, such as that on devaluation in November, 1931.[23] But one must not overlook informal and confidential advisory work, such as Shann's. Moreover, the number of economists in a position to give personal advice increased. The central bank took a professor as economic adviser (L. G. Melville), while another who had graduated to academic work from statistics (L. F. Giblin) returned to government service as acting Commonwealth statistician in 1931. The state government of Tasmania appointed the professor in the University as part-time economic adviser; and in 1932 the Commonwealth government created the position of economist in the Bureau of Statistics. Subsequently, when this economist (R. Wilson) became statistician, he was given the additional title of "Economic Adviser to the Treasury," and other economists were added to the Treasury staff. In 1938 the government of New South Wales, which had already been obtaining regular reports on economic conditions from university economists, arranged for a university economist to act as adviser to the Treasury.

A federation, in which financial adjustments are made between the central government and the states, has a special use for economists, namely, as advocates to prepare and even to present statistical material and argument relating to the states' financial needs. Since 1933 the Commonwealth government has relied on a Grants Commission to investigate the claims of the weaker states and to recommend the amounts to be distributed by way of special grants. The commission has from the beginning had an economist among its personnel, and the three claimant states (Western Australia, South Australia, and Tasmania) and the Commonwealth Treasury have all come to rely in some measure upon economists for the preparation of their respective "cases." While not the most satisfactory work for an academic econo-

[22] W. R. MacLaurin, *Economic Planning in Australia, 1929–1936* (London, 1937), p. 257.

[23] Cf. E. O. G. Shann and D. B. Copland, *The Australian Price Structure* (Sydney, 1933), p. 85.

mist, duties of this type give him a firsthand knowledge of economic conditions and government finance, bring financial success to his government, and establish more firmly his competence to advise the government on matters of general economic policy. The practice has also developed for the various Commonwealth and state governments to make use of the services of economists as advisers at meetings of the Loan Council (which decides the borrowing programs each year and allocates the available funds among the Commonwealth and states), and sometimes to other conferences of Commonwealth and states. For these occasions, too, there is often need for the preparation of a "case"; and sometimes an informal discussion among advisers may suggest a way out of what appears to be a deadlock of the various governments.

With the outbreak of war in 1939, there was a further expansion of economic advisory services, particularly in the Commonwealth government. A Financial and Economic Committee was established,[24] and a professor (L. F. Giblin) was brought to Canberra as full-time adviser. Numerous young economists found employment in the various departments, in many cases with the official designation of "economist," or "research officer." A prominent businessman (Sir Ernest Fisk) was brought in as director of economic co-ordination; but this arrangement does not appear to have been a great success. Three former university economists were given important administrative positions (secretary for Munitions, secretary for Labor, and prices commissioner), and one of these (D. B. Copland) later became economic consultant to the prime minister.

There is no question about "publication of reports" by war advisers. The advisory work of these economists is confidential, like that of any other Commonwealth official. But the idea of an independent research bureau still persists, especially in scientific and university circles. There was recently a suggestion that the Commonwealth and state governments might jointly finance an independent bureau of agricultural economics, an idea which Commonwealth and state ministers found equally unattractive, especially at a time when there was some conflict of opinion among the various governments on agricultural marketing schemes.[25] It was also suggested to a Parliamentary Committee

[24] Professors L. F. Giblin (chairman), D. B. Copland (prices commissioner), and R. C. Mills (University of Sydney), Dr. H. C. Coombs (Treasury economist), Dr. R. Wilson (secretary for Labor), Mr. J. B. Brigden (secretary for Munitions), and Mr. L. G. Melville (Commonwealth bank economist).

[25] The government of New South Wales has since established its own Bureau of Agricultural Economics.

on Social Security that the Commonwealth should establish an independent bureau for research into problems related to the social services. Some find signs of increased government interest in independent economic research in the provision of a special vote to subsidize university research into post-war reconstruction problems. But, meanwhile, the confidential advisory services are carrying on, and the dream of a continuous public appraisal of economic policy by social scientists and of an educated public opinion still seems far from realization.

THE UNSCIENTIFIC ATMOSPHERE OF GOVERNMENT

Politics remains basically unscientific, and this fact carries over into the world of the confidential adviser. Perhaps there is, in some country or other, a statesman who, before initiating any economic policy, has the problems thoroughly investigated by his expert advisers and carefully sifts their findings, even postponing action until he can proceed with the certainty that every relevant fact has been marshaled, every relevant consideration examined. But such a statesman must be something of a curiosity in politics. Major decisions on policy are often—too often—made on the run. Problems may come to a head quickly; and sometimes it is not the problem that impels the politician to action, but the occasion. The need for something to say at an important function, especially if there are other competitors for the limelight; signs of incipient revolt among a bunch of his supporters; a challenge from his political opponents; a visit to a distressed district—these demand that the politician shall, there and then, make up his mind about at least one of the pressing problems of the day. Advising on policy decisions in such circumstances as these does not permit lengthy research and therefore presents a contrast to the work of the academic economist.[26] If the economist's own submissions are to be more than snap judgments, he must take a leaf from the book of the leader-writer and keep ahead of the news. If his judgment is to be backed by research, it must be by research undertaken in anticipation of where the political wind will blow. This means that an adviser must take an interest in the political situation, instead of devoting his whole attention to the scientific analysis of such problems as may be referred to him from time to time or to the study of economic trends. The latter, it is true, may help the economist to foresee some political developments, because future economic problems will often give rise to political issues. But there will not be a perfect correlation between the magni-

[26] This point is also made by Professor Copeland (*op. cit.*, p. 531).

tude of the economic problem and the politician's interest in what the economist has to say about it. The economist is, therefore, in a somewhat paradoxical position; if he desires to utilize scientific economic research as the basis of his advice, he must study more than economics.

In so far as the economist has his own jargon and habits of thought, the problem of communicating his ideas to the politician is a difficult one. But he also shares the technical worries of any official seeking to make his voice heard "higher up." The methods of work of politicians and administrators vary from individual to individual. Some surround themselves with a multitude of counselors and evolve their own decision out of the clash of opposing opinions. Others are influenced by each adviser in turn, and the important thing is to have the last word. Others, again, rely on very few confidants—perhaps a single expert in each field. Methods of absorbing information and views are no more uniform. Some prefer the interview; others the written memorandum—bulky and replete with figures and arguments, or, in some cases, restricted to a single sheet of type. Some set time aside to go into a particular problem with their advisers; others are always too busy to give more than five minutes to any matter at a stretch without being called on long-distance telephone. To all these idiosyncrasies the economic adviser, if he is to be of service, must, like any other official in a similar position, adapt himself, even if this implies a departure from the systematic exposition which he associates with the idea of economic science.

There is one trait, however, which is common to all executives who seek advice, namely, an appetite for definite conclusions rather than for a nice balancing of all the relevant considerations which make a decision difficult. This means that, whenever possible, the adviser must make up his own mind one way or the other, even if (as is often the case) the data are not sufficient to place the matter beyond scientific doubt. There are occasions when the only thing to do is to insist that the available information does not permit a rational decision; but economic science will not make much impact upon policy if the economist is chronically unable to arrive at definite recommendations, merely because the practical problem involves elements that do not fit the framework of economic theory.

This raises the question as to how far the economist is expected to go in practice. He is not expected to make a close study of political tactics; the politician is quite prepared to exercise his own judgment on matters of political expediency. Professor Viner writes:

The economist conditioned to the purity of abstract thought is liable to be unreasonable in his refusal to recognise that the official, in choosing his time for action and his manner and degree of action, must give regard to their impact on his relations with superiors, colleagues, Congress and the public, and to their effect on the prestige of his agency and the morale of his staff.[27]

But in time the economist will either learn to be "reasonable" or leave. What is asked of him is not that he, too, will give weight (in his amateurish way) to all the political elements in the problem but that he will not waste too much of the official's time with proposals which are *patently* absurd from this viewpoint.

Rather more important are the limits of legal procedure and administrative feasibility, which, as Professor Viner points out, are likely to be imperfectly understood by other specialist advisers in addition to economists. "The lack of legal and administrative training on the part of the economist," he says, "may be regrettable, but it is not fatal so long as he is not permitted to decide policy questions all on his own."[28] It is highly desirable, however, that the economist's advice should be based on knowledge of the legal processes involved and should include some indication of suitable administrative arrangements. If the economist has not the training or experience himself, he must seek advice from the proper quarters before finalizing his own recommendations.

One might also ask: How much is the economist expected to know about matters which fall outside the scope of economic theory? The practical man has the vaguest of notions as to where the boundaries of economic science lie. Trade, industry, agriculture, finance, labor, transportation, and marketing—all these may fall within the net of an economic adviser, and he must know as much about technology and the institutional framework as is useful in each particular concrete problem. "Analytical" definitions of the type that have become fashionable among theorists in recent years do not limit the demands which will be made on him.

Finally, there is the question as to whether the economist is expected to pronounce on objectives, as well as on measures to attain given ends. The policy-maker, according to Professor Viner's experience,

insists that he be advised not only on what will be the objective consequences of a specific line of action, but whether or not these are desirable consequences. While he always has some notions of his own with respect to the values which policy should

[27] J. Viner, "Short and Long View in Economic Policy," *American Economic Review*, March, 1940, p. 2.

[28] *Ibid.*, p. 6.

serve . . . . he always demands of his economists that they guide him also in the determination of what is socially desirable, and he expects the economist to acknowledge and to display some professional competence in giving such guidance.[29]

This accords with the current academic conception of the politician, but it has only limited application in Australia. An Australian economist is more likely to be consulted about means than about ends. Most Australian politicians have very strong notions as to "the values which policy should serve." At the same time, the "best" method of achieving a particular objective implies that there is some special criterion by which to judge the merits of different methods, and the economist may be expected to be armed with such a criterion.[30] In this sense, admittedly, the ends of policy are customarily defined vaguely, and the economist is expected to share in their more precise formulation. But it is the exception rather than the rule, in this author's experience, for the economist to be asked to consider the social desirability of *specific* objectives. Indeed, if the consequences of a particular line of action are clear, there is often no division of opinion about its social desirability.

The need for a criterion of social desirability is most apparent when there is a conflict of interests and the benefit of some persons must be set against the damage to others. Anybody acquainted with the hurly-burly of politics might be tempted to interpret the nineteenth-century search for methods of determining the "general interest" as an attempt to offset the pressure of sectional interests, not as a response to the politician's *lack* of values, but as an attempt to provide him with a better set. Without some supreme principle, such as "maximum happiness," the best the politician can do is to mete out rough justice "according to his lights," and the worst, to favor whichever party seems most likely to influence his own position. For a decision on either type of issue the politician will rarely expect help from the economist; and the politician seldom feels the need for a principle which would override his judgment in these matters, though that need may be obvious to the social reformer.

It must be remembered that the whole of the foregoing is based upon a limited range of experience in a single country; it should not be regarded as a series of dogmatic generalizations   Perhaps, in the course of time, as more economists feel free to comment on their actual experiences in government work, a more balanced picture will be made

[29] *Ibid.*, p. 2.

[30] Cf. R. F. Harrod, "Scope and Method of Economics," *Economic Journal*, September, 1938, p. 391.

available. Economists who teach students, as well as those who aspire to advise the practical man, need this type of information, for there is a temptation to form an a priori estimate of the behavior of politicians, as well as of the entrepreneur.

DANGERS TO THE ECONOMIST

The picture we have drawn may well raise the question as to whether an economist can touch pitch without being defiled. Can he maintain his scientific objectivity in so unscientific an atmosphere? Professor Viner thinks that "economic doctrine is now following public opinion and government practice more than it is influencing them"; but he attributes this tendency to the modern economist's preoccupation with short-range problems rather than to "a new subservience of the profession to external opinion."[31] There are, however, undoubted dangers in the economist's becoming closely identified with particular political movements. If effective advising requires relations with the politician or other official as intimate as has been suggested, this does constitute a peril to the economist's independence. And, living in that curious half-world where questions of fact and questions of value continually jostle each other and where decisions are made as often on considerations of political expediency as on the appraisal of economic consequences, there is a strong temptation to slip into the forms of expression which most readily produce assent to one's proposals.

An illustration of the intrusion of noneconomic arguments into the economist's exposition of his views may be found in the emphasis laid by Australian economists on the "inequitable" distribution of the loss of income caused by the depression. It was argued that the concentration of the initial loss, upon export producers and persons previously dependent upon government-loan expenditure, would cause more extensive repercussions than would the same total loss if it were distributed over all sections of the community. This is a proposition in positive economics and can be scientifically examined. It could also be argued that it was inequitable for some sections to bear heavy losses while other sections escaped. This is an entirely different issue. But in Professor Copland's evidence before the Arbitration Court in 1930, the two arguments were fused into one. The "secondary losses," that is, the repercussions from the initial loss, were "due to the present inequitable distribution of the first loss." The "equitable distribution of

---

[31] *Op. cit.*, p. 8.

the first loss" was "a prerequisite of economic recovery."[32] If these words could be taken literally, they would constitute a novel approach to business-cycle theory—the level of activity depending on the degree of social justice. Their real purpose, however, was to appeal simultaneously to the Australian's love of fair play and his desire for recovery.

The economist's case could have been more accurately stated as follows: "The secondary losses are increased by the concentration of the first loss on a section of the community [which is in any case inequitable]. A wider distribution of the loss [which would in any case be more equitable] will facilitate recovery." But the popular appeal of such a formulation would have been less; it would have drawn attention to the possibility of attacking independently the economist's theory of the mechanics of recovery and the alleged equity of making everybody share the loss. It is not suggested that the evidence was, in fact, drafted with such Machiavellian attention to detail but merely that when advice involves persuasion as well as analysis it is difficult to maintain the scientific level of discourse. Of course, the individual economist may be so strongly in favor of a particular policy that its success appears more important to him than the purity of economic science; the time may come when he personally must forsake economics for politics. It is in the interests of economic science that, when this point is reached, it should be openly avowed.

Apart from the danger that the economist may be gradually transformed into a politician without realizing it, advising also constitutes a continuous threat to his professional scholarship. The danger may be illustrated by an Australian student's comment, on his return from overseas, regarding an economist famed for his political activities. "His lectures were very interesting at first—until you realised that he had not read any theory since 1930." It takes a special effort for an economist in an advisory position to keep abreast of the main currents of academic thought. Not only the pressure of other tasks but also the atmosphere in which he works discourages the systematic study of theoretical treatises. For this reason a continued link with a university is an invaluable stimulus. An economist engaged in practical affairs will inevitably count some parts of the world of theory well lost; but, if he is wise, he will not ignore the possibility that contributions to theory may have revolutionary practical implications.

[32] Quoted by E. O. G. Shann and D. B. Copland, *The Crisis in Australian Finance, 1929 to 1931* (Sydney, 1931), p. 100.

COMPENSATIONS

On the other hand, it is difficult to overestimate the value of the experience of practical affairs which economic advising can bring. It gives the economist a much better perspective in which to view his science. If the limitations of present-day economic theory stand out more clearly, so, too, its value in approaching concrete problems is more firmly demonstrated. Professor Copeland lists, among the advantages of government research workers, the fact that "the fields of economic inquiry are less marked out into detailed specialties than in academic life."[33] The contrast is less marked in Australia, where specialization is not carried so far in universities.

Still more striking is the fact that the fields of economic inquiry themselves are hardly marked off from other fields of inquiry in government. Not only do all sorts of other specialists deal with problems of industry, commerce, and finance, but the economist himself is required to deal with matters which escape from the categories of academic economics. To the practical man economics does not cover merely the transactions of the market. His economic problems usually have only one foot in the market and the other in what Professor Robbins calls "the sociological penumbra." The figure is not altogether a happy one, for the economist is likely to find the shadows around the market deeper than those within. Not only the processes of exchange but the other relationships between the parties to exchange come into the picture. Many of the economist's difficulties arise from the wide prevalence of "noneconomic" behavior and the fact that he is expected to take full account of it when developing economic proposals. The upshot is that the economist tends to lose interest in the absorbing academic problem of fixing the exact limits between the various social sciences. He is more concerned over the lacunae between them than over the possibility that they may overlap. He may even be attracted by Mrs. Wootton's suggestion that "the fertility and value of economic studies depends upon a ruthless disregard of present boundaries and definitions,"[34] until he remembers how wide our modern definitions really are.[35]

[33] "Economic Research in the Federal Government," *American Economic Review*, September, 1941, p. 531.

[34] B. Wootton, *Lament for Economics* (London, 1938), p. 261.

[35] Perhaps some readers would include this paragraph under the head of "Dangers to the Economist" rather than "Compensations." It is hoped that they will not assume that the author is completely lost to economic science, without considering the discussion in chap. iii.

Above all, the economic adviser has access to much factual material on a scale, which, in Australia at least, would never come the way of the academic researcher. He may be able to have special information collected, if he can show that it will be useful. But, even apart from this possibility, the information coming into government departments, which are concerned with various aspects of economic policy, far exceeds, of course, the amount that goes out to the public through statistics, speeches, and the like. The economist may not only add to his own knowledge of economic conditions and commercial practices but also find numerous opportunities of working out in concrete terms analyses which, in academic studies, can be illustrated only by imaginary examples. This experience should tend to make him a better economist.

CHAPTER III

TOWARD REALISTIC ECONOMIC THEORY

THE professional equipment of an economist may be said to consist of two parts: a knowledge of economic theory and experience in its application to new problems. The pure theorist may never consider concrete problems, but an economist—as distinct from a mere expositor—must be able to show how economic theory can be applied to new problems, even if only to imaginary ones composed of hypothetical assumptions rather than observed conditions. In this chapter we shall look a little more closely at the first part of the economist's equipment. What is economic theory? In what sense can it be applied to problems? How, in fact, does it assist the solution of concrete problems? What are the limits to its usefulness in this connection? The reader, like the author, is probably tempted to skip a chapter which looks suspiciously like yet another essay on the nature, scope, and method of economics. All the first chapters of the masterly "Principles," the slim volumes on methodology, the brilliant inaugural lectures and presidential addresses, rise up in protest. But, since a good deal will be said in later chapters about the refitting and extension of the economist's theoretical equipment, it is essential to survey briefly what he already possesses.

THEORY AND FACT

Standard works on economic theory usually contain a considerable number of empirical generalizations, in addition to analyses of the implications of given sets of conditions. Under the former heading would fall statements such as the following, chosen at random from the writings of three great economists:

When a trader or manufacturer buys anything to be used in production, or to be sold again, his demand is based on his anticipations of the profits he can derive from it. . . . .

The great mortality of infants among the poor is largely due to the want of care and judgment in preparing their food. . . . .

In districts in which manufactures have long been domiciled a habit of responsibility, of carefulness and promptitude in handling expensive machinery and materials becomes the property of all. . . . .

The accumulated wealth of civilised countries is at present growing faster than population.[1]

[1] A. Marshall, *Principles of Economics* (8th ed.; London, 1922), pp. 92, 195, 205, 321.

In real life production is always a continuous process. . . . .

In modern civilised society the collective wants form a very extensive group. . . . .

When contracts are offered by public authorities or large companies, there is frequently a very keen competition between large concerns that are in a position to undertake the work.[2]

The weariness of labour is by no means in proportion to the number of hours spent on it. When indeed the hours of labour are unduly prolonged, fatigue becomes so great and so deep-seated that the period of rest and sleep does not suffice to remove it. . . . .

The habit of saving is strongly entrenched among the well-to-do. Spendthrifts are rare, and such wasting as does occur is more than balanced by the fresh accumulations of new savers and investors. . . . .

There is an unmistakable tendency to diminishing returns on any plot of land.[3]

These are all statements (true or not) of fact; but they purport to be more than historical or statistical facts relating to a particular date. They affirm certain conditions as part of the world which the economist studies, which will presumably continue for some period of time at least. These generalizations may be contrasted with other statements which affirm logical relationships between certain conditions. We may illustrate this type by quotations from the same works.

Let us inquire what are the conditions, under which a check to the supply of a thing that is wanted not for direct use, but as a factor of production of some commodity, may cause a very great rise in price. The first condition is. . . . .

If there were more than enough land all of about the same fertility, to enable everyone to have as much of it as was needed to give full scope to the capital he was prepared to apply to it, then it could yield no rent.[4]

If copper can be used either for kitchen vessels or in electrical industry, the most economical use of the available stock of copper requires that the coppersmith shall pay the same price as the electrician. . . . .

The need to pay interest at a certain rate will always cut off a number of possibilities of satisfying human wants by the use of durable goods.[5]

From the definition of value, it follows that there can be no general rise in values and no general fall in values. . . . .

If a bank keeps just as much specie as it has notes outstanding, its note issue obviously can be no source of profit.[6]

These are all statements of logical relationships. In some of the sentences quoted the logical connection would be clear only if the other links in the chain of argument were also presented, but any economist will recognize the type of theory to which the statements refer. The purely logical nature of the statement is evident when it begins with

[2] G. Cassel, *Theory of Social Economy* (London, 1923), I, 27, 69, 125.

[3] F. W. Taussig, *Principles of Economics* (3d ed.; New York, 1927), I, 13, 78, 184.

[4] Marshall, *op. cit.*, pp. 385, 428.

[5] Cassel, *op. cit.*, pp. 88, 215.

[6] Taussig, *op. cit.*, pp. 113, 329.

"from the definition it follows" and often when it takes the form "if a bank . . . . then. . . . ." The conditional form, however, may cloak a factual generalization. For instance, when Cassel (or his translator) writes, "If a pit has to be dug, the addition of one more man will make little difference to the day's output unless you give the man a spade," this is another way of saying that tools are needed for digging pits efficiently, which is a generalization about technology. On the other hand, statements which appear to be statements of fact often consist of a proposition in logical analysis. "Let us inquire what are the conditions under which . . . . " might introduce either type of proposition; in the one quoted it is the *logical* conditions which are the object of study. So, too, Cassel's proposition about interest, quoted above, is the result of a logical analysis of the implications of "durable goods" and "interest."

The distinction between factual generalization and logical analysis is not carefully drawn in some of the best-known economic treatises. In some cases one feels that the distinction is not appreciated by the writer himself; in other cases, as apparently in the case of Marshall, this method of writing is deliberately adopted in order to keep pure theory close to the real world. When Walras urged Marshall, about 1872, to publish separately his diagrammatic illustrations of economic problems, he declined to do so "because he feared that if separated from all concrete study of actual conditions, they might come to claim a more direct bearing on real problems than they in fact had."[7] Whether the relationship between fact and theory is best conveyed by a continuous amalgam of the two, in a "realistic" treatment, or by a continuous emphasis on the distinction between theoretical propositions and statements of fact is questionable. Some of Marshall's own pupils noted the danger that his method of writing concealed the difficulties of the subject;[8] probably the difficulties are increased by the impression that all his statements are equally true or can be tested by the same methods.

Pantaleoni preferred to make the distinction clear. He wrote:

Every economic theorem may be expressed in the form of a syllogism having as its major or minor premise the hedonic hypothesis, and for its other premise some matter of fact, which may be a truth borrowed from some other science, or ascertained inductively by the economist himself. . . . . The category of premises of fact comprises chiefly the more or less complex technological data utilised by economic science, consisting of mechanical and chemical laws of those bodies which in economics are re-

[7] A. C. Pigou (ed.), *Memorials of Alfred Marshall* (London, 1925), p. 21.

[8] Cf. Keynes on p. 48 and Pigou on p. 86 of the *Memorials*.

garded as commodities, and of the biological, psychological and sociological laws that govern man and other organic beings. The demonstration of the truth of these premises pertains to the science to which they respectively belong. Economic science can only accept them, until they are modified, or their accuracy is impugned, by the science which originated them. . . . . Sometimes economics requires a groundwork of facts which other sciences, owing to their special nature or trend, omit to investigate; in which case it proceeds itself to ascertain these facts by the induction and generalisation of typical data. These researches after premises for economic theorems are however, though often necessary, and always useful, nevertheless mere prolegomena, or even digressions from the economist's point of view. . . . . It is a mistake to give the name of economic laws, as is occasionally done, to some of the premises of which we have been speaking—not that they are untrue, nor that they are not of capital importance to the economist, but because they pertain to other branches of science, or will certainly do so some day.[9]

Marshall recognized the distinction, even if he did not give it prominence, in his systematic exposition of economics. In his inaugural lecture at Cambridge in 1885 he said that economics was "not a body of concrete truth, but an engine for the discovery of concrete truth"[10]— a dictum echoed by Mr. Keynes in his famous description of economics as "a method rather than a doctrine, an apparatus of the mind, a technique of thinking, which helps its possessor to draw concrete conclusions."[11]

This "technique" amounts to the linking-together of observed or hypothetical facts in a logical structure or theory, which exhibits the facts as causally related to one another. Without theory, said Marshall, "the facts by themselves are silent. Observation discovers nothing directly of the actions of causes, but only of sequences in time. . . . . In order to be able with any safety to interpret economic facts, whether of the past or present time, we must know what kind of effect to expect from each cause and how these effects are likely to combine with each other."[12]

Logically considered, the theory consists of the affirmation that certain conditions, or certain actions, are implicit in certain other conditions, usually referred to as "the assumptions" of the theory. These assumptions must contain not only the relevant environmental conditions but also a general principle of behavior or way of reacting to stimuli. Often an economic theory is expounded incompletely, in that certain assumptions which are essential to the argument are taken for granted instead of being explicitly stated. Then, although the stated assumptions

[9] M. Pantaleoni, *Pure Economics* (London, 1898), pp. 3–5.

[10] *Memorials*, p. 159.

[11] Introduction to any of the "Cambridge Economic Handbooks."

[12] *Op. cit.*, pp. 166, 168.

may be accepted, the "conclusions" of the theory may be challenged as "illogical" by those who do not also make the same tacit assumptions. From this it would seem that the claim of theory to "explain" or "interpret" certain facts rests upon the acceptance of all its assumptions, as well as upon the logical impeccability of the argument that leads to the conclusions.

[But] granted the correspondence of its original assumptions and the facts, its conclusions are inevitable and inescapable. . . . . It is this inevitability of economic analysis which gives it very considerable prognostic value. . . . . Given the data in a particular situation, it can draw inevitable conclusions as to their implications. But if the data remain unchanged, these implications will certainly be realised. They must be, for they are implied in the presence of the original data.[13]

Of course, "the changing facts which make prediction in any given situation possible must be discovered by observation, or empirical investigation";[14] but the mere enumeration of facts cannot, unaided, reveal the future. At the same time, if theory is to be useful in the interpretation and prediction of events in the real world, it must be fed on facts.

Theory can sometimes be enriched by the further examination of its present assumptions. If the analytic method is "an instrument for shaking out all the implications of given suppositions,"[15] there is always the possibility that further industrious shaking will produce some additional conclusions. But many developments in theory are due to the investigation of problems posed by a slight or substantial modification of the assumptions. Pantaleoni held that "the advancement of economic science can be furthered only in two ways, *viz:* by the discovery of new premises pregnant with inferences, or by the discovery of new conclusions drawn from known premises."[16] If the new premises are to be realistic, they must be suggested by empirical investigation or observation. "Only close study of the facts is likely to reveal which assumptions are most likely to have a counterpart in reality."[17]

Finally, economic theory can be applied in practice only through the study of *particular* facts. This may sound too obvious to need any emphasis. The point is, however, that even a theory which contains allegedly realistic assumptions rarely supplies the answer to a concrete problem. Each of the assumptions has to be checked against the specific conditions of the time and place; and some may require to be

[13] L. Robbins, *Essay on the Nature and Significance of Economic Science* (2d ed.; London, 1937), p. 122.

[14] *Ibid.*, p. 123.

[15] *Ibid.*, p. 122.

[16] *Op. cit.*, p. 5.

[17] Robbins, *op. cit.*, p. 118.

given concrete content. The existence of a consumer's scale of preferences may be a realistic assumption, but, for the solution of many problems, we need to know which particular commodities the consumer prefers and in what order. The theory of gold flows may be realistic, but in a particular case we need to know the actual cost of gold shipments if we are to determine how far the exchange rate will move under the gold standard. Realistic theory tells us what facts will be significant in relation to a certain problem, but not the form which the facts will take in the particular case.

HOW THEORY GUIDES EMPIRICAL INVESTIGATION

The "method" of economics is not simply to record all sorts of facts and explore their logical implications (treating the facts as the premises of logical analysis). There are too many facts, and the possible implications of all the various combinations of facts which could be selected are too vast to be contemplated. What economic theory claims to do is to single out, from the overwhelming complex of facts, the ones which are worthy of attention. How can it do this?

The method is to construct theoretical "models"—logical constructions in which certain processes (buying and selling, for instance, at a particular price) are shown as the inevitable implications of certain conditions (such as the possession by the traders of certain stocks, their desires to hold different stocks, the availability of market facilities, etc.). The theory is not intended to be a complete replica of the real world with all its complexities, but a simplified model, representing only certain features of the real world which are believed to be important for the problem under consideration. When such a theoretical model has been constructed, it can be "tested." The economist turns to the real world and checks the assumptions and the conclusions of its theory against such facts as can be observed. He begins to feel some confidence in the theory if it "works"; that is, if he finds, in a number of instances, that the conditions which fit in with his assumptions are, in fact, followed, at an appropriate interval, by other conditions or processes which conform to the conclusions of his theory. If the theory works sometimes, but not often, it is possible either that it is too simple or that it is definitely "unrealistic." It may be possible to improve it by including additional assumptions or by replacing some assumptions by others or, again, by working out some further implications which had been previously overlooked. Since any theory must abstract from some of the conditions of the real world, if it is not to be a complete replica, there is always the danger that some significant factor may be left out of our analysls. "The conditions from which we abstract," wrote Wicksell, "must be relatively unessential, at least as regards the question under discussion. It is not always possible to decide in advance whether the conditions from which we abstract are essential or not."[18] Only experience in the application of theories can show whether or not we have been guilty of oversimplification in our theoretical construction.

With a well-tested theory to guide us, we can take up new problems —either the interpretation of past events or the prediction of the future. Our theory suggests that certain events (say, a fall in prices) will be produced if certain conditions are present (say, technical progress) but that the tendency will be checked if other conditions are also present (such as monopolistic organization of industry). We therefore turn to the facts, to see which, if any, of these various conditions are present. Other facts which have no place in our theoretical scheme we ignore; those that are represented as significant by our theory we classify according to the direction in which they are supposed to work. From the inspection of these facts, arranged within the framework of our theory, we decide what developments are to be expected, that is, what facts will correspond, in practice, with the conclusions of the theory. This may involve a large degree of judgment, particularly if the theory represents the events as the outcome of opposing forces, which have to be balanced one against the other. If the economist can provide a common measure by which to estimate the relative strength of opposing forces in a concrete instance, the scope for personal judgment is accordingly reduced. But, whether the final conclusion can be reduced to arithmetic or must contain a considerable element of opinion, the preliminary work of sorting the facts into relevant and irrelevant and the classification of the former under the headings suggested by the theory are essential parts of the scientific study of concrete problems. Without a theory to guide us, the same work of classification would be necessary, but it would be interminable, because it would have to proceed by trial and error.

Even the practical man usually has some theory in his mind when he approaches a new problem. This preformed theory or conceptual scheme may have been formed subconsciously in the course of past experience, or it may be the result of the systematic study of some particular technique.

---

[18] K. Wicksell, *Lectures on Political Economy* (New York, 1934), I, 10.

This point may be illustrated by analogies from other specialties. A mechanic may be confronted by a motorcar of a make that he has never before encountered. But his knowledge of the general features of motor engines in general provides him with a method of procedure when he sets out to discover the cause of engine failure in this case. So, too, a physician can, within certain limits, diagnose the disease of a new patient, by gradually eliminating the irrelevant and concentrating upon the significant symptoms. But this is possible only because the mechanic and the physician already possess their conceptual scheme of the various factors which might be involved. In dealing with a concrete problem they must investigate the facts, but it is their theoretical knowledge which shows them what facts to look for. Their conceptual scheme of cause and effect may have been built up by empirical study (practical experience) to a greater degree than is true in the case of many economists, but it is, nevertheless, the possession of this theory which facilitates the analysis of the new situation. No amount of practical experience will serve this purpose unless it leads to the formulation of a conceptual scheme, and some useful conceptual schemes can be taught with little recourse to experience other than for illustrative purposes.

The same point may be put by comparing economic theory to a map of an extensive territory. No map can be complete; if it included everything it would be useless, for it would be a full-scale replica of the area covered. The economist's map is drawn in an attempt to pick out the features which are significant for the particular type of problem which economists have traditionally discussed and leaves out, like Mr. Horrabin's political maps,[19] all the features which are considered to be of little significance for the purpose in view. To approach the same problems with no conceptual scheme at all is equivalent to exploring an entirely unknown terrain. To approach them with only the conceptual scheme of a lawyer or accountant is like using a map designed for another purpose. A map which shows only the contours will facilitate the location of rivers but is a poor substitute for a map with the rivers plainly marked.

The diagnostic or direction-finding function of economic theory is apparent in such a practical problem as that of deciding whether a particular industry is monopolistic or competitive. If this problem is tackled severally by a lawyer without any knowledge of economic the-

[19] J. F. Horrabin, *An Atlas of Current Affairs* (New York, 1940); *An Atlas of European History* (New York, 1935); etc.

ory and by a trained economist, we know from experience that they are likely to arrive at different conclusions. The explanation of this is that they have conceived the issues differently and have applied different conceptual schemes. If there is more than one firm, the lawyer discovers monopoly only when there is proof of overt acts calculated to operate "in restraint of trade"; "the law does not make mere size an offence"; the fact that small firms accept the price leadership of a large firm does not constitute legal proof that the latter is exercising monopoly power. Consequently, the lawyer looks primarily for overt acts of the type indicated. The records of American cases under the antitrust laws and of cases before the British courts, as well as the reports of various select committees and royal commissions, show the legal mind twisting and turning in an effort to find a clear and unambiguous application of terms on the basis of their traditional legal interpretation and often arriving at conclusions which shock common sense and appear ridiculous to the economist.

Is competition restricted by the emergence of a few large firms? Is price discrimination monopolistic? Do trading associations with price-maintenance agreements limit competition? To questions such as these economic theory can give clear and definite answers, after defining such terms as "monopoly" and "competition." Economic theory shows that the terms cover a large number of different "market situations," the implications of which differ considerably. It lays down the characteristics (definition) of each market situation and provides a map which shows us *what to look for*, in a particular industry, in our attempts to determine the market situation and its consequences. While the jurist also has his map, with some points in common with the economist's map, it does not include all the data which are essential to this problem.

Two further examples will serve to illustrate the function of theory in indicating what facts are relevant to a particular problem. What will be the effect upon prices of an expansion of public works financed out of central bank credit? In the first place, the effects of the credit expansion upon the policy of the other banks must be estimated, and economic theory indicates the factors which might determine this: e.g., the conventional reserve ratios of the banks and their liquidity prior to the expansion, the clearing practices, the speed with which money passes from cash circulation to credit balances, and the expectation of future stability or instability. Next, account must be taken of the degree of unemployment and the availability of other resources to permit an increase in output of goods in response to the increased expenditure of money. Nor can we ignore the question of the stability of the foreign exchanges. That each of these points must be studied is clear from the pure theory of money and prices. A student of facts who is ignorant of this theory might easily omit one or more of the relevant factors; or, if his inquiry is complete and exhaustive, he might reach the important factors very much later than if he accepted the guidance of theory. In economic policy, decisions have to be made, and time is often the essence of the contract.

What will be the probable yield of an increase of 10 per cent ad valorem in all import duties? The practical man will allow for *some* decline in total imports, when making an estimate; but economic theory indicates several specific factual inquiries which should be made if the magnitude of the decline in imports is to be assessed in advance. In the first place, what imports are meeting competition from local production with a price difference not exceeding 10 per cent? What are the possibilities of expanding production in the local industries and what increase in cost will this involve? To what extent will consumers turn to other articles rather than pay the higher price of imports or local substitutes? If imports are to decline seriously in the first instance, what effects will this have upon exchange rates or monetary conditions and how will that affect imports? Behind each of these questions is a host of others. Admittedly, economic theory produces a "monstrous brood of hypotheses such as might well alarm some Malthus of the speculative world,"[20] let alone the empirical investigator whose task it is to verify them. Some of the queries noted above prove to be very difficult to answer even roughly. But this practical obstacle to realistic economics does not diminish the utility of knowing what questions to ask. It is only by asking that we learn the limits of our knowledge. Practical politics may often not be able to wait for the scientific elaboration of hypothesis and sifting of the facts. This means that policy must often be based on rough judgment rather than on scientific knowledge. The economist's task, in this regard, is to attempt to increase the use of the latter, and this can be achieved only gradually by persistent advance along all the channels of scientific method.

THEORY AS CLASSIFICATION

In these concrete examples the chief function of economic theory emerges as the *classification* of the observable facts according to a sig-

[20] B. Wootton, *Lament for Economics* (London, 1938), p. 65.

nificant scheme. This point may not be apparent from an inspection of economic theory, for it appears to consist of models of *processes* rather than lists of categories within which specific facts are to be arranged. Consider, for instance, the analytic determination of output and price by the intersection of two curves. Here the theory presents an exact result in quantitative terms and shows how this result is produced by definite operations in the market. This does not at first glance suggest that economic theory is mainly a classification of possible happenings, each of which must be explored empirically.

But, when we attempt to predict the output and price of a particular commodity, the intersecting curves are not of much use. The difficulty is that we do not know what the position of the curves will be at the time to which our prediction must refer. For a few commodities demand curves have been statistically "derived" from data relating to a number of years. The most that can be claimed for such "empirical" curves, however, is that they indicate within extremely broad limits the slope which the demand curve had over the period under examination. Even if we are prepared to project these conditions into the future, the margin of tolerance must be very wide. While such empirical curves may be of help in the case of certain commodities, the prediction of output and price must still proceed by a preliminary classification of the possible causes of a movement one way or the other and an individual estimate of the absence or presence (and in this case the strength) of each factor which might contribute to the final result. The classification is provided by the economist's analysis of the factors behind supply and the factors behind demand. This enables us to ignore a host of observable facts as irrelevant and to sort out those that are relevant, according to the influence they may exercise on supply or demand and so upon price.

This does not mean that economic theory consists merely of a list of headings, under which facts can be arranged. Its categories are *significant* only because they are derived from theoretical models of processes similar to those that cause things to happen in the real world. But the processes which theory exposes are described in very general terms, which abstract from the particular form which the conditions may assume in particular cases. The particular form of the conditions must be specifically identified in the analysis of a concrete problem. In this descent from generalities to particulars, which constitutes the application of theory to practice, the role of theory inevitably appears as the provision of a significant list of *things to look for*. This must be borne in mind when we attempt to extend economic theory to include certain processes which at present find no place in its analysis.

THEORY AS TAUTOLOGY

Having discussed the positive function of economic theory as an aid to the study of concrete problems, we may now turn to its limitations. There is one alleged weakness of theory which needs only brief mention, that is, its tautological nature. Pure theory consists in the analysis of selected premises to arrive at the inferences implied in such premises. Nevertheless, it adds to our knowledge for practical purposes since, until the implications of given premises are recognized, they cannot be made the conscious bases of action.

Theoretical analysis thus compensates us, in a certain way, for the fact that our brains are not all-powerful. With all-powerful brains we would need no pure theory to work out the relations and implications of our definitions or empirical premises. We would just have a dictionary in which all our concepts—"perfect competition," "monopoly," "saving," etc.—were clearly defined and after reading it through would perceive at one glance all the most subtle interrelations [and conclusions of economic theory].[21]

Mr. R. F. Harrod lists among the possible contributions of the student of methodology that "he may show that propositions usually deemed to constitute constructive knowledge do not in fact do so, but consist essentially of definitions of the terms employed."[22] One's thoughts immediately turn to the savings-investment controversy of recent years. But "constructive knowledge" is a matter of degree. All pure theories consist in part in the elaboration of the terms employed; this becomes useful or constructive whenever it throws a clearer light upon the object of study.

REQUIREMENTS OF REALISTIC ECONOMICS

The test that we must apply to economic theory, therefore, is not whether its results are contained in its premises but whether it is a serviceable instrument in the study of concrete problems along the lines indicated earlier in this chapter—whether the facts which it rejects as irrelevant are, in fact, insignificant, and those that it selects, important. We have already noted Wicksell's admission that one cannot be sure in advance that one is abstracting only from the unimportant. There is also the danger that, if we misread any of the facts which we

[21] T. W. Hutchinson, *The Significance and Basic Postulates of Economic Theory* (London, 1938), p. 35.

[22] "Scope and Method of Economics," *Economic Journal*, September, 1938, p. 385.

do regard as important, this is liable to cause not only the misinterpretation of the facts we do consider but also the neglect of other facts which really are material to our problem. From this viewpoint the chief criticisms that can be made of present economic theory are its frequent use of frankly unrealistic assumptions and its habitual abstraction from elements which are obviously part and parcel of economic life, as the term is usually understood.

Both these criticisms will be considered at greater length in the following chapters. It will be conceded, for instance, that present-day economics suffers from "theoretic blight," that is, from a tendency to develop theory for its own sake, even if this involves using unrealistic postulates and an increasing remoteness from the real world. It will be argued that the extent of "theoretic blight" is greater than many economists believe and that, if economics is to be more widely used in practical affairs, the more parasitic sections of theory must be replaced by something in less conflict with everyday experience. Unless this is done, economic theory cannot be used to classify the facts into significant and irrelevant, let alone to weigh the importance of those that are selected as significant.

One matter in which economists have long been dodging the shafts loosed by other social scientists is the psychological assumptions of economics. In this connection, too, the practical application of economics demands a revision of our rather primitive theory of motivation, in place of the shrug of the shoulders which is the usual reply of the economist to psychological criticisms. The economist has always felt at a loss to know what to do about it, even though he might admit that his psychological postulates were not always realistic. Fortunately, the case is less hopeless than might appear, and some suggestions will be made as to the way in which the theory of economic behavior can be made more useful.

These weaknesses limit the applicability of economic theory in the sense that its conclusions may be, on occasion, misleading, even if all the things not amenable to economic analysis can be correctly estimated. But there remains the question as to whether economic theory can be extended, along the lines suggested in chapter i, to interpret some of the types of behavior which find no place in its categories and also to facilitate the prediction of changes in the conditions which present theory takes as given. This can best be tested by examining the chapters devoted to these proposed extensions. But two points may be noted here.

The first point arises from our stress on the function of economic theory to guide us in our search for significant facts. In view of the necessity to use economic theory primarily as a basis for classifying observed facts, it is apparent that this also is the chief use to which a theory of economic development and a theory which goes beyond the market will be put. The theories must contain a sufficiently clear model of the processes involved in order to add conviction that the resulting classification of the facts will be significant; but the status and utility of these theories will not depend upon the complexity of the formal logical structure which may be developed out of their assumptions. The second point is the possibility of adding to economic theory in this way without altering its nature. There is no question that these new theories involve an enlargement of the scope of economic theory; but will it still be economic theory?[23] Our discussion of economic theory has concentrated on the aid it lends to the study of facts; we have not considered what marks economic theory off from other sciences.

THE PROBLEM OF DEFINITION

The distinction cannot be made in terms of method, despite the famous doctrine of Mr. Keynes that economics is a method rather than a doctrine. Other sciences use conceptual schemes to aid the study of observed facts, although some of them enjoy superior methods of isolating, for examination, the facts which are suspected of being significant. The theoretical schemes may be more prominent in the sciences which do not lend themselves so readily to experiment and which are concerned with facts that are likely to alter from one observation to the next. But even in the physical and biological sciences, with their accumulated masses of constant facts—many of them accurately measured as well as carefully described—the facts must be fitted into an orderly scheme and interpreted by a theoretical (or logical) structure. And progress is made in all sciences, not only by the observation of facts which, because they do not fit into existing theories, constitute a challenge to further investigation but also by the verification of hypotheses, conceived by the theoretical elaboration of the implications of certain assumptions.

[23] This point has been raised by several readers of an earlier draft of this work, in which the author, in his eagerness to enlarge the theoretical schemes at the disposal of the practical economist, ignored the question of definition altogether. These readers were accordingly left in doubt as to the author's "conception of economics." Since failure to satisfy the reader on this point may prejudice his willingness to consider these new theories primarily in terms of their practical utility, it seems necessary to say something about the definition of economics at this stage.

Can the economist claim any special technique in the construction of his own theoretical scheme? "Economics has no method of investigation peculiar to itself, i.e., *no logical methods of its own*," wrote Pantaleoni. "There is not a single species of logical argumentation that may not, in some instance, be turned to account."[24] Pantaleoni, noting that economics appears to deal with phenomena "contemplated at least incidentally by a hundred other sciences and technical arts," found a distinction, however, in the economist's choice of assumptions. Economics "either recognises in these processes (connected with wealth) the realisation of the hedonic hypothesis, or supposes that they take place under the operation of the hedonic postulate."[25] Embarrassed by the identification of economics with a now outmoded school of psychology, modern economists assert that economic theory has no need of the hedonic postulate; but, nevertheless, a somewhat similar assumption is introduced. Professor Pigou tells us that "the task of positive economics is to display the structure and working of the economic cosmos as an outgrowth of the principle" of maximization, which is defined as "so acting that a more keen desire is always followed in preference to a less keen one, and that, when a desire can only be satisfied at the expense of undergoing an aversion, it will be followed or not according as it or the aversion is the keener."[26] Again, Professor Knight writes that "economic theory deals with . . . . the use of resources or means in such a way as to secure the maximum degree permitted by the means available to any economizing subject, the promotion of whatever interests he may be trying to promote."[27] This problem of maximization presents itself only when our means are "scarce" relatively to our various desires; and our desires are therefore brought into competition with one another. Economy, or maximization, is, therefore, a form "assumed by human behaviour in disposing of scarce means";[28] and "economic analysis turns out to be the elucidation of the implications of choice in various assumed circumstances."[29]

[24] *Op. cit.*, p. 7.

[25] *Ibid.*

[26] A. C. Pigou, *Economics of Stationary States* (London, 1935), p. 4.

[27] F. H. Knight, "Professor Parsons on Economic Motivation," *Canadian Journal of Economics and Political Science*, August, 1940, p. 462.

[28] Robbins, *op. cit.*, p. 15.

[29] *Ibid.*, p. 83, quoting F. A. Fetter, *Economic Principles* (New York, 1922), pp. ix and 12–21.

The great discovery of economic theory is that the maximum effect will be achieved from given resources when they are arranged in such a way that any substitution of a small unit of one type of resources for a small unit of another would reduce the total effect. From this it follows that, in so far as individuals watch the "marginal" uses to which they put their resources and make the necessary adjustments whenever marginal substitution promises an increase in satisfaction, they will achieve the maximum satisfaction that is consistent with their limited resources and competing desires. If we accept the empirical generalization that persons who are confronted with the necessity for choice do, in fact, proceed by the principles of substitution, the elaboration of their implications becomes a method of predicting human behavior. In a particular instance, of course, we need to know not only whether they do proceed by these principles but also what particular ends they desire to achieve and what alternative courses of action are open to them. The assumptions which economists habitually make about these matters will be considered in chapter v.

The range of economic analysis, if this definition be accepted, is extremely wide. This conception of economics, as Professor Robbins reminds us, "does not attempt to pick out certain *kinds* of behaviour, but focusses attention on a particular *aspect* of behaviour, the form imposed by the influence of scarcity. It follows, therefore, that in so far as it presents this aspect, any kind of human behaviour falls within the scope of economic generalisations."[30] But reflection suggests that "scarcity of means to satisfy ends of varying importance is an almost ubiquitous condition of human behaviour,"[31] and it would appear that economics is as wide as life itself. Indeed, Wicksteed claimed that the maximum principle "is not exclusively applicable to industrial or commercial affairs, but runs as a universal and vital force through the administration of all our resources."[32] This observation has been carried to its logical conclusion by Mr. A. MacFie, by showing the importance of "economy" in literature, art, and morals.[33] Professor Knight, on the other hand, has argued that "there can be no mathematical formula for maximum performance in connection with such values as victory or vengeance, beauty, morality, adventure, love, sport, conversation,

---

[30] *Op. cit.*, p. 17.

[31] *Ibid.*, p. 14.

[32] P. H. Wicksteed, *Commonsense of Political Economy* (London, 1933), Book I, p. 3.

[33] *An Essay on Economy and Value* (London, 1936); there is also a similar problem of economy in warfare (cf. E. R. Walker, "War Economy," *Economic Record*, June, 1940, p. 1).

family life, social success, or most of the things that people really care about."[34] Here is matter for extensive debate.

It is significant, however, that hardly any economists display the slightest interest in this wider issue. Economists *do* confine their analysis of the implications of choice to its manifestation in industrial, commercial, and financial matters, even though this limitation is not imposed by the definition we have been considering. Although the definition is based on the notion of scarcity, it would appear that economics is not concerned with all cases of scarcity; either certain ends are excluded from consideration, or certain resources and courses of action are ignored. This affects both the choice of assumptions and the directions in which implications are developed. One thing that distinguishes economics from other social sciences is that the assumed "scales of preferences" do not indicate gentlemen's preference for blondes or the voters' aversion to avowedly clever men. Another is that when the economist studies, say, the effects of currency inflation, such as took place after 1918, he ignores the question of whether some individuals will be driven to suicide and others demoralized by a sudden access of wealth. In some circumstances the implications of the necessity for choice may be stealing or insanity. But conclusions of this type are not regarded as falling within the scope of economics, even if they can be fitted in under the famous "scarcity" definition.

The limitation upon the scope of economic theory is traditional. The economist may study the psychology of choice, but in the past it has been choice in industrial, commercial, and financial matters that interested him. And such is the force of habit that economics is still primarily concerned with these things. But even within this field, only certain kinds of behavior have been made the subject of theoretical schemes by the economist, namely, those that take place in the market: the processes of exchange. This limitation is achieved by assuming, for the purpose of theoretical analysis, that the alternative uses of resources and the alternative courses of action all lie inside the market. The result is that, although economic theory analyzes the implications of tariffs and combinations and transfers of wealth by state action, it does not provide a theoretical scheme to explain the emergence of these data, even if they are due to deliberate human choice under the impulse to maximize certain ends. Consequently, as we have already

[34] F. H. Knight, "Economic Science in Recent Discussion," *American Economic Review*, June, 1934, p. 236.

seen, economic theory is often unrealistic, even within the field of industry, commerce, and finance.

Professor Robbins has argued that, once the stage has been reached where the identity of the problems underlying separate economic inquiries can be detected, the formulation of a definition serves to indicate the problems that remain to be solved.[35] If this identity is found in the need for choice, the gaps to be filled are enormous. From the practical point of view, there is no doubt regarding the need to extend our understanding of behavior in industry, commerce, and finance; the only question is whether "the elucidation of the necessity of choice in various circumstances" can throw light upon actions which have previously been estimated by common sense but not studied by economic theory. Our discussion suggests that in order to bring them within the scope of economic theory it is necessary only to widen the range of the permissible assumptions, and that this does not alter the nature of the science. The value of these extensions can then be judged on their performance. From a methodological point of view, at least, they will be irreproachable.

[35] *Op. cit.*, p. 3. But Professor Robbins might not approve the conclusion drawn from this statement.

CHAPTER IV

THEORETIC BLIGHT

WE HAVE seen that economic theory—that "engine for the discovery of concrete truth"—works by the construction of logical systems, based on assumptions which are held to be significant for the problem on hand. It is not likely to be of use in the discovery of concrete truth if there are logical flaws in the structure of the theory or if the assumptions of the theory are in flagrant conflict with the observed facts of the real world. But the theory must always be simpler than the real world, and, as Wicksell noted, this entails the danger that it may abstract from what is essential as well as from what is insignificant in relation to a particular concrete problem. "There is scarcely any limit," wrote Marshall, "to the developments of economic theory which are possible; but of those which are possible only a small part are useful in having a direct relation to practical issues. Ricardo, who added more to the theory than anyone else, was not fortunate in his choice of cases to be worked out in detail."[1]

To what extent is it a matter of luck as to which cases are worked out in detail? Is there any method which will guide us in our choice of assumptions? It may well be argued that it is this part of economics which gives the greatest scope to genius, to those intuitive flights of constructive imagination which are denied to most people. There is always the possibility of improving a complicated logical argument; and there is room for ingenuity in the perfection of observational techniques to verify particular assumptions about the real world. Originality makes its presence felt in these fields, too. But it is the brilliant hypothesis, giving new prominence to hitherto neglected facts or assumptions that marks out the genius from the competent economist. Of course, genius is sometimes wrong; and, on the other hand, mere competent practitioners occasionally enjoy a brief moment of insight which lifts their work on a particular problem out of mediocrity—the distinction between genius and competence is a matter of degree. It is desirable, on the one hand, to enable the general run of economists to produce bright ideas more frequently and, on the other hand, to facili-

---

[1] A. Marshall, "The Present Position of Economics [1885]," in A. C. Pigou (ed.), *Memorials of Alfred Marshall* (London, 1925), p. 162.

tate their rapid evaluation of the dazzling but sometimes sterile contributions of brilliant theorists. An economist concerned with the formulation of policy has so difficult a task that he cannot afford to dispense with any assistance that may be provided by new theoretical analyses; but he cannot leave it to subsequent experience to show whether the intuition of the theorist has guided him aright or led him astray in the selection of certain elements of a problem as the significant ones for analysis. It would be useful to have at least some working rules or tests of validity to apply to the choice of assumptions which purport to contain the important features of a problem, just as we have statistical methods to aid us in testing particular assumptions by observation of the real world and the rules of logic to guide our analysis of the particular assumptions we have adopted.

THE MEANING OF THEORETIC BLIGHT

There is one test which the practical man applies to all economic theory, namely, that it must not leave familiar features of the concrete world out of account altogether or definitely misrepresent them. One does not expect that theory should attach significance to the various features of the real world according to their prominence to the superficial observer, for "it is not the purpose of science to describe the obvious in elaborate terms."[2] The only function of economic theory is to show the causal significance of less obvious factors which are not of apparent importance. "That which is not seen is often better worth studying than that which is seen."[3] But it is difficult to believe that the economist has put his finger on the clue to a problem if his analysis does not admit the possibility of events being influenced by the concrete conditions which stare him in the face. For instance, if an Australian economist were asked to advise on the probability of a rise in the wage rates for unskilled labor, a discussion of the prospects of an increase in the marginal productivity of unskilled labor, without any reference to the existence of the Commonwealth Arbitration Court, would earn and merit the ridicule of the practical man. In the privacy of his study the economist may examine frankly unrealistic cases in order to discover the significance of a particular element in a wider problem, "all other things being equal"; but in the real world where other things do not remain the same that particular element may have

[2] K. Wicksell, *Lectures on Political Economy* (London, 1934), I, 19.

[3] A. Marshall, *Principles of Economics* (8th ed.; London, 1922), p. 778.

a different significance. It is not merely the fear of ridicule that should prevent the exhibition of such analyses as contributions to the solution of "economic problems."

Yet economists do expose themselves to criticism in this respect. To many people this is just what the term "academic" conveys: a preoccupation with problems from which the most obvious and most challenging features of the real world have been abstracted. But this would seem to be a fault against which the economist could easily guard. We may have no general rules to determine in advance whether the obscure elements of the situation, which a new and untried theory represents as the really important ones, are, in fact, significant; but there should be little difficulty in deciding whether a theory takes account of all the facts which are prima facie relevant.

The fault is sometimes in the formulation of theory and would be corrected if the assumptions were set out more explicitly. In how many expositions of the theory of marginal productivity is there a list of all the conditions which must be fulfilled if wages are to be equal to marginal productivity? If this is done, the inapplicability of the theory at certain phases of the trade cycle becomes obvious.[4] Unstated assumptions may exclude prominent facts from analysis by denying their existence. Re-examination of a theory to make all its assumptions clear may therefore be an essential preliminary to determining whether it does ignore the obvious. But there are too many cases where this re-examination is not necessary.

Why do economists often persist with the elaboration of theories which are patently out of touch with reality? Is it because they believe, with Professor Whitehead, that "in our most theoretical moods we may be nearest to our most practical applications"?[5] Or is it because they love theory for its own sake and desire to facilitate its growth in extent and beauty? If, as Mrs. Robinson says, "the subject matter of economics is neither more or less than its own technique,"[6] there is a temptation to select problems to which the technique is suited and to protect the beautiful "engine" of economic theory against the hard facts which might dull its cutting edge. This type of narcissism has exercised too great an influence over the development of economics in recent years, despite Marshall's warning to be on our guard "lest we

[4] See below.

[5] A. N. Whitehead, *Introduction to Mathematics* (New York, 1911), p. 100, quoted by A. C. Pigou, *Economics of Welfare* (3d ed.; London, 1929), p. 5.

[6] Joan Robinson, *Economics Is a Serious Subject* (Cambridge, 1932), p. 4.

should fall tacitly into the fallacy of regarding what is tractable to our intellectual machinery as equivalent to what is important."[7]

This development of economics under the impulse of theoretic construction, for its own sake, along paths which become ever more remote from the real world, is best described by the term "theoretic blight." From the point of view of one who desires to use economics for the discovery of concrete truth, theories that build on incredible postulates seem a parasitic growth. All this has been said before by "practical" critics. But many economists do not realize how much of economic theory is open to such criticism. An attempt is made in this chapter to illustrate the extent of theoretic blight in modern economics.

CAUSES OF THEORETIC BLIGHT

But first let us consider the process by which it gains a hold. Since the economist's method is to begin with the examination of simple cases and to approach the real world by a series of successive approximations, the temptation to select tractable cases is strong. Wicksell writes:

It may even happen that we must deliberately ignore conditions which are of themselves of the greatest importance, because the problem in question is of so complex a nature that it cannot be rationally treated in any other way. . . . . In all these cases the results are, of course, not even approximately correct; though inquiry is not, on that account, valueless. They constitute rather a necessary *element* in the full and correct solution of the problem under discussion, and are, therefore, to be regarded as useful work, even if it should sometimes prove impossible, for the moment, to complete the reasoning by the inclusion of other factors hitherto omitted.[8]

Wicksell quotes "parallel cases" from the natural sciences, such as "Newton's discovery of the speed of light through the atmosphere, which differed from the actual result by about one third, because the heating of the air under pressure had not been taken into account." Now economists cannot be superior about an error of only one-third in a quantitative estimate. But there is no knowing how large the error due to the omission of certain factors may be. Moreover, the method of successive approximations holds special dangers for the biological and psychological sciences. Where we are dealing with complex living matter, a change in certain conditions may cause a great change in behavior. In moving from a simple hypothetical case to the real world, we may need not merely to complete and correct our conclusions in detail but, instead, may have to recognize entirely different

[7] Quoted by Pigou, *Memorials*, pp. 84–85.
[8] *Op. cit.*, I, 10.

conclusions.[9] If there is reason to believe that successive approximations will lead to an entirely different view of the problem, a first approximation, made by abstracting from elements believed to be important, could only be a dangerous guide to practice.

Economists who are not concerned with practical affairs may take a
more complacent view of first approximations and may consider time
well spent in the elaboration of theories that are remote from reality,
patiently waiting for the day when the approach to the world of concrete facts will be less difficult.

> The two questions which can be asked of a set of assumptions in economics are
> these: Are they tractable? and: Do they correspond with the real world? The first
> question can only be answered by the application of analytical technique to the as-
> sumptions. Some sets of assumptions are too complicated to be managed by the tech-
> nique now at our disposal. But a set of assumptions that is manageable is likely to be
> unreal. . . . . The choice between manageable and realistic assumptions is one of tem-
> perament, not of opinion.

To the criticism that an assumption is unrealistic, "the economist who
has made it must answer: I know very well that the world to which
my technique applies is not the real world, but . . . . when I have got
well used to using my two-dimensional technique I will try to evolve
a three-dimensional or an n-dimensional technique which will be
capable of solving the problems which arise on your assumptions."
This view Mrs. Robinson describes as the optimistic view; the optimistic economists "must get all the results which are just as complicated
but no more complicated, than their technique can produce, hoping
gradually to build up a more and more complicated technique as time
goes by." This view is contrasted with that of the "pessimistic, methodological, Continental economist," who "prefers sitting at the apex
of a pyramid of completely self-consistent, realistic, but intractable assumptions to solving unrealistic problems."[10] The contrast is, however, false. It is not that the complexity of realistic assumptions makes
them intractable but that they are in conflict with the asumptions used
in some of the established theories and, if admitted to the economist's
system, must destroy those theories. The best method of "building up
a more and more complicated technique" is not by solving as many
(unreal) problems as possible with the existing technique but to study
new, and preferably realistic, problems with a view to seeing what

---

[9] This was not altogether Marshall's view. "When we know the action of two economic
forces separately we can predict fairly well their conjoint action." But he accused Mill of
exaggerating the extent to which this can be done (cf. *Principles*, p. 771 and n.).

[10] Robinson, *op. cit.*, pp. 6–9.

changes should be made in the economist's technique. This task will be assisted by the frank recognition of theoretic blight wherever it is encountered.

Theoretic blight may be caused not only by the desire to expand economic theory in those directions to which existing technique is suited, despite their remoteness from reality, but also by admiration of the aesthetic qualities of the conceptual schemes which can be built up from unrealistic premises. It is not only in reaction from contact with the confused thinking of the layman that economists "run back to find peace and contentment in neat equations and elegant equilibria."[11] There is positive satisfaction in symmetry, where it is discoverable, in the analysis of supply and demand, import duties and export duties, wage increases and wage decreases. The aesthetic sense may even inspire a dream to remake the real world in the image of theory, instead of adapting theory to the ugly facts of the real world. Dr. Benham, in writing of Britain's departure from the gold standard in 1931, acknowledges this tendency as a possible source of bias:

> As an economist, I have learnt to love the way a flexible economic system, in which prices and wages are quite free to move and the quantity of money is fixed, automatically responds to changed conditions, to changes in consumers' wants, in methods of production and in factors external to man, such as good or bad seasons. I resent all attempts to hamper and distort the smooth working of this system by keeping particular prices and wages, or prices in general and wages in general, at a higher level than the free play of supply and demand would bring about; I resent opposition to more efficient methods or restriction of the free flow of migration and investment. I suppose I resent all this partly because I would like the real world to correspond more closely to the beautifully-working imaginary world, without "economic friction," which economists describe and explain as a "first approximation." Thus I naturally want greater flexibility. . . . . All the same, I have tried to discount my own bias.[12]

It is refreshing to meet an economist so conscious of this bias; it runs, unacknowledged, through the writings of many.[13]

USEFUL THEORIES FIRST

We may now illustrate the problem of selecting cases for analysis, that is, deciding which combination of assumptions is likely to provide a theory that will prove to be significant in relation to a concrete prob-

[11] E. Cannan, "The Need for Simpler Economics," *Economic Journal*, September, 1933, p. 379.

[12] Frederic Benham, *Go Back to Gold* ("Criterion Miscellanies," No. 35 [London, 1931]), p. 6.

[13] In an unpublished dissertation, "Notes on Some Selected Aspects of Economic Science" (manuscript in Fisher Library, University of Sydney), H. D. Black gives many examples and concludes that "a craving for symmetry together with the practice of mere formal abstraction are likely to hide more truths than they serve to discover."

lem. Reference has already been made to the diagnostic value of the theory of "market situations." Earlier writers distinguished only two market situations, namely, competition and monopoly, and elaborated a theory to deal with each. Subsequently, it was recognized that duopoly presents special problems, and a separate theory (or group of conflicting theories) emerged as a result of attempts to deal with these problems. We have also had theories of "bi-lateral monopoly" and "partial monopoly." More recently it has been recognized that a great proportion of the facts of real life can be explained only by a new group of theories dealing with "monopolistic competition" and "im-

TABLE I

TYPES OF MARKET SITUATION

NUMBER AND SIZE OF SELLER	NUMBER AND SIZE OF BUYER				
	One Large; No Small	One Large; One or More Small	Two or More Large; No Small	Two or More Large; One or More Small	Many Small
One large; no small.....	1	2	3	4	5
One large; one or more small..............	6	7	8	9	10
Two or more large; no small..............	11	12	13	14	15
Two or more large; one or more small..........	16	17	18	19	20
Many small..........	21	22	23	24	25

perfect competition." There has been some unprofitable discussion as to the most appropriate definitions of these terms. The important thing, however, is the recognition of the possibility of distinguishing between a considerable number of market situations; how each is to be christened is of secondary interest. One or two attempts at classification of the various possible situations have been published,[14] but none has done full justice to the great range of possible combinations. Table 1 has been used in lectures by the author; it provides a salutary lesson to the student in the limitations of existing theory.

The situations may differ with respect to the buying side and the selling side. It is assumed in Table 1 that there is no discrimination on

[14] Leonhard Miksch, *Wettbewerb als Aufgabe* (Stuttgart, 1937); also Fritz Machlup, "Monopoly and Competition: A Classification," *American Economic Review*, September, 1937.

either side of the market, that is, no product differentiation or preference by buyers for certain sources of supply and no discrimination by
sellers as between different buyers or groups of buyers. Along the top
line are indicated five different situations on the buying side, distinguished according to the number of buyers and their size. Down the
left-hand column are indicated five situations on the selling side, distinguished according to the same principle. A large buyer or seller is
one who constitutes so great a proportion of the market that he can
exercise some control over price by varying his purchases or sales. A
small buyer or seller is so small that his influence upon price is negligible. The line between large and small will be drawn differently in different industries, according to the elasticity of supply and demand.[15]

The five different situations on either side of the market might conceivably be combined with any of the five situations on the other side.
This gives twenty-five different combinations. The numbers in the
table may be attached to the buying and selling situations indicated
at the top of the vertical column and the beginning of the horizontal
column in which the number is placed. For instance, Market Situation No. 1 is that with one buyer confronting one seller, both necessarily "large" in relation to the market. In No. 5 many small buyers
confront one large seller. In No. 21 one large buyer confronts many
small sellers. The reader will recognize some of these situations, to
which names have been given:

No. 1......Bilateral monopoly
No. 5......Monopoly
No. 10......Partial monopoly
No. 15......Oligopoly (or, when there are only two sellers, duopoly)
No. 21......Monopsony
No. 25......Pure competition (or polypoly)

It is surely only a matter of time before No. 23 is christened "oli-
gopsony." Only in No. 1 does the conventional name refer to both
sides of the market; in No. 21 it refers to the buying side, but the theory assumes many small sellers; in the other cases the name refers to
the selling side, but the theory assumes many small buyers. To the
knowledge of the author, only the six named situations have been
made the subject of theories; economic "technique" has not yet been
applied to the other nineteen. It is only reasonable to assume that
there are twenty-five different situations, possible in practice and sig-

[15] Cf. my article, "Limited Competition," *Economic Record* (Melbourne), December,
1934.

nificant in their differences. On the selling side four different situations have been shown to be significant by the theories developed to explore their implications. No theory has yet been published for the combination which might be described as "partial oligopoly," in which the selling side of the market consists of several large sellers and one or more small sellers, but there is every reason to regard this situation as distinct from the others. On the buying side, published theories still distinguish between only monopsony and competition—one buyer and many—but one may expect that the peculiarities of intermediate cases on the selling side will have their counterparts on the buying side. This is a case in which the desire for symmetry indicates an avenue in which theory might be developed. But there is no conflict with reality, for nobody can deny that these buying situations may well exist. We may, therefore, make our scheme symmetrical, though it does not follow that the theories should be developed symmetrically. Already we have theories for No. 1 and No. 25, which are symmetrical situations, and for No. 5 and No. 21. But it does not follow that, because we have a theory for No. 10, the next step should be to construct a theory for No. 22; there may well be more urgent work to do.

It is possible that out scheme should embrace more than twenty-five market situations; but present theory suggests no other distinction in terms of number and size as being likely to yield significant results. A purely empirical classification might work with a larger number of hard and fast statistical groups, but economic theory suggests that such a scheme would be less significant than that presented here. If cases are encountered in practice which indicate that one of our divisions should be subdivided, the number of situations must be enlarged accordingly. As it is, on the basis of theoretical analysis, we have grouped both oligopoly and duopoly under No. 15. If these two were to be distinguished, we should logically extend our scheme to include thirty-six situations, instead of twenty-five.

When the possibility of discrimination is taken into account, however, the number of situations is increased to eighty-one. All but Nos. 1–5 provide scope for discrimination by buyers as between different sellers, giving twenty situations, if there is no discrimination on the selling side of the market. Similarly, with no discrimination on the buying side of the market, there can be twenty situations with discrimination by sellers as between different buyers. Finally, eliminating the nine situations which include only one party on one or the other side of the market, we have sixteen situations in which discrimination is possible on both sides of the market. This makes fifty-six situations in all to be added to the twenty-five already distinguished in the absence of discrimination. Only three out of these fifty-six situations have been studied theoretically, discriminating monopoly (discrimination on the seller's side of No. 5) and product competition between small firms and between large firms (discrimination on the buyer's side of Nos. 15 and 25).

It is not suggested that all these market situations should be made the subject of theories in the near future. Even if, for the sake of completeness, they should all be examined, the question remains as to which should receive attention first. According to the views of Mrs. Robinson, quoted above, the optimistic economist would tackle all those that responded to his existing technique and hope to devise new methods to deal with the others later on. The other method of attack, advocated here, is to decide which situations are most frequent in the real world and do one's best on them with existing technique. This will reveal the limitations of our technique. The next step is to build new techniques to handle the intractable cases. Such a problem has already arisen with regard to situation No. 1, bilateral monopoly. Surely economic technique will develop more rapidly and more usefully if we do not confine it to the problems in which existing methods work most readily! It is true that progress in the understanding of one situation may provide the key to the analysis of another situation which is of less practical importance. In such a case no economist will be able to resist the temptation to follow up the clue. But that is a different matter from concentrating, as a matter of principle, on the cases which are amenable to the old methods of analysis.[16] Perhaps it is necessary to add that frequency of occurrence in the real world is not necessarily the best test of the practical urgency of studying a particular market situation. But it is a better guide than the tractability of the assumptions.

A very different attitude to that advocated here is adopted by Professor Hicks in his recent work:

It has to be recognised that a general abandonment of the assumption of perfect competition, a universal adoption of the assumption of monopoly, must have very de-

---

[16] In this connection Dr. R. Triffin's *Monopolistic Competition and General Equilibrium Theory* (Cambridge, Mass., 1940) is of particular interest, as it reduces the number of situations on each side of the market to five, even when discrimination is present. Some of the situations which we have distinguished in terms of numbers may be brought under a single category, if analyzed in terms of the degree of external interdependence of the firms. The classification adopted in the text, however, is less remote from the traditional Anglo-American approach to monopoly and competition.

structive consequences for economic theory. Under monopoly the stability conditions become indeterminate; and the basis on which economic laws can be constructed is therefore shorn away. . . . . The situation which emerges may be illustrated from the case of a rise in demand for a monopolist's product. A rise in demand for a product may raise its price or lower it. It is not even certain that output will rise; if the demand as it increases becomes less elastic, output may fall. It is, I believe, only possible to save something from this wreck—and it must be remembered that the threatened wreckage is the greater part of economic theory—if we can assume that the markets confronting most of the firms with which we shall be dealing do not differ very greatly from perfectly competitive markets. . . . . We must be aware, however, that we are taking a dangerous step, and probably limiting to a serious extent the problems with which our subsequent analysis will be fitted to deal. Personally, however, I doubt if most of the problems we shall have to exclude for this reason are capable of much useful analysis by the methods of economic theory.[17]

But this question can be settled only by making the attempt.

THE THEORY OF FLUCTUATIONS NOT IMMUNE

Theoretic blight has been very prominent in the field of cyclical fluctuations. The classical writers do not appear to have arrived at the concept of more or less periodic variations in production, employment, and trade; but they did discuss the problem of the glutted market, which is a phenomenon of one phase of the cycle. Sismondi and Malthus set out to construct a theory to explain how general overproduction, relative to consumption, comes about. James Mill, Say, and Ricardo proved to their satisfaction that there was no such thing as general overproduction, but only partial overproduction, due to errors of judgment by businessmen, which would be swiftly rectified. Ricardo wrote:

M. Say has most satisfactorily shown that there is no amount of capital which may not be employed in a country, because demand is only limited by production. No man produces but with a view to consume or sell. . . . . By producing, then, he necessarily becomes either the consumer of his own goods, or the purchaser and consumer of the goods of some other person. It is not to be supposed that he should, for any length of time, be ill-informed of the commodities which he can most advantageously produce, to attain the objective which he has in view, namely, the possession of other goods, and, therefore, it is not probable that he will continually produce a commodity for which there is no demand.[18]

As Dr. Lutz says, this is "an astonishing example of the strength which systematic and theoretical thought had with these classical economists;

---

[17] J. R. Hicks, *Value and Capital* (Oxford, 1939), pp. 84–85. It should be added that this pessimism is not characteristic of the work as a whole.

[18] D. Ricardo, *Works*, ed. McCulloch (London, 1846), p. 174.

it overcame even their eyesight."[19] Say, in his later writings, wriggled out of his untenable position by defining "production" as "produce which is demanded"; but the theoretic blight affected English writers throughout the nineteenth century. Say's "Law of Markets" cropped up again in the discussion of wage reductions about 1930. To some economists the contention that wage reductions might diminish the demand for goods and services seemed patently absurd, since production is the source of demand; wage cuts by leading to increased employment would increase production and hence demand.[20]

In the works of modern writers the problem of glutted markets has become linked with the decline in investment or the downturn of employment. The theories may be grouped under three heads: (a) the impossibility of a glut, (b) the possibility of a glut, and (c) the inevitability of a glut. It is possible to construct a logical, consistent theory of each type, by selecting appropriate assumptions. Say's Law of Markets is an example of the first type and Marx's theory of crises of the third type. There are many theories of the second type. The distinction between (b) and (c) is that the former makes the glut contingent upon certain conditions not included or implied by the set of assumptions and indicates what those conditions are. If they are added to the assumptions, the glut becomes inevitable, and we have a theory of the third type. Theoretical discussion of cyclical fluctuations consists largely of the exposure of logical flaws in proposed explanations. Where the flaw is not the inclusion of contradictory assumptions, but an inconsistency between the assumptions and the conclusions, the theory can be reconstructed by modifying the assumptions, as well as by asserting a new conclusion. Ricardo himself acknowledged that "if every man were to forego the use of luxuries, and be intent only on accumulation, a quantity of necessaries might be produced for which there could not be any immediate consumption."[21] But he thought this unlikely, particularly in England.

The multiplication of theories, which makes some economists sensitive and certainly does not improve the popular reputation of economics, is due largely to the wide range of conditions revealed by empirical studies. Theoretic blight is evident when economists seek to construct theories with the least possible room for irrational factors

[19] F. Lutz, *Das Konjunkturproblem in der Nationalökonomie* (Jena, 1932), p. 23.

[20] See my *Australia in the World Depression* (London, 1933), chap. vi, for a discussion of this argument.

[21] *Op. cit.*, p. 176.

and frictions, irrespective of the prominence of these elements in the real world. Concrete conditions rather than the desire to display theoretical virtuosity should determine the direction in which the theory of fluctuations is developed.

From this viewpoint Mr. Harrod's brilliant essay is open to criticism, for it shows some traces of theoretic blight. Writing of his theory, he claims "on its behalf that a larger number of the special phenomena of the trade cycle are accounted for as the necessary consequences of its central propositions than are accounted for by any other theory."[22] One of the central propositions is that "Crusoe is alive to what he is doing and acting with deliberation and knowledge. It is assumed in these pages that he acts in his own best interest."[23] The fact that it is possible on this assumption and with a careful selection of other assumptions to produce a theory of fluctuation does not provide any evidence regarding the relative importance of businessmen's errors and other factors in the causation of particular fluctuations in the real world. It is true that Mr. Harrod introduces psychological factors as possible reinforcing forces at some points of his theory and that he records his opinion as to the facts: "To suppose that in the short period decisions how much current output to produce there is systematic error in one direction enduring throughout the whole phase of the boom or the whole phase of the slump by all or most entrepreneurs seems to me altogether far fetched."[24] Yet one cannot but be impressed by Mr. Harrod's desire to show that the psychological factors are not necessary to the theoretic scheme. Thus, in commenting on Mr. Keynes's *General Theory*, he writes:

> In the recent volume the marginal analysis has come into its own again. This is a great improvement. There is no longer any reason to suppose . . . . that the entrepreneurs misjudge their proper course of action throughout the boom and slump.[25]

Or again, in discussing the growth of profits during the boom, he writes:

> The burden of the argument in this section has been that the shift to and from profit is connected with very deeply rooted conditions in our economic system. It is too often treated in a superficial way as due to some temporary lag or some careless misdemeanour. The banks behave improperly with regard to credit; the wage-earners fail to press for a timely rise of wages. I have connected it with the relation of average to marginal costs of production and with the behaviour of elasticity of demand, matters not easily tampered with.[26]

[22] R. F. Harrod, *The Trade Cycle* (Oxford, 1936), p. vii.

[23] *Ibid.*, p. 2.   [25] *Ibid.*, p. 71.

[24] *Ibid.*, p. 76.   [26] *Ibid.*, p. 87.

But these are questions of fact. Although Mr. Harrod may show that on certain assumptions the rise in prices and in profit in the boom would result from well-informed reasoned behavior, this logical connection does not prove that they can arise in only this way or that erratic behavior does not play an important role in the fluctuations of the real world. Mr. Harrod argues, in effect, that, but for his theoretical construction (that is, but for his choice of assumptions and analysis of them), economists would be forced to attribute more weight to "temporary lags" and "careless misdemeanours." Three years later, following the Oxford economists' direct questioning of a group of businessmen, Mr. Harrod wrote: "It has been impossible not to be struck by the devastating completeness of entrepreneurs' uncertainty about matters usually assumed to be known in the text-books."[27] To construct a theory which makes no use of this fact may be an intellectual tour de force; but it does not promise a correct interpretation of the march of events.

The multiplicity of theories of fluctuations need not be a subject for shame among economists. If in the real world the course of successive waves is influenced by different factors in varying degree, so that the turning-point of prosperity to recession, for instance, is caused in one way in one historical instance and in another way in the next historical instance, then any theory which deduces a pattern of fluctuation from a few assumptions must be inadequate. If there is no regular pattern in the real world, but only a series of episodes in which the dominant role is played by a different actor on each occasion, or, at least, if the changes in cast follow no recurring pattern, the most useful type of theory is the eclectic or pluralistic one. But not that sort of eclectic theory in which *all* the possible causes of fluctuations are represented as operating in the appropriate phase throughout each historical cycle, for this would not describe reality. What is needed is a theory explaining the various mechanisms by which an impulse to expansion or contraction of activity can be initiated or propagated; also the mechanisms by which such a movement may be accelerated or checked. There are already at hand theoretical models of what may be called "self-reversing mechanisms," which exhibit precise relationships of the type indicated by the generalization that boom conditions sow the seed for a subsequent depression. The theory would also distinguish the conditions essential to the maintenance of economic activity at a high level and set out the rates of capital expansion (if any) which can

[27] *Oxford Economic Papers, No. 2*, May, 1939, p. 5.

be maintained without setting up forces which inevitably interrupt expansion. Mr. Harrod's essay has undoubtedly added much to our understanding of such mechanisms, as have other constructions of theories of the trade cycle. But the very conception of "the trade cycle" may be wide of the mark. The type of theory suggested here, which details the various possible mechanisms, would conceive the whole problem somewhat as Mr. Kaldor has represented the boom: "like a peculiar steeplechase where the horse is bound to fall at one of four obstacles. If it survives the first, it might be checked on the second, the third or the fourth. It is probably a rare horse which survives until the last hurdle."[28] But there are probably more than four mechanisms to be considered as obstacles to steady economic development.

Such a classificatory theory has greater diagnostic value than a nicely rounded explanation of the cycle. If we know a number of different conditions which may in theory produce or affect fluctuations, we know what to look for in any concrete instance. The practical problem is, of course, extremely difficult. The mechanisms depicted by two theories may work against each other instead of in the same direction. For instance, it is conceivable that the Hobson effect (an increased flow of consumers' goods due to "overinvestment") may offset the Hayek effect (an increased demand for consumers' goods due to "overconsumption"), so that their joint result is to prolong the boom while their separate effects would be to end it. And sometimes the only available facts may appear to be equally consistent with different theoretical mechanisms. *But these difficulties cannot be solved by taking as our guide the tidiness of theory instead of the factual evidence.* If there is, in fact, a regular fundamental pattern of fluctuation in the real world, lurking beneath the superficial variability of historical fluctuations, the pluralistic form of the theory will not prevent us from finding it. Even if we have not yet in our apparatus a conceptual model of the fundamental mechanisms, the continuous checking of all our models against the observed facts is more likely to suggest the true theory than premature allegiance to a theory which is complete in itself but omits certain common facts of experience. Thus the pluralistic type of theory of the mechanisms of fluctuation will be superior as a guide to concrete truth, not only in the event that successive fluctuations are dis-

[28] N. Kaldor, "Stability and Full Employment," *Economic Journal,* December, 1938, p. 657. The same author has since presented us with an ingenious model of a complete cycle but does not claim that its logical simplicity renders it more realistic than less tidy competitors (see "A Model of the Trade Cycle," *Economic Journal,* March, 1940).

crete episodes, some of which have certain factors in common, but also, if, as seems less likely, these fluctuations are due to a single cause or group of causes. One reason is that the pluralistic theory is less subject to theoretic blight.

Theories of the various particular mechanisms of fluctuations are not, however, free from this disease. Sometimes they carry over from value theory concepts which already owe their popularity to the ease with which they fit into existing theory rather than their correspondence with the real world. In other cases concepts which would not be unrealistic under stable conditions are used in the analysis of instability, without consideration of the possibility that they may not be applicable to unstable conditions.

THE CONCEPT OF NORMAL PROFIT

As an example of the former, we may take the concept of *normal profit*, which figures prominently in both the theory of competitive equilibrium and the theory of fluctuations. According to Mrs. Robinson:

> Normal profit is that level of profit at which there is no tendency for new firms to enter the trade, or for old firms to disappear out of it. Abnormally high profits earned by existing firms are regarded as inducing new firms to begin to produce the commodity, and abnormally low profits, by leading to a cessation of new investment, are regarded as leading to a gradual decline in the number of firms in the industry. Such an account of the matter is somewhat artificial, in so far as the expansion of an industry is concerned. An increase in the demand for a commodity attracts new entrepreneurs to the industry directly, by opening up some new possibility of profitable investment, rather than indirectly, by making their mouths water at the sight of the high profits of the existing firms. The abnormal profits are a symptom rather than a cause of the situation in which new firms will find it profitable to enter the trade. But the artificial device of regarding the abnormal profits as a causal factor is of great assistance in simplifying the formal argument, and provided that its artificiality is recognised, it seems permissible to make use of it.[29]

Here again, observation of the real world suggests that theory is on the wrong track, but the theorist considers it permissible to continue, provided we realize that the theory is unrealistic. Why continue? Because on this artificial assumption the formal argument can be simplified. Even then we have to exclude from profits the additional receipts which are attributable to the superior skill or luck of the individual entrepreneur; otherwise the great variety in profits within an industry would not easily fit into the notion that profits are normal in equilibrium and that abnormal profits attract new firms into the industry.

[29] Joan Robinson, *Economics of Imperfect Competition* (London, 1933), p. 93.

But is it not the big prizes, due perhaps to the possession of exceptional ability, which attract firms into an industry rather than the general level of profit, after allowing for the "rent of entrepreneurship," as Mrs. Robinson calls it? Writing of the profits of enterprise in the sense of innovation, Professor Monroe suggests that

what successful enterprises obtain as a result of their activities is as varying a quantity as the quality of the plans they devise and apply. It does not settle at any level, even as an average, and stay there until other entrepreneurs learn of it and bring it down by their numbers. There is nothing to attract or repel the would-be pioneer except his own hopes and his own taste for the sort of work. It is impossible to speak of any level-ling tendency. Everything depends upon the elements of the particular situation. The profits of enterprise are conjunctural.[30]

This point has wider application than Professor Monroe gives to it, even if his statement of it seems rather extreme. Product competition, as distinct from price competition, proceeds by innovation, if not in the exploitation of new commodities, at least in the differentiation of existing ones. Only in pure competition, under static conditions, is it possible to draw a line between the "rent of entrepreneurship" and profit. In most industries in the real world, where competition is "imperfect" or "monopolistic," the distinction is untenable. Accord-ingly, "normal profit" cannot play the role ascribed to it by Mrs. Robinson. This conclusion will not be easily accepted by those who see in it only the wreck of much of existing economic theory.

The concept of normal profit was a prominent feature in Mr. Keynes's 1930 theory of the trade cycle, but under the name of "the normal remuneration of entrepreneurs," the word "profit" being re-tained for their abnormal earnings. Mr. Keynes defined "the normal remuneration of entrepreneurs at any time as that rate of remunera-tion which, if they were open to make new bargains with all the fac-tors of production at the currently prevailing rates of earnings, would leave them under no motive either to increase or decrease their scale of operations."[31] Consequently, when firms make "profits" they have an incentive to increase output.

This concept of normal profit is not identical with that used by Mrs. Robinson, since she treats normal profit as a fixed sum for each entre-preneur. Presumably Mr. Keynes would regard it as increasing with the output of each firm. Otherwise aggregate employment would only expand by workers' or rentiers' becoming employers. But the point to which attention must be drawn is that any change in the entrepre-

[30] A. E. Monroe, *Value and Income* (Cambridge, Mass., 1931), p. 256.

[31] J. M. Keynes, *A Treatise on Money* (London, 1930), I, 125.

neurs' views as to just how much would make it worth while to give a particular amount of employment alters their "normal remuneration." Whenever employment is expanding, entrepreneurs must be making abnormal profits, by definition. But we do not know whether this is due to a rise in actual profits or to a fall in normal profit. Similarly, if actual profits rise, we cannot be sure that employment will increase unless we are assured that normal profit has not risen also. There is no way of establishing independently the level of normal profit; all we know is that, if employment is going to be steady, then actual profit is normal profit. Thus the theory is based on a concept chosen, not with a view to facilitating the task of checking the applicability of the assumptions to a concrete case but with a view to constructing a theoretical model. Indeed, it is impossible to check the assumption of normal profit, because it is by definition simply a figure above, below, or equal to actual profits, according to whether output is about to rise, fall, or remain constant.

In the 1936 version of his theory Mr. Keynes abandoned the concept of normal profit, feeling that it was "not sufficiently defined [in 1930] if we allow for the possibility of changes in the scale of output" and that the exclusion of abnormal profits from income involved a peculiar definition of saving.[32] However, the same tendency to build a theory on concepts which fit in with existing theoretical schemes but which cannot possibly be checked against concrete facts was again evident. Mr. Keynes asked us to conceive of an "aggregate supply price" schedule, showing for any level of employment "the expectation of proceeds [from the sale of the output] which just make it worth the while of the entrepreneurs to give that employment." We must also imagine an "aggregate demand" schedule showing the proceeds expected from the sale of the output resulting from the employment of various numbers of men. Then, if at a given level of employment "the expected proceeds are greater than the aggregate supply price, there will be an incentive to entrepreneurs to increase employment, and, if necessary, to raise costs by competing with one another for the factors of production" up to that level of employment at which the expected proceeds are equal to the aggregate supply price.[33] From this it would seem that, if Mr. Keynes is not to work with the concept of normal profit, he must have, instead, a supply curve and a demand

[32] J. M. Keynes, *The General Theory of Employment, Money and Interest* (London, 1936), p. 61.

[33] *Ibid.*, p. 25.

curve, intersecting at the point of equilibrium. But in practice the points on his supply-price curve are as elusive as his earlier concept of a normal profit. We can determine whether the expected proceeds are above, below, or equal to the aggregate supply price only by deciding whether employment is about to increase, decrease, or remain constant.

Mr. Keynes's important practical conclusions could be reached without this laborious shadow sparring. In the library of the Australian Parliament at Canberra there is a copy of the *General Theory*. The first three hundred pages, in which the theory is worked out, are of virgin whiteness; the last eighty pages, with the practical applications, are well thumbed and heavily scored. Parliamentarians could not follow the supply and demand functions; yet they know that, if businessmen find they are selling more goods, this leads to an attempt to give more employment. Mr. Keynes's discussion of fluctuations in investment would have the same bearing upon practical policy if he abandoned his concept of an aggregate supply function and concentrated upon a more realistic model of business behavior.[34]

THEORY OF WAGE REDUCTIONS

We may now consider an example of theoretic blight arising from the attempt to apply, to the analysis of fluctuations, concepts which are consistent only with stable conditions. One of the most contentious points in the theory of fluctuations is the effects of general wage reductions in a period of depression. Professor Pigou's treatment of the question in his *Theory of Unemployment* is marred by his persistence with a theoretical analysis whose assumptions are obviously false in at least the early stages of depression. The traditional view has been that "the demand for labour is elastic" in depression as in prosperity; consequently, a general reduction in wages was supposed to cause an expansion of employment and to check the depression. The principal opposition to this view is based on the observation that wages are a source of demand; it is therefore argued by some that general wage reductions are neutral, reducing purchasing-power by as much as they reduce costs, and by others that wage reductions make the depression worse, reducing purchasing-power by more than they reduce costs. Professor Pigou does not bother about the more extreme view but

---

[34] It is remarkable that so original a brain should be bound by the form of the theoretical schemes on which it was trained, even when challenging their practical conclusions. Preoccupation with the problem of building a theory in terms of the traditional concepts would seriously limit the performance of most men in the creation of new conceptual schemes.

agrees that the more moderate view, "in spite of its paradoxical appearance, deserves investigation."[35] His "investigation" amounts to a proof that a fall in money wage rates involves some fall in "real wage-rates" on the assumption that nothing has happened to nonwage-earners' incomes. Accordingly, he concludes that "the system [since the wage reduction] is not in equilibrium. Additional labour *must* be employed." This appeal to equilibrium is based on Professor Pigou's earlier indorsement of the marginal-productivity theory of wages and employment: "The quantity of labour demanded at any given rate of real wage is such that the value in terms of wage goods of its marginal net product . . . . approximates to that rate of wage." This is the position in equilibrium. If the real wage is higher than the marginal net product of labor, equilibrium at that wage can be restored only by a reduction of employment; if the real wage is reduced to below the marginal net product, equilibrium can be restored only by an expansion of employment. And the desire for profit drives the employer toward the equilibrium position at which profit is maximized.

Nowhere, to the writer's knowledge, has Professor Pigou detailed the assumptions on which this marginal-productivity theory rests. But Professor Paul Douglas, who has even measured marginal productivity and calculated from it the elasticity of demand for labor, gives a list in his book *Controlling Depressions*. Assumption No. 1 is that "management knows how much the last workers add."[36] For Professor Pigou's version the employer must know "the value of the marginal net product in terms of wage goods"; that is, not merely the physical marginal product, but its value. Perhaps no employer *thinks* in terms of marginal net products, but he behaves as if he did, provided that he balances changes in total costs against changes in expected receipts, when deciding whether to employ more labor or not. In other words, the first assumption of the marginal-productivity theory is that the employer can estimate the variations in total costs and total receipts which will accompany changes in employment. Without this he does not know whether or not he can increase his profit by taking on additional employees. In short, the marginal-productivity approach seems inappropriate to conditions in which the employer does not know the demand curve for his product.

In discussing Australian wage policy in the depression, the writer considered it more appropriate to work on the assumption that "out-

[35] A. C. Pigou, *The Theory of Unemployment* (London, 1933), p. 101.
[36] (London, 1935), p. 224.

put and employment vary as sales or orders vary, but not in anticipation of increased sales."[37] This assumption is much more consistent
with Professor Pigou's own comments on the conditions of the real
world in depression than is the essential assumption of his marginal-
productivity theory. "The great complexity of modern economic
structure," he writes in another connection, "makes it extremely difficult for any dealer to estimate correctly either the total final buyers' demand for any product a little while ahead, or the extent of the prepara-
tions that other dealers are making to meet it."[38] Until recently the
writer was sufficiently under the spell of theory himself to incline to the
view that the marginal-productivity theory is a useful approach to the
problem of wages and employment in a period of stability. Yet the
Oxford economists' examination of businessmen suggests that even this
was a case of theoretic blight.

> Our questions revealed that the great majority of entrepreneurs were in profound
> ignorance with regard to the elasticity of demand for their product. Time and again
> with regard to this magnitude of cardinal importance, which economists are apt to as-
> sume to be known as a matter of course, we found that the entrepreneur was often
> unable to make any conjecture at all. And our sample erred, if at all, by being biassed
> in favour of well organised and efficiently conducted businesses.[39]

If this be true, it involves the "wreck," not only of a portion of Professor
Pigou's theory of unemployment, but also of much of the accepted theory of value and distribution, or, at least, the recognition that the theory is not a very useful technique for the discovery of concrete truth.[40]

CONCLUSIONS

These examples demonstrate that theoretic blight is encountered
in the economics of exchange and fluctuations alike and that it is deep
rooted, as well as widespread. Further traces of the disease will be discerned when we come to consider the psychological assumptions of economics. It would seem, therefore, that a not inconsiderable portion of
economic theory is unsuited to the function which it is expected to perform in the study of practical problems, namely, the classification and

[37] *Australia in the World Depression*, p. 175. For a detailed discussion of this problem, see
my article "Wages Policy and Business Cycles," *International Labour Review*, December,
1938.

[38] *The Theory of Unemployment*, p. 120.

[39] R. F. Harrod, "Price and Cost in Entrepreneurs' Policy," *Oxford Economic Papers*, May,
1939, p. 4.

[40] The discussion of wages policy has progressed a good deal further than the arguments
discussed here, and Professor Pigou's own position has been modified as a result of the debate.

arrangement of observable facts into a significant scheme. The conceptual schemes are there, but many of them are little more useful, in the analysis of a concrete situation, than the crude, half-formed theories of the "practical man."

What are the implications of this for policy formulation and for the future development of economic science? In the first place an economist dare not base practical advice on theoretical models of cause and effect which he knows to be flagrantly unrealistic. It is essential, therefore, that he should recognize theoretic blight whenever it is present in the constructions which economic theory offers for the interpretation of events. While a wide knowledge of concrete fact reduces the danger that unrealistic theories will be taken as a guide to practice, it is probable that a clear understanding of the nature and causes of theoretic blight will help restrict the ravages of the disease. From this viewpoint the destructive criticisms contained in this chapter may serve a constructive purpose.

The second implication of the prevalence of theoretic blight is the opening of a wide field of future work for the economic theorist in the construction of models which are free from the disease or, at least, are less remote from known facts than those criticized above. It would be wrong to suppose that the distressing frequency of theoretic blight constitutes a case for the rejection of economic theory as a guide to policy or a field for research. Any impression of hostility toward economic theory which might arise from the juxtaposition of so many destructive criticisms[41] should be corrected by the previous insistence upon the value of the analytic approach and by the optimistic essays in the formulation of new theoretical schemes in later chapters. Economic policy requires not less, but better, theory.

Apart from the extensions of economic theory which will later be proposed, there is need for a systematic overhaul of the existing body of theory. Where the asssumptions are found to be unrealistic, the problems must be worked out again with assumptions that promise better service in the analysis of concrete situations. The resulting theories will be less tidy than the constructions at present in favor; and in many cases the chain of argument will not be capable of great elaboration in general terms, without dissolving into a classification of the various possible things that may happen under certain conditions.

[41] Several academic colleagues consider my treatment of theoretic blight too harsh; perhaps the disposition to chastise others for one's own secret faults is partly responsible for my unwillingness to bate a jot.

But this will be a greater aid to the interpretation and prediction of events than a pretty theoretical model based on patently false assumptions. If the theories are untidy, so is the real world. If, on certain limited assumptions, the solution of the theoretical problem is indeterminate, so, too, the outcome of a particular set of conditions in the real world will be one thing or the other, according to the action of other factors which we are, as yet, unable to take into account. Any theoretical problem can be made determinate, if we introduce sufficient appropriate assumptions; but it will often be impossible to supply the necessary realistic assumptions in the form of generalizations; instead, we must be content with the facts in a particular concrete instance. It is more useful to have a theory which, though indeterminate in itself, gives some hint as to what particular events the final result may turn on than a theory which, by the premature adoption of unrealistic generalizations, establishes a determinate solution for an imaginary problem. If the uniqueness of concrete situations permits but a limited degree of generalization, it is better that our theory should reveal the scope for variation.

It is not enough to lament the "unnatural divorce between theory and fact"[42] or to plead for reconciliation. A happy remarriage would not be possible if "mutual incompatibility" were the true source of trouble. But it was theory who deserted fact, and not even his mental cruelty justified this. Admittedly, fact is difficult to live with being capricious and disorderly; but theory promised to honor and obey. Even if she only married the brute to reform him, she must adapt herself to his changing moods.

This systematic revision of existing economic theory is not attempted here. It is over a hundred years since Malthus set out "to prepare the general rules of political economy for practical application,"[43] and some time will be required and the work of many minds before it will be possible to write a general treatise that is free from theoretic blight. Those who feel that this task should take precedence over the exploration of the new territory surveyed in the following chapters will have plenty to occupy their attention. But, if we confined our attention to these familiar problems, the gulf between theory and policy would still be distressingly wide.

---

[42] E. F. M. Durbin, "Methods of Research—a Plea for Co-operation in the Social Sciences," *Economic Journal*, June, 1938, p. 196.

[43] T. R. Malthus, *Principles of Political Economy* (London, 1936), p. 21.

CHAPTER V

THE PROBLEM OF BEHAVIOR

WE NOW enter a field which, according to Professor Robbins, is "the happy hunting ground of the charlatan and the quack" or, at best, "of minds averse to the effort of exact thought."[1] It is only to be regretted, however, that the specialism of modern studies arouses suspicions of any student who claims competence in both economics and psychology. Anyone choosing to work in the borderland runs the risk of being regarded by economists as a psychologist off his beaten path and by psychologists as an economist off *his* beaten path. This chapter makes no attempt to effect a general synthesis of the two subjects. Its purpose is to consider whether the assumptions which existing economic theory make about the principles of human behavior are sufficiently realistic to be of value as a guide to practical problems. We are not concerned with the question as to whether economic theory should be modified in the light of new "fashions" in psychology,[2] even though so reputable an economic theorist as Professor J. M. Clark has recorded his view that "the only way in which the economist can keep his studies from duplicating the psychologist's work is by taking his psychology from those who have specialised in this field."[3] More important for our purpose is the suggestion, which might come from any observing individual as well as from a student of psychological textbooks, that economics ignores the complexity and irrationality of human nature and that the economist's map of the world is unnecessarily misleading.

CONVENTIONAL ECONOMIC PSYCHOLOGY

Our first task is to determine just what assumptions the economist does make about human nature or, more exactly, what psychological assumptions are implicit in modern economic theory. Reference has

[1] L. Robbins, *Essays on the Nature and Significance of Economic Science* (1st ed.; London, 1932), p. 83. The reference to "the charlatan and the quack" was toned down to "minds averse to the effort of exact thought" in the second edition (p. 83), no doubt as part of the author's attempt "to eliminate certain manifestations of high spirits no longer in harmony with present moods" (Preface to 2d ed.).

[2] It is this, in particular, that Professor Robbins deprecates (*ibid.*, p. 84).

[3] J. M. Clark, *Preface to Social Economics* (New York, 1936), p. 95.

already been made to Pantaleoni's statement that every economic theory involves as its major or minor premise "the hedonistic hypothesis."[4] This was the utilitarian theory of human motivation, according to which man seeks pleasure and strives to avoid pain, it being his constant endeavor to maximize his pleasure and to minimize his pain. Modern economists attempt to show that economic theory has now liberated itself from utilitarianism and that its psychological assumptions can be couched in such general terms as to render it impervious to any further changes which may take place in psychology. "The hedonistic trimmings of the works of Jevons and his followers were incidental to the main structure of a theory which—as the parallel development in Vienna showed—is capable of being set out and defended in absolutely non-hedonistic terms."[5] We shall return to Professor Robbins' conception of the very simple psychological foundations of economic theory later.

For the dominant viewpoint in English economics on this matter it is still safe to go to Marshall:

> Everyone who is worth anything carries his higher nature with him into business, and, there as elsewhere, he is influenced by his personal affections, by his conceptions of duty and his reverence for high ideals. . . . . But for all that, the steadiest motive to ordinary business work is the desire for the pay which is the material reward of work. The pay may be on its way to be spent selfishly or unselfishly, for noble or base ends, and here the variety of human nature comes into play. But the motive is supplied by a definite amount of money: and it is this definite and exact money measurement of the steadiest motives in business life, which has enabled economics far to outrun every other branch of the study of man.[6]

Marshall stresses at length the other motives but claims that they do not lend themselves to measurement through their effects in the same way as does the search for wealth. This implies that the economist's scheme, based on the assumption that men seek their own financial advantage (corrected for other nonfinancial but still self-interested advantages) abstracts from other motives; and, in applying the economist's scheme to a particular concrete problem, special attention should be paid to the need for modifying its conclusions in the light of any information about other motives in the particular case. This is the use made of the psychological assumption of self-interest.

But Marshall conceded that the operation of self-interest in the pursuit of wealth may be restricted by custom. "It is not to be supposed

---

[4] See above, chap. iii.

[5] Robbins, *op. cit.*, p. 85.

[6] A. Marshall, *Principles of Economics* (8th ed.; London, 1927), p. 15.

that we assume every action to be deliberate, and the outcome of calculation. In ordinary life people do not weigh beforehand the results of every action." Nevertheless, he argues,

the side of life with which economics is specially concerned is that in which man's conduct is most deliberate, and in which he most often reckons up the advantages and disadvantages of any particular action before he enters on it. And further it is that side of his life in which, when he does follow habit and custom, and proceeds for the moment without calculation, the habits and customs themselves are most nearly sure to have arisen from a close and careful watching of the advantages of different courses of conduct.[7]

This is the notion of *rational* self-interest. Marshall's method again is to abstract from impulsiveness and lack of calculation, on the one hand, and from custom and inertia, on the other. Only by this process of abstraction can he build his theory of supply and demand with its principle of substitution: cheaper methods for expensive ones; more strongly desired goods for less strongly desired ones. But Marshall was careful to qualify his statement of this principle by saying: "*As far as the knowledge and business enterprise of the producers reach*, they in each case choose those factors of production which are best for their purpose."[8]

It will be seen that Marshall assumed the search for monetary gain, corrected for estimation of other advantages, as the motive of action in the business world and assumed further that this motive was applied intelligently and systematically. Without these psychological assumptions, his theory must have developed differently, if at all. But he attempted to show, by citing common experience, that the assumptions were not chosen merely for their convenience; he claimed that they were valid for a wide range of economic behavior. This raises two questions. We have to consider not only whether these psychological assumptions are even less realistic than Marshall supposed but also whether they are selected primarily to fit in with a desired development of theory. If the answer to both questions is in the affirmative, some considerable reconstruction of economic theory is called for.

On these two questions we have a frank avowal by Mrs. Robinson:

The fundamental assumption on which the present simple technique of analysis is based is that each individual person acts in a sensible manner from the point of view of his own economic interests. The striking unreality of this assumption has sometimes tempted economists to deny that they are making it. . . . . Now if individuals act in an unpredictable manner, as electors are alleged to do, the technique of analysis must give way to a purely statistical technique, from which there is nothing to be hoped. And if individuals act in a predictable manner, but from a wide range of complicated motives, the economist must await the verdict of the psychologist on what

[7] *Ibid.*, p. 21.   [8] *Ibid.*, p. 341; Marshall's italics.

those motives are. Meanwhile the optimistic economists are working out their analyses on the simple assumption, and resolutely refusing to despair of evolving in the future a technique which will allow them to assume the existence of whatever other human motives have an influence in the economic sphere.[9]

The same author also writes of the time "when the technique of economic analysis will be sufficiently advanced to analyse the results of neuroses and confused thinking."[10] Whereas Marshall thought that "the same bent of mind that led our lawyers to impose English civil law on the Hindoos" and "led our economists to work out their theories on the tacit assumption that the world was made up of city men,"[11] Mrs. Robinson argues that this is methodologically correct or perhaps that the theories should first be worked out on the supposition that the world is made up of university dons.

SELF-INTEREST OR SCALES OF PREFERENCE?

In view of such statements as these, it is not surprising that the "impression has been widespread that a predominantly 'self-interested' or 'egoistic' theory of the motivation of economic activities was a logical necessity of economic theory."[12] But it is urged by some economists that this "widespread impression" is based on a failure to understand the nature of modern economic theory. For instance, Professor Robbins attempts to show that the notion of economic man, seeking always his own rational self-interest, "is only an expository device—a first approximation used very cautiously at one stage in the development of arguments which, in their full development, neither employ any such assumption nor demand it in any way for a justification of their procedure."[13] Professor Knight admits that "even reputable economists have, at least until recently, been careless in their use of such expressions as 'rational self-interest.' "[14] But he argues that economic theory does not rest on an attempted "distinction between *self-interest* and other types of interest." The distinction is one "of ethical import," and

if one general methodological position has been stated and hammered home in the literature of modern economic theory more consistently and persistently than any

[9] Joan Robinson, *Economics Is a Serious Subject* (Cambridge, 1932), p. 10.

[10] *Economics of Imperfect Competition* (London, 1933), p. 16.   [11] *Op. cit.*, p. 762.

[12] T. Parsons, "The Motivation of Economic Activities," *Canadian Journal of Economics and Political Science*, May, 1940, p. 189.

[13] *Op. cit.*, p. 97.

[14] F. H. Knight, "Professor Parsons on Economic Motivation," *Canadian Journal of Economics and Political Science*, August, 1940, p. 461.

other, it would surely be the emphatic pronouncement that the economist has absolutely nothing to do with ethical (or other evaluative) distinctions. . . . . Economics accepts and deals with human preferences " as they are," and specifically as they are manifested in action, without any implication of condemnation or approval upon them. . . . . [It] deals with the use of resources or means in such a way as to secure to the maximum degree permitted by the means available to any economising subject, *the promotion of whatever interests he may be trying to promote*.[15]

This appears to be the same view as that taken by Professor Robbins of the fundamental psychological assumptions of economic theory, namely, that "different goods have different uses and that these different uses have different significances for action, such that in a given situation one use will be preferred before another, and one good before another." The assumption of "scales of valuation" or "preferences" involves no ethical judgment and theory of human motivation. "Why the human animal attaches particular value in this sense to particular things, is a question which we do not discuss. That is quite properly a question for psychologists or perhaps even physiologists." Economists work "not by assuming some particular psychology but by regarding the things which psychology studies as the data of their own deductions."[16]

Leaving aside the question of ethical judgment, we may note that the chief advantage of the concept of "scales of preference" is that it shifts the emphasis away from financial gain as the principal motive to behavior. It makes no difference to the possibility of constructing a theory of exchange whether money ranks high or low in one's scale of preferences, as compared with public reputation, joy in work, or Sabbath observance. But it does make a difference to the theory itself. A formal analysis can be based on the assumption of a scale of preferences for a, b, c, d, and e, where a, b, c, d, and e are all "unknowns." But a theoretical model of a real process or a conceptual map to guide our study of the facts must give the scales of preference some empirical content. And this is recognized by the writers of textbooks, who work chiefly with scales of preference in which money gains rank exceedingly high.

It is sometimes argued that the concept of scales of preference enables economists to swallow at one gulp all the difficulties associated with the pursuit of other objectives than money. In discussing this question we need some agreed term to apply to these other objectives; we shall therefore refer to them as "nonfinancial" motives. Although this term is not entirely satisfactory, it will serve at least to distinguish

[15] *Ibid.*, pp. 461–62; my italics.   [16] Robbins, *op. cit.*, p. 86.

certain aims from Marshall's "material reward of work—a definite amount of money."

Professor Robbins argues that just as "every first-year student since the days of Adam Smith has learnt to describe equilibrium in the distribution of particular grades of labour in terms of a tendency, *not* to the maximisation of *money gains*, but to the maximisation of *net advantages* in the various alternatives open," so, too, all other nonfinancial considerations can be included in arriving at the net advantages of various courses of action.

> The valuations which determine particular transactions may be of various degrees of complexity. In my purchase of bread I may be interested solely in the comparison between the bread and the other things in the circle of exchange on which I might have spent the money. But I may be interested too in the happiness of my baker. There may exist between us certain liens which make it preferable for me to buy bread from him, rather than procure it from his competitor who is willing to sell it a little cheaper. In exactly the same way, in my sale of my own labour or the hire of my property, I may be interested only in the things which I receive as a result of the transaction; or I may be interested also in the experience of labouring in one way rather than another, or in the prestige or discredit, the feeling of virtue or shame in hiring out my property in this line rather than in that. All these things are taken into account in our conception of scales of relative valuation.[17]

But, if the reader turns to the references given by Professor Robbins to illustrate his point, it will be found that the method by which "all these things are taken into account" is to proceed on the assumption that they are absent and then to qualify the conclusion by saying that the result will be different, in so far as the economic agents are influenced by these other motives. In the case of such motives as an interest in the conditions of work as well as the pay, or in the repercussions of family ties as well as wage differences upon the mobility of labor, the nature of the difference in behavior can be, and is, clearly set out. But the textbooks give no analysis of the consequences of such motives as an interest "in the happiness of my baker" or "the feeling of virtue or shame in hiring out my property," except that they will be somehow different from the consequences of the motives assumed in the theory. For purposes of analysis, conventional economic theory abstracts from behavior in response to motives other than money and such other advantages as can be measured in money. The concept of scales of preference comes down to Marshall's theory of motivation, so far as the producer and businessman are concerned, at least. In the case of the consumer, the scales of preference, with which economic theory works,

[17] *Ibid.*, pp. 95–96.

are for only those goods and services which can be obtained by exchange.

Since economic theory abstracts from certain forms of behavior, it is only to be expected that actual behavior in the world of industry, trade, and finance will often deviate from that which economic theory alone would lead us to expect. Three sources of deviation may be distinguished, namely, the pursuit of nonfinancial ends, inefficiency in the selection of means, and experimental or exploratory behavior, arising from uncertainty over ends or means.

THE PREVALENCE OF NONFINANCIAL MOTIVES

The mere fact that such herculean efforts have been made to bring disregard for profit, preference for prestige, desire for vengeance, sportsmanship, lust for power, and generosity all into the fold of "scales of preference" is sufficient evidence of the frequency with which behavior escapes from the pigeonholes to which the usual theory of economic motivation assigns it. Often, it is true, these purposes can be achieved through financial channels. But they promote activities which conflict with the maximization of monetary gains—sentiment interferes with business—with sufficient regularity to expose the economist's analysis as inadequate. If behavior is to be predicted with greater accuracy, the assumptions of economic theory must be modified to include other motives than the conventional one.

One's first reaction to this proposition may be despair. It may seem hopeless to attempt to do any better with such heterogeneous material as is provided by these "nonfinancial" motives than economic theory has in the past. It will be remembered that Marshall thought it was the availability of the monetary measures of motives that "enabled economics far to outrun every other branch of the study of man."[18] But the difficulty of imagining a more systematic treatment of the implications of these other motives as integral assumptions of (rather than exceptions to) the theory arises largely from the individualist bias of economic tradition. This is apparent in Professor Robbins' work. It is *his* interest in his baker's happiness or *his* personal interest in "the experience of labouring in one way rather than another" that complicates economic analysis. But in so far as these interests are due to group pressure, as is probably the case with "the prestige or discredit in hiring out property in this line rather than that," we are confronted

[18] *Op. cit.*, p. 15.

by patterns of social behavior. Provided that in these nonfinancial motives individuals reflect a common tradition or code, there is a possibility of predicting their action, in particular circumstances, from the group pattern, just as we can predict their action if they seek only to maximize their financial achievements. Economic theory has concentrated on the latter form of behavior and largely ignored the possibility of explaining other forms, except, perhaps, as the precipitate of variations on the theme of self-interest, which was Marshall's view of custom and habit. It must be remembered that, when the foundations of modern economic theory were laid, it was usual to explain all behavior by reference to the individual's assessment of the advantages of various lines of conduct.

The suggestion that the economist should explore the possibility of social patterns of "nonfinancial" motives comes simultaneously from anthropology and psychology. The anthropologists, in their study of primitive communities, have definitely established that many acts which to us appear capricious and irrational are the result of conformity to recognized social norms, enforced by group pressure and public opinion more often than authoritarian law. In primitive communities to act as an "economic man" would be as great a deviation from the normal, as inexplicable and capricious, as the pursuit of "nonfinancial" ends appears to those who are dominated by the viewpoint of economic theory. Alongside the abstraction known as "economic man" may be placed "institutional man." He, too, is an abstraction, but in the opposite direction from "economic man." "Institutional man" does not seek to achieve the greatest results from given means, by exchange, but behaves instead in conformity with custom and socially indorsed ethical standards.[19] Psychologists, concerned not with the description of social norms but with the explanation of the development of personality and individual behavior, have grown increasingly dissatisfied with the instinct theory. Instead of seeking the explanation of human conduct in a few organic dispositions, psychology is turning more and more to the social forces which determine the formation of the personality and modes of behavior.

Another converging line of thought will be found in the work of Professor Parsons, who conceives of sociology as the attempt "to develop an analytic theory of social action systems in so far as these systems can be understood in terms of the property of common-value in-

---

[19] See H. Pinney, "The Institutional Man," *Journal of Political Economy*, August, 1940, p. 543, and references there cited.

tegration."[20] This fearsome expression covers codes of conduct: "normative patterns which define what are felt to be, in the given society, proper, legitimate or expected modes of action or of social relationship."[21] The relevance of this concept to economics is that, "so far as the patterns are effectively institutionalised, action in social relationships is not random, but is guided and canalised by the requirements of the institutional patterns."[22]

It seems to be a fair criticism of the attitude of many economists to say that they assume only one social pattern, namely, the pursuit of "rational self-interest" (meaning profit in the case of the businessman; maximum satisfaction in wants in the case of the consumer). Any other form of behavior, such as the pursuit of "nonfinancial" ends, is regarded as a random deviation from this pattern. The possibility that it is due to conformity to some other institutional pattern is not considered. Within its own logical framework, economic theory must, of course, ignore what is definitely excluded by its assumptions. But in dealing with practical problems there is no reason to treat these forms of behavior as capricious, simply because they are not included in the conventional economic scheme.

The extent to which the pursuit of "nonfinancial" ends does conform to a social pattern in modern society is, of course, a matter for empirical investigation. Merely to posit such patterns of conduct and to build an elaborate analysis upon them would be yet another example of theoretic blight. Economic theory cannot contribute much to our understanding of these tendencies toward conformity in "nonfinancial" motivation until the effectiveness of certain norms is established by observation.

This task is essentially one for collaboration between economists, anthropologists, sociologists, and psychologists. The economist who is continually checking his theories against the facts is unhappily able to indicate numerous individual instances of behavior that fail to conform to his analysis; the anthropologist is acquainted with institutional patterns to which apparently irrational individual behavior conforms in more primitive societies; the sociologist (of Professor Parsons' school, at least) seeks to display the role of normative patterns in all societies; and the psychologist investigates the process by which the

[20] T. Parsons, *Structure of Social Action* (New York, 1937), chap. xix.

[21] T. Parsons, "Motivation of Economic Activities," *Canadian Journal of Economics and Political Science*, May, 1940, p. 190.

[22] *Ibid.*, p. 190.

individual develops into a social being, with his personality shaped by "social forces." Each has an interest in "nonfinancial" motives, from the viewpoint of his own science; and the problems that each desires to solve are somewhat different. If their help is to be secured in the solution of the economist's problems, it is the economist who must frame the problem and bring it to their notice. Otherwise these other social sciences will never get round to supplying just the information the economist requires for the interpretation of concrete situations in which "financial" and "nonfinancial" motives are mixed together.

There have been many pleas for collaboration among the social sciences, but even when the workers are gathered together under one roof, as in the London School of Economics, this does not automatically secure a joint attack on borderline problems. The initiative must come from workers who, because they are conscious of the limitations of their own specialty and have some knowledge of the methods of other specialties, recognize specific points at which liaison would be useful, from their own point of view, and are able to formulate their problem in such a way that it is also recognized as a problem for the other social sciences.[23] The most important outcome of our discussion of "nonfinancial" motives, therefore, is to indicate one of these points at which liaison should be established with other social sciences, in order to improve the application of economic theory to practical affairs—one of the tasks suggested in chapter i.

From collaboration of this sort we might hope to obtain some new postulates for economic theory. These postulates would take the form of an affirmation that in a particular society men are driven, by social pressure, to conform to certain practices other than to seek the maximization of money gains, for instance, a preference for dealing with small independent shopkeepers, a preference for additional leisure rather than additional income, the hereditary transmission of occupations irrespective of the state of the labor market, a refusal to deal with members of certain racial or other groups within the society. Much of Veblen's work—often considered as social satire rather than economic theory—assumes new importance if considered as an attempt to work with the new psychological postulates suggested by the anthropological researches of his day. The attempt must be continued, as better estimates of these social patterns become available.

---

[23] The collaboration between specialists would be greatly aided if more workers could undergo a systematic training in several social sciences, with a view to specializing in borderline problems.

It must be recognized that these social patterns, and the economic theories in which they can be incorporated, will be of only local application, for the particular social norms will probably vary from one society to another, if we may generalize from the results of anthropological surveys. It may be that in the modern world no social pattern is so widespread as the pursuit for money gains and that in this sense existing economic theory has greater generality than any of the new theories that may be constructed on the basis of other social patterns. But concrete problems arise in their own local social setting; and even "world problems" cannot be solved by ignoring local peculiarities. The theory which is of only local application is an equally important part of the economist's equipment as the theory of more general application, because the latter alone is an inadequate guide to the local situation.

Another source of local variation is the strength of the social pattern and the frequency of individual deviation from it. Thus the growth of "commercialism" in medicine represents the prevalence of deviations from the institutional patterns of professional ethics. The range of phenomena that can be explained in terms of "institutional man" depends upon the degree to which the social system is "institutionally integrated," and that varies from one society to another and from time to time.[24] It may be hoped that anthropology, sociology, and psychology will, in the course of time, throw more light upon the conditions under which conflicting patterns develop in a society and pure individualism, in the sense of a departure from all social norms, becomes sufficiently widespread for the norms to lose their predictive value. The more urgent task, however, from the viewpoint of economics, is to determine the degree of conformity to any observed institutional patterns, other than the pursuit of money, in the particular community in which economic analysis is to be applied for the solution of concrete problems.

INEFFICIENCY AND ERROR

If we put aside the problem of the empirical content of the scale of preferences or the relative strength of "financial" and "nonfinancial" motives, doubts arise as to whether it is legitimate to assume that human behavior is the outcome of a rational comparison of the various possible lines of conduct according to an explicit scale of valuation.

Economists have been somewhat careless in their use of the term

[24] Cf. Parsons, "Motivation of Economic Activities," p. 202.

"rational," as well as in their application of the prefix "self" to "interest." Professor Robbins finds considerable difficulty in discussing
whether economic theory assumes "rationality," partly because "rationality" has various meanings. "It is not possible to regard" a preference "as rational unless it is formulated with a full consciousness of
the nature of the sacrifice which is thereby involved."[25] On the other
hand, Professor Knight says that "motives are usually assumed to be
accurately known, but it is not necessary to the theory that the subject
be conscious of them at all." The theory only "assumes that any individual's motives are correctly expressed in action. . . . . As careful
writers have emphasized, economic theory abstracts even from the
factor of *error* on the part of the subject in translating his actual wishes
into action."[26] He does not label this type of assumed behavior as
"rational"; though common usage would sanction this application of
the term.

The assumption is, therefore, that, either as the result of a scrutiny of
the motives and alternatives which are present to consciousness or as a
result of some unconscious process, the resulting behavior is that which
would give due weight to all relative considerations and promote the
individual's "interests" to the maximum degree possible in the circumstances. It is, perhaps, permissible to describe this process, conscious or unconscious, as "efficient."

There are several reasons why behavior is often less efficient, in
practice, than economic theory implies. For instance, many choices
are made under the pressure of custom or imitation; and one may never ask one's self if he really prefers the result to some other conceivable
course of action which has never been essayed. It may be argued that
this implies a preference for peace at all costs—including the cost of
making up one's mind. But even this verbal solution provides no escape, for in many cases one does not even envisage the possibility of
acting differently or of changing one's consumption habits. And, if
our attention is attracted to the question as to whether some other
goods would not give greater satisfaction or some other activity be
more interesting, our resultant action must itself be largely exploratory.

Even when the possible courses of action are scrutinized in advance,
however, and one is balanced against another, the decision may be
the result of confused calculation. As Wicksteed[27] and, more recently,

[25] *Op. cit.*, p. 155.   [26] *Op. cit.*, pp. 462–63.
[27] P. H. Wicksteed, *Commonsense of Political Economy* (London, 1933), Book I, chap. iii.

Reddaway[28] have pointed out, consumers will often be more influenced by conventional notions of extravagance and fair prices than by the relative marginal utilities (or rate of marginal substitution) of different channels of expenditure. Reddaway was amused when his Australian friends considered that the difference in postage by air mail and ordinary mail to England far outweighed the saving in time. Wicksteed, on the other hand, considered it a commonplace that one might spend 3/6 on a book but not 2/6 on taxi fares and 1/- on the book, even if one wanted to take it to read on a journey. Indeed, Wicksteed's account of the irrationalities of the consumer is one of the best in print. He even admits what Professor Robbins denies, that where there is a scale of preferences it may continue to be internally inconsistent, so that $A > B$, $B > C$, but $C > A$. Professor Robbins argues that this would soon be eliminated by "internal arbitrage operations."[29] So it would *if* consumers were more "rational."

These are examples of personal inefficiency in effecting the most satisfactory compromise between one's competing desires. The theory of consumer demand, whether couched in terms of marginal utility or of marginal rates of substitution, abstracts from this sort of inefficiency. It shows how efficient people would behave under given conditions but gives no hint of the errors which are likely to be made in practice.

Although discussion so far has been directed toward the behavior of the consumer, it is equally relevant to the problem of entrepreneurs' behavior. The usual textbook analysis of the equilibrium of the firm assumes not only that profit is the sole objective but also that it is pursued efficiently, in the sense that, of the available courses of action, the most profitable is, in fact, followed. But it is generally recognized that, in practice, many entrepreneurs do not make the maximum possible profit. There are communities where it is the exception rather than the rule for an entrepreneur to know how much profit he makes. For instance, one consequence of wartime price control in Australia is likely to be a revolution in bookkeeping. Many traders, for the first time in the history of their firm, have now found an incentive to keep accurate accounts. Were it not for the supervision of the prices commissioner, they would still be behaving quite differently from the entrepreneur of the textbooks.

[28] W. B. Reddaway, "Irrationality in Consumers' Demand," *Economic Journal*, September, 1936, p. 419.

[29] *Op. cit.*, p. 92.

It is often not possible to say whether an entrepreneur's failure to make the maximum possible profit is due primarily to the pursuit of other conflicting ends ("nonfinancial" motives) or to inefficiency in the pursuit of profit. Observation suggests that both conditions are sufficiently frequent in their occurrence to justify the construction of theories which include them among the assumptions. Such theories must be as different from conventional equilibrium theory as the behavior of the businessman is different from that of the textbook entrepreneur.

We have already noted that much behavior is conventional, in the sense that we never face up to the question of whether we really prefer it to doing other things or even consider whether there are other conceivable ways of spending one's time. In business the counterpart of this is failure to experiment or to take advantage of visible opportunities of profit. This clearly fits in with the usual notion of inefficiency, which includes both the apathy which leaves opportunities unexplored and the making of mistakes. It is the negative side of Marshall's occasional but fundamental qualification of the businessman's behavior: "according to his energy and ability."

Of course, the irrational or inefficient entrepreneur is not unknown in economic theory. He is occasionally introduced to simplify the analysis when the assumption of complete efficiency would produce no determinate conclusion. For instance, Bertrand's theory of duopoly, as expounded, *inter alia*, by Professor Chamberlin, assumes general stupidity by both sellers. Each proceeds on the assumption that if he undercuts his competitor the latter will not retaliate and continues to operate on this assumption, although it is proved false every time he tries it in practice. Cournot's solution is open to the same objection, although the retaliation takes a less obvious form. Professor Chamberlin states that, although these two theories yield different conclusions, they "complement, rather than oppose, each other, each flowing from a particular assumption. . . . . No presumption in favour of either the one or the other seems to be created by the general hypothesis that each seeks to maximise his profit."[30] As several writers, including Chamberlin, have pointed out, an intelligent pursuit of profit is consistent with neither assumption; and it may be argued that it is more likely to be personal prejudice or some other "nonfinancial" motive rather than profit which prevents collaboration between duopolists in practice. "The unreal atmosphere which surrounds our current theories of oligopoly may be ascribed to the fact that the assumptions are

[30] E. Chamberlin, *Theory of Monopolistic Competition* (Cambridge, Mass., 1933), p. 37.

too often chosen for their analytical convenience, rather than for their actual relevance to the real world of to-day."[31] But, although in the study of oligopoly some economists have, in effect, jettisoned the concept of the "rational" economic man, because it would not imply a determinate equilibrium within a given market situation but would only suggest the development of a new market situation, in many parts of theory it has generally been the other way around, since the concept of efficient "economy" usually provides a tidier theoretical structure and more precise conclusions.

In applying economic theory to a concrete problem, therefore, it is always necessary to consider whether or not the theory implies a greater degree of personal efficiency or rationality (or, in the case of oligopoly, a less degree) than is likely to be encountered in practice. Some attempt must be made to allow for failure to "count the cost" of alternative lines of conduct and for errors of judgment. The question is whether this allowance must be made by sheer common sense or whether it is possible to discover any tendency toward uniformity in inefficiency, which might be made the basis of more realistic theoretical models.

It might be thought that the admission of this type of irrationality will make a wreck of existing theory and that the range of individual possibilities is too great to permit any generalization as to the results of behavior when errors are present. But a clue has already been given to this problem by the observation that nonfinancial motives may conform to a code. Is there any central tendency of errors which can be made the subject matter of a useful theory?

Professor Pigou has already shown, in his study of *Industrial Fluctuations*, that a common bias in errors during one phase of a cycle provides a plausible explanation of certain phenomena. He also attempts a classification of the factors which promote errors by entrepreneurs.[32] This type of discussion has gone somewhat out of fashion in business-cycle theory[33] but bids fair to be rehabilitated as a result of the increasing use of the concept of "expectations" in economic analysis. Some "errors" of judgment lead to actions which, in their turn, produce repercussions which appear to justify the original "error" or in

[31] R. Triffin, *Monopolistic Competition and General Equilibrium Theory* (Cambridge, Mass., 1940), p. 78.

[32] A. C. Pigou, *Industrial Fluctuations* (London, 1927), chaps. vi and vii.

[33] See A. MacFie, *Theories of the Trade Cycle* (London, 1934), for a recent renewal of interest.

other cases to make it much worse. Professor Hicks has developed the concept of "elasticity of expectations" to classify the different consequences which may emerge from different estimates regarding the temporary or permanent nature of an observed price change and the possibility of its being the commencement of a trend or "the cumulating point of a fluctuation."[34] He suggests that we must "assume a good deal of variation in different people's elasticities of expectations" and that "people who have been accustomed to steady prices, or to very gradual price movements are likely to be insensitive in their expectations; people who have been accustomed to violent changes will be sensitive. . . . . A community which has been exposed to violent disturbances of prices . . . . may have to be regarded, in consequence, as being economically neurotic."[35]

Generalizations of this type are based, of course, on observation and undoubtedly permit the construction of somewhat more realistic theories than an assumption of complete rationality. But their use in other branches of economic theory is practically unknown—perhaps because it is less difficult to be rational under the static conditions which are assumed for the analysis of most problems other than economic fluctuations. Yet even the most superficial observation suggests that there is widespread inefficiency in consumers' choice and in the day-to-day administration of many businesses.

These errors of judgment and the varying elasticity of expectations might be made the subject of a more systematic study to determine the extent to which they are influenced by social factors, as contrasted with pure individualism. The efficiency of labor and of management is often diminished by social influences, such as traditional labor practices and traditional group attitudes of employers toward their employees. It would be surprising if similar social factors did not sometimes influence the type of mistakes made by consumers and businessmen generally.

We cannot, however, appeal to the other social sciences for help, as in the case of "nonfinancial" motives. The outcome of our discussion of errors is not to indicate points at which liaison should be established with workers in other specialties but to suggest a particularly difficult field of research for empirically minded economists. It is impossible to

[34] J. R. Hicks, *Value and Capital* (London, 1939), p. 205. Elasticity of expectations of price is defined as "the ratio of the proportional rise in expected future prices to the proportional rise in current price." It may be noted that "optimism" in a boom is identified with an increasing elasticity of price expectations (cf. p. 296).

[35] *Ibid.*, pp. 272–73.

say in advance whether sufficient regularity will be discovered to enable economists to go very far in the analysis of "the results of neuroses and confused thinking."[36] But any advance in the direction of realistic analysis will increase the predictive value of economic science and diminish, even if only slightly, the scope for personal opinion.

EXPLORATORY BEHAVIOR

The third source of deviation from the forms of behavior which economic theory would lead us to expect is man's capacity for experiment, with both new ends and hitherto untried means of achieving accepted ends.

Professor Knight writes:

> We all know that we generally do not know at all accurately what we want, and in considerable measure act to find out. And our interests are to a considerable extent explorative in a more intrinsic sense; the motive of action is in part curiosity as to what the result will be, and hence depends on partial ignorance of the result when the action is performed. It is undoubtedly a general principle that ends are more or less defined in the process of realisation, and that the interest and value in an action centres in this redefinition as well as in the achievement of any result given in anticipation.[37]

Behavior of this type cannot be explained in terms of any existing scale of preferences.

A similar problem arises in the case of the businessman. According to the traditional view of the entrepreneur, he, too, is frequently engaged in exploratory action, designed to discover methods of maximizing profit. "The advantages of economic freedom," wrote Marshall, "are never more strikingly manifest than when a business man endowed with genius is trying experiments, at his own risk, to see whether some new method, or combination of old methods, will be more efficient than the old."[38] Even assuming that profit is the *objective* of his experiments, his exploratory behavior cannot be represented as the *selection* of the most profitable methods or the choice of means to achieve a given set of ends. That can come only later, after the results of the experiments have been considered. Although economic theory assumes that much behavior must be exploratory, its assumptions permit no explanation of the direction which the explorations take, that is, the actual form of this part of behavior.

[36] Joan Robinson, *Economics of Imperfect Competition* (London, 1933), p. 16.

[37] F. H. Knight, "What Is Truth in Economics?" *Journal of Political Economy*, February, 1940, p. 25.

[38] *Op. cit.*, p. 406.

The explanation is, of course, that economic theory has been concerned with the conditions of equilibrium rather than the path by which equilibrium may be reached or the cul-de-sac into which individuals may be led in their attempts at maximization. From this point of view it may seem permissible to attribute experimentation with various means as a temporary stage in the approach toward equilibrium. Although not prominent in economic literature, the problem of experiments in the choice of goods for consumption and of types of work as an occupation can be treated in the same fashion, if we assume that the fundamental conditions (human dispositions and qualities of goods or the nature of the work) are stable. Not the experiments are the center of interest but the adjustments which follow the experimental demonstration that certain courses of action are more profitable or more desired than others.

But, when conditions are unstable, the hope of ever establishing equilibrium in practice recedes. A great proportion of actual behavior in the real world, if businessmen are "on the job," must for this reason be experimental. It follows that the predictive power of economic theory is greatly reduced, if it must confine itself to the equilibrium implied in certain conditions but never realized, and if it must ignore the exploratory activity which, although theoretically preliminary to equilibrium adjustments, may be at least as frequent in practice.

Moreover, desire for novelty is itself an impulse to experiment. On the side of consumption we have the modern desire for excitement. The speed with which one craze follows another may indicate, not an instability of wants in any fundamental sense, but a lack of self-knowledge, an attempt to find satisfaction in one thing after another. Rapid technical change greatly enlarges the scope for such experimentation, and business enterprise does its best not only to cater to it but also to incite it by continued stimulation.

In each of the other two types of deviation from the norm which might be predicted from economic theory, we found some hope that the empirical discovery of social patterns of behavior might make possible a more scientific approach to the interpretation of individual behavior. Is there a similar hope that the choice of experiments, whether in the course of an attempted adjustment to given conditions or in the search for direct satisfaction from the experimental activity itself, may be socially determined? In some cases a social pattern may be discernible. For instance, experiments in the production of new commodities or in the adoption of new practices will often be imitated by other firms, even before the results, in terms of sales or profits, are known. Similarly, much experimental consumption consists of trying out the goods which leaders of style and fashion have recommended. For the greater part, however, experimental behavior is thoroughly individualistic, in method as well as in objective; and it is difficult to imagine how it could be brought within the framework of a conceptual scheme, without doing violence to the facts. It is even doubtful whether much can usefully be said about the range of possibilities open to the experimenter; the real individualist invents his own experiments.

The chief aid to be had from the concept of social patterns in this connection is the observation that some societies are more tolerant of experiment than others. It should be possible, by empirical study, to determine whether the mental climate is favorable or unfavorable to innovation in the time and place under consideration and to estimate, accordingly, the margin of error that is likely to arise from this source, in applying the conventional assumptions of economic motivation to concrete problems.

This review of the three different types of deviation from the principle of behavior which underlies most of present-day economic theory shows the need for extreme caution in the prediction of events. It is on the psychological side, above all, that economic theory must be supplemented by sound common sense. At the same time we must continue to put up with considerable differences of opinion among economists on any practical issues that turn on people's "psychological reactions" to particular proposals. It has been suggested that the range of uncertainty might be somewhat diminished if economists would explore the possibility of determining the actual social patterns to which some, at least, of these "psychological reactions" conform and use these social norms as bases for more realistic theories than those at present at their disposal. This line of approach is more particularly hopeful in relation to the so-called "nonfinancial" motives, which often upset conclusions drawn from conventional economic theory. It also suggests a reconsideration of the psychology of exchange, to which we now turn.

EXCHANGE AS A SOCIAL PATTERN

To consider economic behavior as a social pattern, instead of as the outgrowth of the maximization principle or the rational pursuit of one's interests, involves a considerable departure from the usual view-point of economists. Yet reflection suggests that the assumption that each individual seeks to maximize his own advantage is not sufficient psychological foundation for a theory of exchange. Where a multiplicity of individuals is concerned, their dealings with one another may include not only trade but also appropriation and gift. In this respect a society differs from a single individual. When we consider the behavior of an individual, confronted by various possibilities of consumption and various uses for his time and resources, the assumption that he seeks to maximize the satisfaction of his desires leads to the notion of marginal substitution of one thing or one activity for another, until "equilibrium" is attained. This conception of an "internal" process of exchange is analogous to trade between several individuals. Historically this concept of the individual economy was probably suggested by the observation of exchange in the social economy. But it is only in the individual economy that exchange is the sole method of giving effect to the principle of maximization. An individual can substitute only one collection of goods for another, one line of action for another, even if it be inaction. He cannot, in his own individual economy, perform any operations analogous to the compulsory transfer of goods from one person to another, without any recompense or exchange. "Coercion is an exercise of power over others."[39] Nor is there, in the individual economy, any operation analogous to the gifts such as may be made between different persons.

The theory of exchange between individuals can be made the logical outgrowth of the maximization principle only by explicitly abstracting from the possibility of appropriation and gift. This is listed by Professor Knight among the essential assumptions of the theory of exchange:

> We formally exclude all preying of individuals upon each other. There must be no way of acquiring goods except through production and free exchange in the open market. . . . . The people are formally free to act as their motives prompt in the production, exchange and consumption of goods. They own themselves; there is no exercise of constraint over any individual by another individual or by society; each controls his own activities with a view to results which serve him individually.[40]

It is one thing to adopt an assumption for the purpose of argument. But how, if at all, are these activities prevented in practice? When we

[39] T. Parsons, *The Structure of Social Action* (New York, 1937), p. 767. My debt to Professor Parsons' work in this connection will be evident to sociologists. I can only hope that I have made its importance for economics sufficiently clear, by working out some further implications.

[40] F. H. Knight, *Risk, Uncertainty, and Profit* (Boston, 1921), p. 77.

assume that they do not occur, we imply one or both of two other conditions. On the one hand, we might presuppose a *disposition to trade* stronger than any disposition to appropriate goods and services or to give them away.[41] On the other hand, we might assume the existence of *social controls*, which operate to prevent appropriation or gift. These controls might include group pressure operating through institutional norms or a legal system backed by the power of the state.

The former assumption, namely, a trading propensity stronger than the urge to take or give, does not fit in well with the fact that "much of the product of society—possibly one-half or two-thirds of it—reaches its final recipients by gift."[42] The problems raised by this type of behavior are largely ignored by economic theory, except in public finance, where gift and appropriation loom large. Professor MacGregor reminds us that Jevons' *Theory of Political Economy* "has practically no reference to wife or child, friend, relative or social interests,"[43] although in practice "the private economy" is really closer to "the public economy" than to the business economy. The relationships between the members of the family are not settled by exchange. It would be too much to assume, therefore, that where exchange does occur it is due to a native preference for this type of activity over appropriation and gift.

What economists do generally assume—tacitly more often than explicitly—is that, of these three impulses, the tendency to give is strong only when there are personal ties or sentiment, as in the family or charity. Neglecting conduct within this field, we are left with appropriation and exchange. It is generally assumed that the former impulse is the stronger of these two but that it is prevented from finding more than limited expression by the legal and institutional framework of society. On this assumption it is possible to construct a theory of exchange as the outgrowth of the principle of maximization. But it must then be admitted that, whenever personal ties or sentiment are present in business or whenever legal or institutional norms permit a wider range of activities then those involved in pure exchange, economic behavior may deviate considerably from the paths laid down in economic theory. Consequently, realistic theory must take account of these personal ties and institutional forms of control.

[41] Cf. Adam Smith's famous postulate: "the propensity to truck, barter and exchange one thing for another" (*Wealth of Nations*, Book I, chap. ii).

[42] H. J. Davenport, *Economics of Enterprise* (New York, 1923), p. 494.

[43] D. H. MacGregor, *Public Aspects of Finance* (Oxford, 1935), p. 38.

It may be noted that the distinction between gift, exchange, and appropriation is sometimes vague. If exchange involves a "nominal" payment on one side, this comes close to a gift or appropriation, according to whether the giving or receiving side exerts more influence on the terms of the transaction. In the determination of terms of trade different results will be reached according to the preference of one party to avoid higgling or to make a generous settlement rather than obtain the most favorable rate of exchange in the ordinary sense of the word. On the other hand, the terms of exchange may be influenced by the exercise by one party of pressure on the other through some other interest distinct from the exchange or by group pressure in the form of some conventional standard of behavior. In the theory of pure exchange there is no room for these factors, except as conditions limiting the range of possibilities that are open to the parties concerned. For instance, we may assume that employers are obliged, by fear of sabotage, to offer a particular wage. We can then work out the number of employees that they will engage, in the light of this and other conditions, and also the number of employees that will seek work at this wage. The *result* of the coercion, namely, a lower limit to wages, is then assumed as a constant factor in the situation, and the theory of exchange enables us to explore the adjustments which will be made, as each individual attempts to secure the maximum advantage from this rigid price, by modifying the volume of exchanges. But economic literature is not rich in analyses of this sort; the modification of the exchange process through coercion or generosity is considered, if at all, as a special case. If it were customary to give weight to such factors in all theoretical models relating to exchange, the economist's general picture of the world would be rather different from what it is. And the problem of determining just what effect coercion, etc., will have upon the minimum price—a problem not to be solved by the theory of exchange—would make more insistent claims on the economist's attention.

This discussion suggests that many of the things that happen in industry, trade, and finance are explicitly excluded from economic theory by an arbitrary selection of assumptions. It is assumed, for purposes of analysis, that people accept the operations of the market and allow it to work without any attempt to influence its verdict one way or the other. It is assumed, moreover, that they do not attempt to alter the conditions of the market—except in so far as they can improve their own position by the ordinary activities of the market.

These assumptions are inconsistent with the practice of economists in studying the *effects* of such deliberate interference with the market as tariffs, price control, and collective bargaining. And they are inconsistent with the facts of economic life in the ordinary meaning of the term.

What happens if we remove these assumptions and admit the possibility of action outside the market and the use of force, on the one hand, and brotherly love, on the other, inside the market? Some may fear that this would mean the wreck of existing economic theory. It certainly means the collapse of some of the boundaries that have been used to limit the scope of economic theory. And it opens the way to the development of a new theory to cover some, at least, of what goes on beyond the market in the world of industry, trade, and finance. The main outlines of this theory, which may be called the theory of extra-market operations, will be sketched in the next chapter.

CHAPTER VI

BEYOND THE MARKET

IN THE preceding chapter it was argued that among the implicit psychological assumptions of conventional economic theory there is the supposition that people act only through the market. Other forms of behavior may be observed; but economic theory abstracts from them for the purposes of its analyses and assumes that people seek their ends only by buying and selling, hiring and borrowing. Or we may say that economic theory considers the pursuit of ends (financial and nonfinancial) which can be achieved through market activities and does not study human behavior in so far as it consists of the pursuit of other ends. For instance, going to church or doing physical exercises of a morning or agitating for a change in the divorce laws is usually regarded as "noneconomic" behavior, because these ends cannot be achieved through the market. Thus Professor Schumpeter draws a distinction between "economic life," on the one hand, and political activities which "do not aim immediately at the acquisition of goods through exchange or production," on the other, although, as we shall see in chapter viii, he admits that the distinction is not always clearly marked.[1]

It is not suggested there that the economist should enlarge his field of study to cover *all* such phenomena. But there are ends which may be pursued both inside the market and outside it. When the latter course is followed, we have a special type of behavior, which may be distinguished from those forms of behavior which are causally remote from the market, as well as from those that are observed in the market. This special type of behavior differs from noneconomic behavior (as usually conceived) with regard to its ends and from market behavior with regard to its methods. In selecting the term "extra-market operations" to represent this type of behavior, one hopes to convey both shades of meaning. Extra-market *activities* might be taken to cover all behavior outside the market; extra-market *operations* are only those extra-market activities which are directed toward ends which may be sought and are sought also through operations in the market.

---

[1] J. H. Schumpeter, *Theory of Economic Development* (Cambridge, Mass., 1934), p. 5; *Business Cycles* (New York, 1939), I, 11.

The term "extra-market adjustments" might provide an attractive contrast with the adjustments which the market makes to given data and at the same time emphasize that we are concerned with responses to the same total situation as that to which the market adjusts itself. But the term "operations" suggests a more active form of behavior than does the term "adjustments." As Veblen says, "It is characteristic of man to do something."[2]

Our principle of distinction between extra-market operations and other noneconomic activities, therefore, is found in the impossibility of pursuing certain ends in the market, while our distinction between market operations and extra-market operations turns on the possibility of pursuing other ends outside the market as well as inside. According to Professor Robbins, "in so far as the achievement of *any* end is dependent upon scarce means, it is germane to the preoccupations of the economist";[3] but the body of economic theory, as usually taught, deals only with the achievement of ends through market operations and generally ignores not only other methods of achieving those ends but also all ends which cannot be achieved in this way. In other words, the criterion of "scarce means" is interpreted, in practice, to cover only goods and services which are exchanged in the market.

Our distinction raises the question as to why certain ends are sought through the market as well as outside it, while other ends are sought only outside the market. That, although a matter of great historical and philosophical interest, will not be pursued here. The distinction is here considered merely as a means of improving the economist's equipment for the study of concrete problems.

The study of extra-market operations, as defined above, is necessary on three grounds for economists who would advise on policy. In the first place, as we saw in chapter ii, practical men do not regard extra-market operations as lying outside the field of economic behavior, and the economist is expected to show some competence to consider them. Second, any economic explanations or predictions which ignore the possibility of extra-market operations run the danger of being unreal-

[2] T. Veblen, *The Place of Science in Modern Civilisation* (New York, 1930), p.74. Veblen rejects "the hedonistic conception of man" as "a lightning calculator of pleasure and pains, who oscillates like a homogeneous globule of desire of happiness under the impulse of stimuli that shift him about the area, but leave him intact. . . . . Self imposed in elementary space, he spins symmetrically about his own spiritual axis, until the parallelogram of forces bears down upon him, whereupon he follows the line of the resultant. When the force of the impact is spent, he comes to rest, a self-contained globule of desire as before."

[3] L. Robbins, *Essay on the Nature and Significance of Economic Science* (2d ed.; London, 1937), p. 24.

istic. Finally, extra-market operations are an important source of change in the data of the market itself; and when we come to consider the possibility of a theory of economic development, which may aid the economist to predict data changes as well as market reactions to the data, we shall find that the theory of extra-market operations has something to contribute. The pressure of practical affairs makes it impossible for the economist to wait hopefully until some other specialist provides such a theory; but there are also two other good reasons why economists should themselves make the attempt. One reason is that a knowledge of how the market works is an important prerequisite to understanding why people reject its verdict and prefer to operate outside it. The other reason is that, although extreme cases of extra-market operations present a great contrast with market operations, it is, nevertheless, impossible to draw a hard and fast boundary between these two types of behavior. The one shades imperceptibly into the other.

EXAMPLES OF EXTRA-MARKET OPERATIONS

Some examples may render the last point clearer. Racketeering may be generally classed as an extra-market operation. The threat of violence to person or property is used as a means of extracting payments; and, although the payments are nominally for the service of protection, there is no misunderstanding as to their real nature. Even Marshall has observed that

the feverish pursuit of wealth may induce men, capable of great work, to drift into distinctly criminal courses. . . . . The National Cash Register Company, whose technical achievements are in the first rank, has been convicted for malicious libels in regard to competitors; and for causing its agents to injure internal parts of rival machines when in use, and similar practices.[4]

We should class these as extra-market operations, along with some of J. D. Rockefeller's attempts to prevent the construction of pipe lines in competition with the railways under his control: "His agents frightened the farmers over whose lands the pipes must pass, by stories of poisonous leakages and unquenchable fires, and gangs of railway employees attacked the workmen laying the pipes."[5] The sit-down strike is clearly an extra-market operation, amounting to the forcible occupation of the employer's property; and the use of pickets in ordinary strikes is also outside the market. The various methods used by arms

---

[4] A. Marshall, *Industry and Trade* (London, 1920), p. 537 and note.

[5] H. G. Wells, *The Work, Wealth and Happiness of Mankind* (London, 1932), p. 450.

manufacturers to discourage international agreement on disarmament may be regarded as extra-market operations designed to promote or maintain their commercial interests.

Nor should we hesitate to classify as extra-market operations the day-to-day attempts of businessmen and their organizations to obtain legislation favorable to themselves. This type of political business activity is an international phenomenon.

> The government is not a neutral arbiter in economic matters, but tends to reflect the aims of those groups which are in the best position to influence governmental decisions. Few would deny that the policies of Canadian Governments since Confederation have been predominantly shaped by business men. . . . . Permanent lobbies in Ottawa, innumerable special delegations, the molding of public opinion through newspapers and other media, contributions to party funds—all these investments have yielded an abundant return.[6]

Lobbying by various sectional interests, including large business units or organizations, has long been a feature of politics in the United States.[7] Not only the process of legislation but also the activities of regulatory bodies, such as the Interstate Commerce Commission, are subject to campaigns and various forms of pressure in the normal course of business. "The recognised judicial character of its work does not render the Commission immune from efforts to influence its judgments. The struggles of contending economic groups and political influences give rise to actions intolerable in a court of law and to repeated efforts to obtain favourable decisions through the use of propaganda."[8]

In Australia organized producer interests are represented in Canberra when parliament is sitting, outside as well as inside the legislature. The Associated Chambers of Manufacturers—the principal protectionist pressure group—maintains a permanent office in the national capital; and the Associated Chambers of Commerce has followed this example. The reports of the Australian Tariff Board indicate the time, care, and expense which businessmen devote to the preparation of evidence in support of, or opposition to, changes in rates of duty. Another form of political activity is to attempt to influ-

---

[6] L. G. Reynolds, *The Control of Competition in Canada* (Cambridge, Mass., 1940), p. 272.

[7] See E. B. Logan, *Lobbying* (Suppl. to *Annals of American Academy of Political and Social Science* [1929]). A more recent study is D. C. Blaisdell, *Economic Power and Political Pressures* ("Temporary National Economic Committee Monographs," No. 26 [Washington, 1941]).

[8] E. P. Herring, *Public Administration and the Public Interest* (New York, 1936), p. 194; the whole of chap. xii is relevant.

ence the regional distribution of defense contracts. State governments will readily view the granting of contracts to firms in their territory as a legitimate interpretation of the public interest and ally themselves with private interests to bring pressure to bear on the federal government.

In Great Britain, too, organized pressure groups are a prominent feature of the political scene. The National Farmers' Union, for instance, had a political fund amounting to over £68,000 in 1937, in addition to the still larger general fund. Dr. Jennings gives many examples of the pressure exerted by this body on the government and on private members of parliament in connection with specific pieces of legislation.[9] Other prominent business organizations in that country include the Mining Association, the Chamber of Shipping, the National Federation of Iron and Steel Manufacturers, and the Federation of British Industries. To be effective they must not only perfect the technique of political influence but also compel the loyalty of the members whose "interests" they represent. On the other hand, there are labor organizations with varying degrees of political power. The operations of these various organizations are designed, generally speaking, to alter the conditions of the market so that it will yield greater financial returns to the people they represent.

All these examples of political activity are sufficiently related to everyday business operations to warrant our description of them as attempts to gain ends similar to those that are also sought in the market; and they all involve operations *outside* the market. They may, therefore, be referred to as extra-market operations, in contrast to the market operations which are the customary subjects of economic theory. We may now consider some examples of borderline cases—forms of behavior which do not fall easily into either class.

BORDERLINE CASES

The establishment of codes of fair competition under the National Recovery Act would, no doubt, be classed as extra-market operations, for they involved not only agreement among competitors but also the indorsement of the government. The actual trade practices which are covered by the codes (by approval or prohibition) fall into three classes: market operations, extra-market operations, and *mixtures*. In the first class would fall the various methods of costing and determination of selling price; when a code forbids selling below cost, it forbids a

9 W. I. Jennings, *Parliament* (London, 1940), p. 211.

particular market operation. Other market practices which the codes attempted to control include price differentiation, discounts, credit terms, repurchase agreements, distribution of coupons, provision of containers, and payment of delivery costs. In the second class would fall such practices as "coercion," boycotting or black-listing, threats of litigation, violence or threats of violence, espionage of competitors, and defamation of competitors. But the following practices do not fall neatly into either of the first two classes: "collusion to withhold instruments of production from competitors," purchases in excess of requirements in order to hinder competitors, imitation of trade-marks, threats of repudiation of contract, deferring payment of products purchased in order to obtain better terms in future, and "enticement" of competitors' employees. These practices take place in the market; yet they are not simple market transactions.[10] The working of the market itself is influenced by special factors which savor more of personal or political relationships than of pure exchange. The technique of economic theory does not deal adequately with them, because they involve activities which are not covered by its assumptions.

Another group of borderline cases are those in which market activities of a sort are undertaken with the deliberate intention of modifying the conditions of the market or of obtaining some result outside the market. For instance, it might be argued that bribery is a market operation: "Every man has his price." The return asked of the corrupt official is often a small change in the law or the award of a public contract or preferential treatment in some regulatory activity of the government. In these cases the paying party is not content with the results of the market under existing conditions; he desires to alter the data of the market or to obtain direct benefits by means of the extra-market operations of another party; but in order to obtain the latter service he must make a market transaction.

Bribery is outside the law, but the same difficulty of definition arises with some actions which are strictly legal. For instance, the American Telephone and Telegraph Company has paid authors and arranged for the publication of books calculated to improve the public relations of the company and distributed many copies free.[11] This involved market activities; but it may be suggested that the acquisition of goods and services by exchange was of minor importance compared with the

[10] For a general review of the trade practices covered by the codes see C. A. Pearce, *N.R.A. Trade Practice Program* (New York, 1939).

[11] N. R. Danielian, *A.T. & T.: The Story of Industrial Conquest* (New York, 1939).

desire to influence public opinion. Again, the common practice of large industrial concerns of requiring their employees, as a condition of employment, to sell any patents to the company for a nominal fee involves only market activities. The purpose, however, is often to prevent technical improvements from becoming known to competitors, even though the company does not intend to adopt them itself. Patents are put to sleep in an attempt to control the development of a portion of the data of the market.[12]

These borderline cases sometimes involve the intrusion of extra-market operations into the market in order to modify its working; in other cases the methods of the market are extended into the field of politics and other extra-market activities. The result is a mixture of market and extra-market operations. When confronted by a concrete problem of this type, the procedure of the economist is to apply his market theory and to correct its results by a common-sense appraisal of the particular extra-market operations which are visible in the case under consideration. In problems in which extra-market operations dominate the scene and market theory has little or no relevance the economist has no technical competence at all. This is because he has no recognized theory of the purely extra-market operations. If he did possess such a theory, the mixed cases would call, not merely for the correction of market theory by common sense, but for a synthesis of market theory and the theory of extra-market operations. Such a synthesis can be achieved only by those who are masters of both theories. Thus the existence of borderline cases reinforces our argument that the economist should develop the theory of extra-market operations himself.

THE EXTENSION OF CONTROL

It will be noted that the examples quoted above all refer to the behavior of an economic unit in relation to other economic units. In some cases the unit is an individual; in other cases, a group or firm. If we consider a firm or other organization, there is also the problem of internal control or management. When we speak of market adjustments we concentrate attention upon the external behavior of the firm; but the adjustments usually involve internal changes. These internal problems are studied under such names as "business management," "personnel management," "industrial management." It is in-

[12] Cf. J. D. Bernal, *Social Functions of Science* (London, 1939); see also W. H. Hamilton, *Patents and Free Enterprise* ("Temporary National Economic Committee Monographs," No. 31 [Washington, 1941]).

teresting to note that the methods adopted to deal with such problems may be classified along lines analogous with our division between market and extra-market operations. Some of the problems of management may be considered as problems of exchange. All production may be regarded as an exchange of certain materials and labor against the finished product. Pareto used the term "transformation" to cover exchange of goods between individuals and production of certain goods by working on other goods; and he used the same method of analysis for both.[13] Professor Hicks approaches the problem of production in exactly the same way.[14] Not only are the factors of production exchangeable against the final product, but one factor of production can be substituted for, that is, exchanged against, another in the productive process. In the same way it may be argued that the consumer carries on a sort of internal exchange, substituting units of some commodity for units of others in his own consumption, until he arrives at the most satisfactory combination of commodities in appropriate quantities. In the cases of the firm and the individual alike, this internal exchange must take account, not only of the "technical" substitutability and complementarity of various goods viewed as factors in productive yield or consumer's satisfaction, but also the terms on which these various goods and services can be acquired. It is the latter consideration which, in the opinion of many economists, distinguishes an economic problem from a purely technical one. But, as Professor Parsons has pointed out, when there is a plurality of individuals (as in the firm) the possibility of the coercion of one by another as well as exchange between them is present.[15] In other words, the problem of management is not entirely a problem of internal exchange, analogous to market operations. And the literature of industrial management (even in textbooks of general economics) covers many activities more analogous to extra-market operations, but internal to the firm.

A useful classification of these internal activities is contained in a survey by the United States National Resources Committee of the organizational structure of the American economy.[16] Four "major organizing influences" are distinguished: the market mechanism, ad-

---

[13] V. Pareto, *Manuel d'économie politique* (Paris, 1927), pp. 175 ff.

[14] J. R. Hicks, *Value and Capital* (London, 1939), p. 78.

[15] T. Parsons, *The Structure of Social Action* (New York, 1937), p. 767; see also above, chap. v.

[16] *The Structure of the American Economy*, Part I: *Basic Characteristics* (Washington, 1939), p. 97.

ministrative co-ordination, canalizing rules, and accepted common goals. "The role which each influence plays at different times and at different places will vary; but hardly any significant event occurs without some element of organisation being contributed by each of these four influences." The committee views the employment of the nation's resources as a whole and does not lay much emphasis upon the distinction between internal management and external operations, although it implies that the market mechanism controls only the latter.

> While administration plays the role of coordinating the activities of individuals within economic units, the market functions to coordinate the activities between economic units. . . . . It is not the sole influence coordinating the activities of separate economic units but operates within the framework established by canalising rules, in conjunction with the greater or less influence of accepted goals, and supplemented by threads of administrative control running between economic units.[17]

But the report quoted studies these "controls" chiefly as they operate *inside* the economic unit; and their growing importance in the whole economic scheme, as compared with that of the market mechanism, is attributed to the development of large corporations, often interlocked, and of "economic interest" organizations which influence the policies of individual units.[18] In other words, the effective unit of control (combining smaller "specific productive" units) has grown larger and larger.

It should be noted, however, that the extra-market operations that are studied in the present chapter are not attributed to the enlargement of the economic units but are regarded as the extension to the field of external relations of those forms of behavior which are common in internal administration. The principles of exchange apply in both fields; but in both fields exchange is modified and often replaced by collaboration based on common ends, common habits, or the exercise of power. It has been observed that the administration of a very large corporation, such as American Telephone and Telegraph, assumes the characteristics of government rather than business and that even its dealings with other firms and individuals become increasingly a matter of politics.[19] Professor Arnold has suggested that only confusion has emerged from the continued attempts to describe industrial empires in terms of property rights and business transactions and that, although exactions by business organizations are more readily tolerated than similar exactions by governments, there is little difference in fact.[20]

---

[17] *Ibid.*, p. 108.   [18] *Ibid.*, pp. 155 ff.   [19] Cf. Danielian, *op. cit.*

[20] T. Arnold, *The Folklore of Capitalism* (New Haven, 1937).

The prevalence of extra-market operations, as here defined, is therefore recognized, though neither economic nor political theory has previously been extended to take them fully into account.

AN AID TO THE STUDY OF FACTS, NOT A SUBSTITUTE

It is perhaps necessary to emphasize that the function of the theory of extra-market operations is analogous with the function of market theory, namely, to guide the economist in his search for significant facts. It is not to provide, once and for all, a comprehensive account and explanation of every particular operation which takes place outside the market instead of inside it. Like market theory, it is an explicit conceptual scheme under which observed facts can be grouped.[21] It represents certain forms of behavior (in this case, outside the market) as the logical consequence of a given set of conditions or data, including a principle of behavior. To explain a particular extra-market operation in the real world, it is necessary to show that the conditions assumed by the theory coincide with the conditions observed in the concrete case under consideration; then the conclusions of the theory (the implications of the data) should agree with the consequences of these conditions in the real world. The theory is not a substitute for the study of the real world but an aid to its interpretation. It tells us *what to look for*. A good theory is one that directs our attention to the facts which are really significant for the problem in hand. A bad theory is one that directs attention to insignificant facts or promotes a search for facts which do not exist.

Our theory of extra-market operations, then, will be used, in practice, in the following manner. We may want to know whether, in a particular case, businessmen will accept the verdict of the market or attempt to obtain "protection" against it by legislative action. The theory should show the various conditions under which each course of action will be followed. In the particular instance, therefore, we must "look and see" which of these conditions is present in the real world. The procedure is similar to that followed in applying market theory to a concrete case.

An economist who, when dealing with a particular problem, finds it necessary to supplement the conclusions of market theory by a "common-sense" appraisal of extra-market operations does not, in fact, approach the problem without any conceptual scheme, any more than the person without economic training approaches a problem of mar-

[21] See above, chap. iii.

ket behavior without some theoretical preconceptions. In both cases a conceptual scheme of sorts is implicit but not explicit; and it is likely to be an amalgam of personal prejudice and unexamined generalization. In the study of market behavior the economist prefers to use a conceptual scheme which has been stated explicitly and tested logically. Similarly, it would seem better to have out in the open the conceptual scheme which he applies to extra-market operations and to subject it to the same logical criticism.

DIVISIONS OF THE THEORY OF EXTRA-MARKET OPERATIONS

"There is scarcely any limit to the developments of economic theory which are possible; but of those which are possible only a small part are useful in having a direct relation to practical issues."[22] This is equally true of the theory of extra-market operations. Beyond a certain point, elaborations of the theory are practically useful only if related to concrete conditions. Like the revision of economic psychology advocated in chapter v, much of the theory will be shaped by local factors, and it is not useful to push its elaboration in general terms to the same extent as has been done with market theory. Our own exposition of the theory will consequently be little more than an outline of the various types of theoretical construction which promise to be useful. Particular attention will be paid to the relations between the concepts of the theory of extra-market operations and those of the theory of the market.

The theory of extra-market operations falls generally into three sections. The first section is an analysis of dissatisfaction with the working of the market, for this is the motive behind such extra-market operations as are deliberately preferred to market operations. It would be wrong to suggest, however, that people always have before them the need to choose between these alternative forms of behavior. One or the other may be followed habitually, until dissatisfaction with its results reaches breaking-point and stimulates a search for a more satisfactory method of action. Or the break may come only when the possibility of an alternative channel of behavior is brought to one's notice by some external event. Nevertheless, if complete satisfaction with the market were universal, there would be no need for a study of extra-market operations.

The second section of the theory consists of a classification of the

---

[22] A. C. Pigou (ed.), *Memorials of Alfred Marshall* (London, 1925), p. 162; the same quotation was used in our discussion of "Theoretic Blight."

various types of extra-market operations and of the ways in which they furnish, or at least promise to furnish, greater satisfaction than can be achieved, under existing conditions, in the market alone. This part of the theory is analogous to a survey of the technological data of general economic theory; and the same problem arises as to how much detailed description is required. Without some study of technology the economic theory of production, for instance, could not exist. By limiting the technological data to a few formal relationships, such as marginal substitutability of resources, the theory can be developed in very general terms. But most teachers of economics feel impelled to give the theory some contact with real problems and to illustrate the more formal assumptions of "pure" theory. On the other hand, it is not considered desirable to make technological details of particular trades a principal object of study, except in some special fields, such as the foreign exchanges, where this does tend to happen. We shall follow a similar plan, carrying out study of the technology of extra-market operations only as far as may be necessary to give life to the bones of pure theory.

Finally, the third section of the theory attempts to classify the conditions under which dissatisfaction with the market does or does not boil over into the theoretically available channels of extra-market operations. The need for this section arises from the observation that people often continue with one form of behavior when it is evident, at least in the opinion of the outsider, that the other form of behavior would be more advantageous to them. It is in this section, too, that we shall correct the undue emphasis on rationality which might otherwise emerge from the first two sections of the theory.

Extra-market operations are undertaken because they promise better results than can be achieved by strict adherence to market activities under existing market conditions. These results are assessed in relation to the ends which would otherwise be pursued through the market. An analysis of dissatisfaction with the market, therefore, requires first an examination of these ends.

Financial and nonfinancial motives.—The immediate end of much market activity is to obtain a sum of money; "the steadiest motive to ordinary business work is the desire for the pay which is the material reward of work."[23] Money, however, is itself usually a means to some

[23] A. Marshall, *Principles of Economics* (8th ed.; London, 1922), p. 15; quoted above also (chap. v).

other end; after it has been obtained it is expended on various objects or held for future use. For the purpose of market theory it is rarely necessary to go behind the financial motive (though it may be necessary to supplement it by taking account of nonfinancial motives). Expenditure may be directed to the cultivation of one's higher faculties, self-indulgence, objects of "pecuniary emulation," charitable objects, or one's basic physiological needs; this does not affect the analysis of the implications of the profit motive. Even if, as Marshall suggested, many businessmen seek money primarily as a mark of successful achievement, the theory of market behavior is not in need of modification on that account, as long as the desire for distinction does not involve the sacrifice of financial gain.[24]

In the theory of extra-market operations, however, the more fundamental ends cannot be ignored. In so far as they can be attained *directly* by extra-market operations, without the intermediary of money, it is not sufficient to compare the *financial* results of market and extra-market operations. For instance, to organize a trade-union might yield an individual no financial return and might even diminish his personal financial success in the labor market; but it might satisfy the desire for power and prestige far better than the earning of a considerable income by strict attention to business. On the other hand, the market, while providing a certain financial return, may do violence to other desires, particularly for social recognition. For instance, it is argued that low wages are a less important cause of industrial unrest than the inferior status of wage labor, which must work under supervision.[25] The heterogeneity of human motives is therefore of greater importance for the theory of extra-market operations than for general economic theory. This renders more difficult the construction of a compact theory: it must cover a wider range of possibilities than does the theory of the market.

Even in market theory, as we have seen,[26] nonfinancial motives demand more attention than is usually accorded them. The desire for personal prestige may sometimes be satisfied by large-scale production, even though a smaller enterprise would yield greater profits. Continued operation at a loss is not unknown; the motive is sometimes altruism toward the employees. Behavior in the market is influenced by all that Veblen summed up in the term "the instinct of workmanship"

---

[24] The qualifications were elaborated in chap. v.

[25] Cf. H. de Man, *Psychology of Socialism* (London, 1928), p. 93.

[26] Above, chap. v.

and by professional ethics and moral codes, as well as by the calculation of monetary gain. Nor is the desire for power and dominion a
negligible factor in market activities. Very often these motives may
be more easily satisfied through extra-market operations; or the difficulty of expressing them in the market may on occasion encourage the
search for an alternative field of endeavor. The analysis of extra-market operations under the impulse of such motives as these is extremely
difficult; and the prospects in this part of the field are not promising.
In the first place we cannot hope to take them fully into account until
the psychological investigations suggested in chapter v have borne
fruit. Moreover, we are dealing here with ends which are commonly
sought as much outside the market as within; we are approaching the
borderline between extra-market operations as we have defined them
and those other extra-market activities which even the practical man
would consider to be "noneconomic."[27]

In our analysis of dissatisfaction with the market, therefore, we shall
concentrate attention upon the money motive and those more fundamental ends for the achievement of which money is the *usual* instrument.

Equilibrium theory implies dissatisfaction.—For the theory of extra-
market operations it is essential to assume dissatisfaction with the results of the market on the part of the individuals in question. This assumption is reasonable enough on empirical grounds and should not
shock the theoretical economist. For equilibrium theory itself assumes, in effect, that dissatisfaction with the results of the market is a
universal feature of economic life. Equilibrium theory assumes that,
if there were any alternative market adjustment which promised a
greater return, this would, in fact, be undertaken. The implication is
that, even where equilibrium has been reached, the economic subject
is not completely satisfied with the returns from his market activities,
though he cannot see any other market activities which would be more
satisfactory under existing conditions. It follows, therefore, that everybody has a motive to undertake extra-market operations if he knows of
any which would yield better returns than the best returns available
within the market. From this viewpoint equilibrium theory suggests
that the problem is not why people sometimes abandon the market
but why extra-market operations are not more common than they are
in practice. However, equilibrium theory does not necessarily assume
that this chronic state of dissatisfaction is very intense; the dissatisfac-

---

[27] See above, at the beginning of this chapter.

tion must merely be strong enough to overcome any obstacle to another market adjustment if that promised better returns. Whether the obstacles to extra-market operations are of similar magnitude is another question.

The statement that equilibrium theory assumes a chronic state of dissatisfaction with the results of the market may appear strange when placed alongside the proposition, so common in economic writings, that total satisfaction is maximized in equilibrium or, if one objects to summing the satisfaction of different individuals,[28] that each individual in equilibrium draws the maximum satisfaction from the given conditions of the market. There is, however, no contradiction. The maximum satisfaction which is associated with market equilibrium is the maximum possible in the market *under existing conditions;* it is quite consistent with violent dissatisfaction with these conditions or with the limited returns which the market consequently yields to the individual. Insufficiently careful expositions of welfare economics may sometimes give the impression that, in equilibrium, individual satisfaction is maximized in an absolute sense; but the relativity of the "optimum" to the existing conditions of the market is too obvious to need elaboration here.

Equity and exploitation.—It is true that economists have sometimes used langue that implied that the results of market operations should at least give no reasonable ground for dissatisfaction. For instance, J. B. Clark argued that the economic system would be inequitable—and the results of the market questionable—if one man could draw more out of the common stream of production than he contributed, while another drew less than his specific contribution. He satisfied himself on this point, however, by identifying the marginal productivity of labor with labor's specific contribution to the total product; since labor's remuneration was equal to its marginal product (in equilibrium), labor received back the equivalent of its specific contribution, and similarly with the other factors of production.[29]

This type of sophistry is no longer fashionable. It is not possible to determine the specific contribution of any one factor to the fruits of co-operative production. Moreover, there is no certainty that the marginal productivity of a factor will yield a living wage. "It is quite conceivable," wrote Wicksell, "that the output of a society may be large enough for all, but that the *marginal* productivity of labour is

[28] Cf. Robbins, *op. cit.*, p. 138.

[29] J. B. Clark, *The Distribution of Wealth* (New York, 1908).

none the less so small that labour has only a slight economic value."[30] Even if marginal product were the specific product of a factor, it would be difficult to argue that a wage below subsistence level was equitable.[31]

In their search for a precise terminology, economists are sometimes led to the use of words which are pregnant with associations quite foreign to the analysis in hand. For instance, one source of dissatisfaction with the results of the market is the belief that one is being exploited. Karl Marx deliberately made use of this emotional association when he defined exploitation as working for longer hours than was necessary to produce one's own wages. The working day he divided into two parts: necessary labor, which sufficed to support the worker himself, and surplus labor, the product of which was the object of the class struggle. "What distinguishes the various economic types of society from one another (distinguishes, for instance, a society based upon slavery from a society based upon wage labour) is nothing other than the way in which surplus labour is extorted from the actual producer, the worker."[32] The ratio of "surplus" labor to "necessary" labor was defined as the "rate of exploitation." Marx had no scruples about working on the emotions as well as on the intellect. But modern economists, such as Professor Pigou, claim that there is no place for emotion in the cold temple of science.[33] It is surprising, therefore, to find them also using the term "exploitation of labor" and still more surprising that it should be defined as paying a wage below the marginal product of labor.[34] This use of the term, apparently introduced by Professor Pigou, seems to have become common. According to Mrs. Robinson, "what is actually meant by exploitation is, usually, that the wage is less than the marginal physical product of labour valued at its selling price."[35] These writers, however, would probably disclaim any intention of implying that workers have nothing to complain of if they do receive wages equal to the marginal product of labor.

[30] K. Wicksell, *Lectures on Political Economy* (London, 1934), I, 143.

[31] In such a case Wicksell favored paying only the marginal-productivity wage as wages and subsidizing the workers personally out of a levy on the income of the other factors; "it would be better to do this than to insist that every labourer employed should earn the subsistence wage," since, on his assumptions, "that might have the result that many labourers would be unemployed, and with their families, would become entirely dependent upon poor relief" (*ibid.*, p. 141).

[32] *Capital*, trans. Paul (London, 1928), p. 214.

[33] A. C. Pigou, *Unemployment* (London, 1913), p. 11.

[34] A. C. Pigou, *Economics of Welfare* (3d ed.; London, 1929), p. 556.

[35] Joan Robinson, *Economics of Imperfect Competition* (London, 1933), p. 282.

Attention may also be drawn to Professor Pigou's unhappy adoption of Marshall's expression, "fair wages" to mean wages "about on a level with the payment made for tasks in other trades which are of equal difficulty and disagreeableness, which require equal natural abilities and an equally expensive training."[36] On this definition, "fairness" is a relationship between the wages of different groups of workers and not between the worker and his employer. There is no reason, therefore, to expect that workers will be satisfied with "fair" wages in this sense; they might not amount to a "fair wage for a fair day's work" in the common meaning of this phrase.

The kindest interpretation one can place upon the choice of such terminology is that the economists in question are not conscious of the emotional associations which these words arouse among working people. The worst interpretation would be that the terms are intended to carry the full ethical implications which the plain man would attach to them: that marginal-productivity wages are just and that wages equal to the rates paid for similar work are all that any worker has a right to expect. Rather than give the opportunity for such an interpretation, the economist should eschew such terms. In any case, even if particular rates of remuneration are considered by an outside observer to be just, this does not prevent the employer or the worker from being profoundly dissatisfied with them.

Nonfinancial motives.—Dissatisfaction with the market has been considered, so far, primarily in terms of financial returns, because market theory is concerned primarily with the implications of the desire for money. In the case of the consumer, however, the market problem is to get the best value for his money in goods and services. The same parallel may be drawn between market and extra-market operations as in our consideration of financial returns: market theory, as usually expounded, assumes that the consumer is never completely satisfied with the results of his total outlay. This is implicit in the suggestion that any substantial reduction in particular prices leads to some modification of the proportion of expenditure on different things. But consumers' dissatisfaction with the market is a less fruitful source of extra-market operations than producers' dissatisfaction, because the extra-market operations open to an individual in the acquisition of finished goods, as contrasted with money income, are mostly illegal (e.g., shoplifting), while joint action requires an organization or the acceptance of com-

[36] Marshall, quoted by Pigou in *Economics of Welfare*, p. 549.

mon goals, which is more difficult to obtain in the case of consumers.[37]

It is also necessary to supplement the discussion of producers' dissatisfaction by reference to the other conditions associated with the market, such as hours of work, congenial surroundings, and freedom from supervision. Equilibrium theory assumes a desire to maximize *all* the advantages of a particular occupation or employment of capital and infers that a market adjustment will be made whenever, owing to a change in the data, any of the associated conditions can thereby be improved.[38] From this it would follow that there is a general incentive to undertake extra-market operations whenever they promise better nonfinancial conditions and not merely when they promise better financial returns.

If this were all that could be said about dissatisfaction with the market, the center of interest would shift immediately to the next division of the theory. The assumption of general dissatisfaction, with no indication of its intensity or of any variations in intensity over place, occupation, or time, would not give any guidance as to *where* in the economic system extra-market operations might be expected. We could inquire, in any particular case, whether there is evidence of great dissatisfaction and accept such evidence to show that extra-market operations may be attempted. But that is not the same thing as obtaining from our general theory at least a hint as to where we are likely to find such intense dissatisfaction. To make this possible, the analysis of dissatisfaction must be carried further.

Acute dissatisfaction caused by losses.—There is plentiful empirical evidence to support the proposition that dissatisfaction is disproportionately intensified by a reduction in financial returns or a worsening of conditions. That is to say, the satisfaction associated with an improvement in one's economic position is often nothing compared with the dissatisfaction associated with a subsequent loss of that improvement. It is a common observation that people often do not appear any happier as a result of an increase in income. There may be, temporarily, considerable jubilation; but that soon passes, as new financial responsibilities are assumed and familiarity with an improved standard takes the edge off the pleasure it used to give. On the other hand, however, decline in income, involving a considerable alteration in one's way of

[37] Cf. Persia C. Campbell, *Consumer Representation in the New Deal* (New York, 1940).

[38] Though, as we have seen (chap. v), the analysis is rarely worked out fully.

life, not only imposes an initial shock but often leaves behind a load of discontent.

The psychological explanation of the former social fact is found in the mobility of attention. At a particular time a person's hopes and ambitions are centered on certain unsatisfied desires, which (if he is a normal person) are not so distant as to be impossible, An increase in income brings the accomplishment of some or all of the more urgent of these hopes; and their accomplishment gives rise to self-congratulation, as well as the joy of experiencing a long-anticipated pleasure. However, attention soon shifts to new hopes, previously too ambitious to be seriously entertained but now, at the higher level of income, near enough to constitute an urge to their pursuit. As interest is aroused in these new ambitions, the recently won successes drop into the background of the mind and come to be taken for granted. This is particularly true in a society divided into social classes on the basis of income and where individual progress from class to class is common. Each rung of the social ladder brings another rung within reach; and it is the rung just above that is interesting, not those that lie beneath. And this is true of any part of the ladder, except near the very top. A similar tendency is visible in the housewife's budget. The margin of indifference, inside which relative prices are not carefully scrutinized and the marginal-utility theory is not strictly applicable, shifts with the size of the income.

A decline in income, however, does not involve a symmetrical adaptation of ambitions and interests. In the first place, the hopes associated with the previous income level become lost causes and remain for long an object of regret. In the second place, items in the standard of living which had come to be taken for granted and had sunk comfortably into the background of interests must now be relinquished. The wants they satisfy are brought brutally into the center of consciousness; these wants include the maintenance of one's position in a particular social class, with its personal ties as well as its social distinction. Moreover, there is the unpleasant positive task of getting used to more modest circumstances and the new way of life that they entail. If it is a relapse to an old way of life, rather than an unfamiliar new one, the transition is not necessarily any easier; it may be complicated by the personal humiliation of returning to what one had spurned in the past. Finally, there may be added the fear of still further deterioration in the social scale in place of one's former hopes of further progress. Sometimes the readjustment is successful; and people gradually

discover in a more modest way of life, free from ambition, a contentment that was lacking at a higher, but still insufficient, social position.
But that is not the usual outcome. Generally people will make great
efforts, outside the market if need be, to ward off the pressure toward
a lower income.

Resistance to change.—The causes of individual losses are varied. Apart
from personal factors, such as illness or incompetence, and catastrophic
events, such as "acts of God," these causes work through the market.
An industry is depressed, or new competition springs up, or costs of
production are increased by wage and price movements. These
changes in the conditions or functioning of the market may be met
in part through market adjustments: changes in the amount or kind of
goods produced, changes in one's occupation, changes in selling price
or the wages demanded. It is when these market adjustments still leave
the economic unit worse off than before the change in conditions that
there is a strong incentive to any extra-market operations that promise
better results.

It is also worth observing that the resistance to market adjustments
will generally be stronger, if more than mere money income is threatened by the changes in question. When small retail shops meet the
overwhelming competition of chain stores, the appropriate market adjustment might be for the small retailer to seek a position as employee
in a large store. Indeed, his money income might thereby be increased. But this would involve the loss of his "independence" and the
acceptance of an inferior status in the larger organization. Hence he has
a special motive to support legislative restrictions upon chain stores or
to undertake other extra-market operations with a view to retaining
his own business. Again, the small farmer, who must abandon his
holding to make way for extensive cultivation loses more than his
money income; he may lose his whole "way of life." Why should he
respect the limits of market transactions in his attempt to escape this
fate? Upon consideration it appears that many of the factors which
are prominent in the analysis of the "imperfect mobility of labor and
capital" also have their place among the motives behind extra-market
operations designed to remove the need for mobility.

One general cause of changed market conditions is technical progress. In a later chapter we shall have more to say about Professor A.
G. B. Fisher's analysis of the economic implications of technical progress and of the market adjustments which are necessary if the community, as a whole, is to take full advantage of its increasing power to

produce.[39] For our present purpose it is convenient to draw on and extend Professor Fisher's discussion of the principal resistances to the necessary adjustments, for these resistances usually take the form of extra-market operations. Adopting the viewpoint of society as a whole, Professor Fisher describes as "unintelligent" the "desire to avoid the necessity for changes in the character of work and investment."[40] But, when we adopt the viewpoint of the worker or the investor, "it is scarcely surprising that both these groups are ready to take energetic steps, by government intervention or otherwise, to protect themselves against the necessity for change."[41] If it is a question of improving one's position, the chief obstacle to the market adjustment may be sheer inertia or dislike for change. But too often technical progress necessitates a change which involves a decline in income, even if not so great a decline as will be experienced by the individual who chooses to remain in, or on the edge of, his old occupation. Several case studies have been made in the United States to discover what happens to workers displaced from their usual employment. The results suggest that only a minority finally better their position; a considerable portion undergo a more or less prolonged spell of unemployment; and, of those who do subsequently find employment, many— sometimes the majority—must accept a lower level of earnings than that to which they had been accustomed.[42]

These cases in which the market destroys one's previous livelihood and hopes present the strongest incentive to extra-market operations but do not always lead to this result, because suitable extra-market operations may not be readily available. A similar motive is effective, however, in cases where the market is less cruel to the individual but the opportunities for extra-market operations are greater or more obvious. Even a small decline in the profitability of a particular industry indicates the market verdict that labor and capital should be diverted to other, more profitable industries. But the diversity of experience among those individuals who do transfer their investments or abandon their former occupation (as distinct from losing their capital or their job altogether) emphasizes the risks which surround any others who might attempt to respond to the "indicators" of the market mechanism.

[39] *The Clash of Progress and Security* (London, 1935), chaps. i and ii; see below, chap. viii.

[40] *Ibid.*, p. 75.   [41] *Ibid.*, p. 84.

[42] For a summary of these studies see National Resources Committee, *Technological Trends and National Policy* (Washington, 1937), pp. 83–86.

The deterrent is a double one. "There are the uncertain risks associated with the new type of work or investment; but also there are the certain losses associated with the abandonment of the old."[43] The former class of risk appears to be all the greater in periods of general depression or widespread disturbance. In more prosperous times successful readjustment by others is more frequently observed by the individual; and the fear of insecurity is accordingly less pronounced. The motive for extra-market operations is correspondingly weaker in prosperity than in depression.

The resistance to the adjustments implicit in progress may also take the form of barriers to the entry of new capital or labor into the industries, for the products for which demand is increasing.[44] If the inward movement can be checked by restrictions (through extra-market operations), the increased demand will raise the incomes of those who are already ensconced in the industry. It may be that the inward movement threatens to reduce the absolute level of earnings in the industry and not merely to prevent them from increasing. The rules of professional associations and the laws which they induce parliaments to make for the control of entry illustrate the practical expression of this motive. Like other types of market adjustments, the inward flow of resources is not always caused by technical progress. Any factor depressing a particular industry or encouraging emigration tends to cause a flow of labor, and sometimes of capital, into some other employments, thereby creating a motive to extra-market operations to keep the new competition out.

A similar motive is supplied by the emergence of new competition in goods, as distinct from labor and capital. The most familiar example is that of cheap imports, which may be due to a hundred and one causes, ranging from improved transport to a depression in the exporting country and from an increase in efficiency in the exporting country to a fall in the value of its currency. But even within a national or regional market new domestic competition may arise without any inflow of resources into the menaced industry. All industries are, in varying degree, in competition with one another; and technical progress or depression in one industry may lead to a price policy which cuts into the sales of another industry.

In all these cases the common factor is structural change, whether due to progress or not. Progress is one of the causes of structural change, and only one of the causes of acute dissatisfaction with the

[43] Fisher, *op. cit.*, p. 83.   [44] *Ibid.*, p. 86.

market. This analysis of resistance to change, therefore, has wider significance than Professor Fisher has given it.

If the opportunities for extra-market operations were equal in all industries, we should expect them to be most frequent in industries which were adversely affected by structural changes. Economic theory of the usual type, therefore, comes to the aid of the theory of extra-market operations by facilitating the prediction of tendencies to structural change. When the economic system undergoes general fluctuations in prosperity, so that practically all industries may be depressed simultaneously, the general dissatisfaction with the market is, of course, intensified. But, in so far as economic theory throws light on the varying impact of a general depression upon different industries, it again indicates where to expect a particularly strong motive to extra-market operations. Conversely, since recovery, or even a prolonged boom, affects different industries differently, economic theory should help us to predict where the pressure for extra-market operations is most likely to be reduced. For instance, if it were not for differences in opportunity, we might expect extra-market operations to be more frequent in the capital-goods industries than in the consumers'-goods industries. But there are many other factors determining the relative severity of fluctuations in various industries. The main point is to note the assistance which ordinary economic theory may lend the theory of extra-market operations.

Frustration of common aims: solidarity.—In the above discussion we have followed the usual practice of economic theory and concentrated attention upon the pursuit of individual ends. The question arises as to whether the fact of "commonly accepted goals" has any important implications for the theory of extra-market operations. For instance, if the fullest utilization of technical progress along the lines indicated by Professor Fisher were a common goal for all members of the community, irrespective of the sectional losses it might involve, then the resistance to the necessary market adjustments and the corresponding incentive to extra-market operations would be diminished accordingly. There would be less tendency for "increasing State intervention to take the form of buttressing and succouring those economic activities which do not offer reasonable possibilities of adaptation to the changes of economic climate which are inevitable in the circumstances" and more support for extra-market operations designed to secure greater flexibility of the economic system.[45] This assumes that individuals recognize the role of their own personal difficulties in the whole process of progress, which, as Professor Fisher suggests, is still far from being the case. In this connection it may be observed that it is an essential task, in modern warfare, to convince the individual that the economic disabilities, imposed on him via the market, are indicators of adjustments which should be made in the interests of the common goal of victory. Otherwise extra-market operations will be undertaken to protect sectional interests and, incidentally, to obstruct the adjustments which are necessary in "total war."[46]

Apart from times of war and national catastrophe, commonly accepted goals are usually confined to sectional groups. For instance, in countries in which labor "solidarity" is strongly developed, particular workers are prepared to undertake extra-market operations even when they are not personally affected. "Sympathy strikes" are not uncommon. Again, practically the whole of organized labor in Australia, and not only the trades affected, opposed the wartime extension of female labor into new fields unless male rates of wage were paid. Another example is the common attitude of farmers to changes affecting even some of their number. Professor Fisher suggests that it is curious that farmers should favor schemes to increase land settlement, for most professional organizations prefer to restrict rather than to encourage the entry of large numbers into their occupation. The only explanation he can offer is the farmer's desire for a supply of cheap labor and his "profound misconception of the reasons which in fact make land settlement desirable."[47] But it is very common for a member of a group to identify his interests with those of each other member of the group. Admittedly, the farmer is misguided in his assumption that the creation of facilities for new farmers makes the position of every farmer more secure. But the fundamental cause of his willingness to support such measures is the sentiment of rural solidarity rather than lack of economic education, though that lack may be a factor strengthening the sentiment of solidarity.

The relationship between the interests of the individual and those of the community, large or small, of which he is part will be further con-

---

[45] As urged by C. M. Wright, *Economic Adaptation to a Changing World Market* (Copenhagen, 1939), p. 243.

[46] Cf. E. R. Walker and R. M. Beecroft, "New Developments in Australia's War Economy," *Economic Record* (Melbourne), June, 1941.

[47] *Op. cit.*, p. 53.

sidered in our discussion of the objectives of economic policy.[48] Here
we note merely that commonly accepted goals are more likely to be
furthered by extra-market operations than by spontaneous co-ordination of market activities. The latter were referred to by Adam Smith in
his famous dictum that "masters are always and everywhere in a sort of
tacit, but constant and uniform combination, not to raise the wages of
labour above their actual rate."[49] So, too, some Australian consumers
refuse to buy cheap Japanese goods because they believe this competition is inimical to the national interest. But extra-market operations,
such as the formation of trade-unions and employers' federations and
support of tariff increases, are generally regarded as more effective expressions of group interests than the spontaneous co-ordination of
market behavior.

There is one further point to be made before we begin the consideration of the various types of extra-market operation. Dissatisfaction
with the market arises from past or expected results, and it is often not
possible to determine the most important factor among those which
produce unsatisfactory results. In the cases where it is plain that the
fault lies with a certain set of conditions which can be readily distinguished from the totality of market data, the dissatisfaction is likely
to be directed specifically at these particular conditions rather than
the market mechanism in general. If the unfavorable conditions themselves can be traced to the deliberate policy of individuals or groups,
that is, to extra-market operations, there is a challenge to the dissatisfied persons to have recourse to similar methods in "self-defense."
Consequently, many cases of extra-market operations appear, not as
reactions against the market as such, but as counterattacks to regain
a position threatened by other people's extra-market operations. The
demand for retaliatory tariffs is a case in point. Although the field of
struggle appears to shift out of the market altogether in such instances,
the link with the market remains; and the extra-market operations can
still be considered as competition "carried on by other methods." This
imposes a limit to our theory of extra-market operations. We do not
attempt to deal with those political and other extra-market struggles
which are not closely related to the market, by an attempt either to
modify the results of the market or to evade its verdict on matters
which could be, and often are, decided in the market.

[48] See chap. xi.

[49] *The Wealth of Nations* (London, 1933), Book I, chap. viii. But Smith made many excursions into the theory of extra-market operations.

II. CLASSIFICATION OF EXTRA-MARKET OPERATIONS

Given a strong impulse to reject the verdict of the market, an individual or firm (or, more generally, an economic unit) must consider the other means at its disposal. Similarly, a theory which is to guide our study of the facts must set out the various possible courses of action and indicate the conditions under which one is preferred to another. If we consider the methods by which various extra-market operations promise better results than can be obtained from the market under existing conditions, it should then be possible, in a particular concrete case, to determine which of the methods would be preferred, on the assumption that their relative efficiency is the only factor in choice. This involves abstraction from the social and psychological factors which to some extent control the use of extra-market operations. Some operations are illegal, while others, though not illegal, incur social disapproval. Some may be dismissed as too risky, yet others may exercise an attraction for particular persons because they give scope for exploratory behavior. These factors—the "other things" which are not equal but which vary from time to time, from place to place, and from person to person—will be considered in the third division of the theory. By abstracting from them at the present stage we should be able to see more clearly the *modus operandi* of extra-market operations.

But, since our exposition of the theory is to be kept in general terms, it will not be possible to study the actual processes in any detail. As in the psychological investigations suggested in chapter v, the results of further studies will vary considerably in different localities or in different occupational contexts. There is nothing to be gained by the construction of a theoretical model, showing all the details of an extra-market operation, in complete abstraction from the local facts which will largely determine its form. All we require at this stage is a classification of the principal types of extra-market operations and of the general channels through which they can improve upon the results obtainable from the market. In approaching a concrete problem we shall then know the avenues that should be explored; we shall be in a position to ask whether, under the actual conditions of the case, the best results can be achieved by an economic unit which adopts measures falling under one or more of the various types of extra-market operations which our general theory distinguishes.

The various extra-market operations can be classified on two different principles: either according to the form which the behavior takes (e.g., physical violence may be distinguished from agitating for a change in the law) or according to the channel through which results are to be achieved (e.g., making the market work more favorably may be contrasted with evading it altogether). It is useful to establish both classifications and to consider the position of particular actions in relation to each of them.

The second principle gives a smaller number of classes and may be studied first. The classes may be distinguished by asking what are the *intermediate* objectives of extra-market operations. By definition, the ultimate objectives are the same as are sought by market operations; but, in pursuing these ultimate objectives, economic units seek to achieve, inside or outside the market, certain intermediate objectives. In the case of market operations the intermediate objectives may be, for instance, a certain set of prices or scale of production. In the case of extra-market operations we may distinguish *four* intermediate objectives:

a) To circumvent the market and to obtain money, goods, or services without offering anything in exchange

b) To alter the external data of the market so that, without any change in the principles of market behavior, the resulting prices, production, incomes, or the associated conditions of work, etc., will be different from those obtainable with the original data

c) To modify the principles of market behavior so that the same external market data will give rise to prices, production, incomes, or associated conditions different from those reached with the former principles of behavior

d) To influence the scope for extra-market operations by other economic units.

The last of these will be ignored in this division of the theory. It will be considered in our third division, along with other factors which influence the actual use made of various possible extra-market operations. This reduces our classes to three.

The distinction between (b) and (c) is somewhat arbitrary, since the principles of behavior might be stated in the form of data: the ends sought by the various economic units and their methods of choosing between competing ends. But the distinction is commonly made in market theory, and it is equally convenient in the theory of extra-market operations. It may be noticed that the line between (c) and (a) might occasionally be difficult to establish, as when the principles of market behavior are modified to permit goods to be obtained for a "nominal" payment.

But, generally speaking, the distinctions are clear enough. As an example of (a) we might instance transfers of wealth through fiscal policy, living on charity, or the profession of burglary. Examples of (*b*) are abundant: the formation of a cartel, the imposition of a customs duty, the prohibition of sales of alcohol. And under (*c*) we would classify coercion to modify price policy and the prevalence of generosity rather than self-interest in business relations.

Techniques of extra-market operations.—Our other principle of classification turns on what people actually can do to achieve the above-mentioned intermediate objectives. There are so many different things which they can do that this classification might be developed in considerable detail. To be serviceable, however, it must be manageable. We therefore distinguish four major classes, which are intended to cover everything; and within each class we distinguish two subclasses, which do not, however, purport to exhaust all the possibilities of the class in which they fall. Some of the subclasses cover a wide range of activities.

1. Violence by one economic unit against another
    a) Violence to person, including physical compulsion or restraint
    b) Violence to property; forcible dispossession or destruction
2. Specific instructions by one economic unit to another
    a) Backed by individual power: including threats of violence or of damaging business policies, such as price-cutting or boycott
    b) Backed by authority in an organization, including the power of the government or its agencies over the subjects of the state or the power of majority stockholders over others or the power of a bank over its debtors
3. Informal influence (without explicit instructions or rules) of one economic unit over the decisions and behavior of another
    a) Control of psychological conditions in which decisions are made, including the parade of power without direct threats, pressure for immediate decisions, appeals to sentiment
    b) Control of relevant information
4. Establishment (or alteration) of general rules, binding on other economic units
    a) Enforced by an organization
    b) Enforced by social approval or disapproval

This classification may well be improved as a result of further study, particularly through its experimental use in dealing with concrete problems of extra-market operations. The latter is the real test; and, if we remain at the level of generalities, attempts to improve the classification will be directed toward symmetry and the avoidance of overlapping. But it does not follow that an elegant classification is a more useful analytical tool or that the borderline cases that can be imagined a priori will cause serious inconvenience in empirical investigations. Admittedly, the four classes, distinguished above, shade into one another; but overlapping is likely to cause less trouble than would gaps between the various classes. It will also be observed that operations falling into one class may react upon those falling in other classes. This has a bearing upon our earlier inclusion of a fourth intermediate objective of particular extra-market operations, namely, to influence the scope for other extra-market operations. Consideration of this, too, may be postponed to the third division of the theory.[50]

Taking this classification as it is, we may now examine each class in relation to the three intermediate objectives already distinguished and illustrate the type of operation which may be brought under each class. We shall also express an opinion regarding the relative frequency or importance of the various types in practice, while recognizing that practice will be different in different places, times, and circumstances.

1. Violence often involves the evasion, or even the destruction, of the market. Forcible appropriation of goods or money and the attacks of John D. Rockefeller's employees on the workers who were laying pipe lines are sufficient examples. But the destruction of industrial property is often to be regarded as an alteration of the data of the market, designed to make the market conditions more favorable in the future. The kidnaping or murder of a competitor (practiced only in certain trades and countries) is also designed to alter the market data. It is difficult to see, however, how the practice of violence can achieve the third type of intermediate objective, namely, the modification of the principles of market behavior, without breaking up the process of exchange altogether. It is not proposed to investigate the technique or

---

[50] It is perhaps necessary to comment on the relationship between the above list and the National Resources Committee's list of "controls" which regulate "the complex organization of resources" in the American economy. As noted above, four controls are distinguished: the market mechanism, administrative co-ordination, canalizing rules, and the acceptance of common goals. (*Structure of the American Economy*, Part I, p. 97). Although some of our classes deal with somewhat similar concepts, the purposes of the two lists are quite different. The National Resources Committee considers the market as a mechanism controlling the total distribution of resources in the economy as a whole; we are concerned with the market as a mechanism through which the individual economic unit seeks its own ends. Similarly, we are not here concerned with the co-ordination of many economic units or their parts through "administration" or "rules," but only with the attempt of one economic unit to give orders to another or to subject it to rules, so as to advance the interests of the first unit. The National Resources Committee does not include violence among its controls, because in a generally peaceful community violence does not play an important part in the total organization of resources. But in the smaller world of the individual economic unit violence may loom large. In the third division of the theory, of course, we shall be concerned with the controls which regulate extra-market operations; and in that connection our viewpoint will approach more closely that of the National Resources Committee.

"productivity" of violence here. Indeed, its study presents special difficulties and dangers—particularly where direct observation is required. And in any case the extent of its use will depend more on legal and moral controls than upon the rewards which it offers to those who employ it.

2. Specific instructions from one economic unit to another may theoretically apply to almost any form of activity. Accordingly, they may be designed to achieve any or all of the three intermediate objectives. When a bandit orders his victim to hand over his cash or demands a ransom, this is action to achieve market objectives without recourse to the market. So, too, when compensation is sought through a lawsuit. But the dissolution of a trust or labor union, by order of a court of law, alters the data of the market, so that future transactions will yield different results. And when a city government resumes land at an arbitrarily fixed price, this involves a different principle of behavior from that usually observed in the real estate market.

The power to issue specific instructions is based, in the case of the bandit, on his superior armament and his willingness to use it. His threat of violence enables him to establish a relationship of authority over his victim. Other threats may serve in other circumstances, for instance, a large firm may order a small competitor to sell his business, *or else*. Here the power to issue an order rests on the superior resources of the large firm, which can ruin the small firm by price-cutting.

In the other examples mentioned, however, the specific instruction is issued by an authority constituted through an organization; and this may be regarded as the more normal type of extra-market operation within this class. The greatest of all organizations is, of course, the state; but less important organizations may have considerable powers over their members. Political parties, trade associations, religious organizations, and labor unions are examples. But a similar relationship of authority may exist as a result of agreements between businessmen or financial relationships between firms and their customers. When one economic unit is heavily indebted to another, it is likely to receive instructions from it. This even happens in cases where one unit—say, a large processing works—is the only market for the produce of other units. These relationships of authority are similar to those that exist when individual units are bound by the rules of an organization.

The only distinction between class 2 and class 4 is that a specific instruction applies to a single occasion, whereas a general rule requires a definite form of behavior whenever the prescribed conditions are present. Apart from this there is no reason for considering separately the techniques of establishing an organization to issue instructions and one to enforce general rules. The problems which are common to both types of extra-market operations will be considered below under class 4.

It is worth noticing, however, that the frequency with which one economic unit obtains obedience to specific instructions from another may raise difficulties in the use of the concept of an economic unit. If one unit is under the continuous supervision of another, it becomes in effect part of it and is no longer regarded as a separate economic unit for the purposes of economic theory, whatever view the law may take of it. But subjection to an occasional specific direction, either from an organization or from a powerful individual unit, does not constitute a sufficient loss of autonomy to render the concept of an economic unit inapplicable. The distinction is, of course, one of degree.

3. Informal influence of one unit over another may have results similar to specific instructions, leading to the circumvention of the market, alteration of the data, or a modification of the principles of behavior. This is most clearly seen in the case of a parade of force which, even in the absence of any overt threats or instructions, may induce the weaker unit to anticipate the wishes of the stronger, whatever they involve in terms of the three intermediate objectives distinguished above. But our second example, namely, pressure for quick decisions, is designed rather to modify the principles of behavior, making it less rational because there is not sufficient time to weigh all relevant considerations. An appeal to sentiment is usually directed to a similar objective.

Control of relevant information, including the spreading of false rumors, does not alter the fundamental conditions of the market, but it does alter the data available to the economic unit which it is intended to influence. From the viewpoint of the market conditions as a whole, the behavior of the economic unit is thereby rendered less "rational," though this behavior may not be less rational in relation to the information at its disposal.

This class may also provide a convenient receptable for cases where advice is offered by one individual to another, which is sometimes a profitable extra-market operation for the one that gives the advice. But it is introduced for the sake of completeness rather than for its probable importance in practice. Perhaps its chief interest from the theoretical viewpoint is that there are some market operations, such as advertising, which almost qualify for inclusion here. We have followed the convention of treating advertising as a market operation, because it is taken into account, more or less, in market theory. It is, however, a favored method of achieving influence over the behavior of other economic units and might be regarded as being a borderline case between market and extra-market operations.

4. The establishment (or modification) of general rules is probably the largest of our four classes of extra-market operations and has come to be of particular interest with the growth of state "intervention" in economic affairs. But it covers much more than attempts to influence legislation, as can be seen from the two subclasses which we have distinguished. General rules might also include personal habits; but these may be ignored, since they can rarely be altered by other economic units, except through social pressure.

Any of the intermediate objectives of extra-market operations may be gained through the application of rules. For instance, rules requiring the payment of taxes or contributions to other organizations or even charitable gifts achieve a transfer of wealth without any recourse to the market. Rules establishing import restrictions or the conditions on which capital may be borrowed or commodities which cannot be sold to the public or the legal hours of work or patent rights all determine in some degree the data of the market. Finally, rules may influence principles of behavior in the market: the one-price system as against higgling and price differentiation, hard bargaining as against "economic chivalry,"[51] maximization of profit as against regularity of operation.

Organizations as instruments.—It is in this fourth class of extra-market operations that the study of technique will most repay the economist. Consider, first, the wide range of rules which can be enforced by organizations of all sorts, from the state down, and even by organizations extending beyond the state, such as international cartels. Since these organizations also provide the authority for a large number of specific directions, the study of their growth and functioning is particularly important in relation to extra-market operations.

As far as the state is concerned, the field is already occupied by the sciences of law, politics, and administration; and the economist must draw upon them. But much of the ground must be worked over again, before the extra-market operations can be disentangled from other extra-market activities that are stimulated by another set of motives,

[51] Pigou, *Memorials of Alfred Marshall*, p. 323.

for, despite Veblen's dictum that "representative government means, chiefly, representation of business interests,"[52] students of government have been chiefly concerned with forms and administration rather than with the technique by which businessmen may manipulate governments. And so with the study of law. It is said that "one cannot examine nineteenth century legislation without perceiving that organized pressure from groups having a common economic interest is the sole explanation of many things upon the statute book,"[53] Nevertheless, jurists do not generally envisage law as an instrument for the pursuit of business interests but as a system of social control. It is interesting to notice that the view of law favored by Dean Pound has much in common with the "scarcity" definition of economics. "The legal order . . . . may well be thought of as a task or as a great series of tasks of social engineering; as an elimination of friction and precluding of waste, so far as possible, in the satisfaction of infinite human desires out of a relatively finite store of the material goods of existence."[54] But extra-market operations to change or apply the law in the interests of a single economic unit might better be described as "private engineering." It is not the business of the economist to rewrite jurisprudence. But, if the jurist does not provide the type of analysis needed for the study of these extra-market operations, the economist must also study the processes by which the legal order is modified, as well as those by which it affects or circumvents the market. Dr. Odegard's study of the Anti-saloon League illustrates the type of examination which might be undertaken on a larger scale, in connection with political movements more closely related to ordinary business objectives.[55]

The sciences of law and government concentrate their attention upon the supreme organization, the state. But similar problems arise within all other formally constituted organizations, however small, which impose obligations on their members to obey general rules or explicit instructions. Sometimes the state itself supervises the exercise of authority within these organizations, such as restricting the demands made by a trade organization if they involve "restraint of

[52] T. Veblen, *The Theory of Business Enterprise* (New York, 1940), p. 286.

[53] Roscoe Pound, *Interpretations of Legal History* (Cambridge, Mass., 1930), p. 113.

[54] *Ibid.*, p. 156.

[55] P. H. Odegard, *Pressure Politics* (New York, 1928). I have not yet had an opportunity to examine S. D. Clark's *The Canadian Manufacturers' Association: A Study in Political Pressure and Collective Bargaining* (Toronto, 1939).

trade" or supporting the organization in disciplining its members, as in German cartel law. But there is a wide range of methods and activities in which the state, at least in democratic countries, takes no interest. By grouping different organizations under more or less homogeneous types, such as labor unions and trade associations, some general principles may be discovered regarding the methods of establishment, discipline, and choice of policy of each type.[56] But the range of variation between individual organizations is considerable.

It is particularly difficult to discern any uniformity in those organizations which are constituted by the direct relationships between one unit and another, such as banker and customer, factory and supplier of raw materials, employer and employee. For some purposes these organizations must be considered as single units in themselves, and we are not concerned with their *internal* relationships when they are acting as units. But, when an employer instructs his employees how to vote, he is dealing with them not as parts of his productive unit but as other economic units covered by his organization; and this is regarded as an extra-market operation. Similarly, if a bank requires a customer to employ nonunion labor, this is a rule imposed by one economic unit upon another. The theory of extra-market operations can do little more than warn the economist not to ignore the possibility of such forms of behavior; there is little point in trying to formulate precise generalizations about them.

Social norms as instruments.—Equally important in the control of human behavior are those less formal rules which rest upon social approval or disapproval and may never be promulgated by an overt organization. Reference has already been made, in chapter v, to these social "codes" of behavior and to the need to establish their actual patterns, as an aid to the prediction of market behavior under varying conditions. Here, however, our main concern is with the extent to which these codes may be modified in the interests of certain economic units. At present our knowledge of the origin and development of such codes and the extent to which they can be altered by policy is but fragmentary, especially as their patterns are by no means clearly established. We also require, in this connection, that understanding of individual deviation from social codes to which attention was drawn in chapter v.

Attempts are made, of course, to control these codes through ethical teaching in the home, in school, and in church; and the possibility

[56] This has been attempted by many writers on labor unions.

arises that such teaching may be indirectly influenced by private or sectional interests. A Canadian historian has observed that in a period of rapid economic development in Canada, when the traditional mores were breaking down, "religious denominations tended to act as a conservative force. In promoting the good, they were preserving the traditional. Thus, apart from financial considerations, their interests tended to become identified with the economically sheltered groups in the community."[57] But it is apparent that this type of extra-market operation does not, as a rule, promise results comparable with those that can be achieved through a change in the rules of a powerful organization.

Reviewing the various types of extra-market operations covered by our classification, the most important would appear to be specific instructions and rules, imposed by authority in a legally constituted organization. But, if there is little restriction upon the use of violence, this may be a highly "productive" type of extra-market operation; and even an apparently peaceful community may give scope for the use of threats to back specific instructions. The choice of extra-market operations, however, does not depend upon their promised results alone. Account must also be taken of the limits of practicability, social controls, and other obstacles to action. These factors will now engage our attention.

III. IRRATIONALITY AND SOCIAL CONTROLS

In the first division of the theory we found the source of extra-market operations in dissatisfaction with the market. It is clear, moreover, that, other things being equal, these extra-market operations are most likely to be undertaken where dissatisfaction is intense—a matter on which existing economic theory throws some light. But these other things are not equal, and among them is the theoretical possibility of achieving better results through extra-market operations. Accordingly, a study of the "productivity" of different types of extra-market operations, in general terms, forms the second division of the theory. It reveals the various channels into which dissatisfaction may flow. But there are forces which complicate behavior in practice. There are strong deterrents to certain types of extra-market operations, which require consideration in a third division of the theory. Often there is a reluctance to abandon the market, even temporarily, despite one's dissatisfaction with its results; and sometimes the choice of particular

[57] S. D. Clark, "Economic Expansion and the Moral Order," *Canadian Journal of Economics and Political Science*, May, 1940, p. 212.

extra-market operations is impulsive and irrational, showing little evidence of attempts to balance the relative productivity of different types of behavior.

Irrational extra-market operations.—The last point requires special emphasis. One of our principal criticisms of conventional economic theory is its failure to explore the implications of impulsiveness and personal inefficiency in economic affairs. It would be no less a weakness in the theory of extra-market operations if it represented all behavior as due to a careful assessment of the possible lines of conduct and to an efficient comparison of their relative productivity in terms of the ends sought. Unfortunately, the scope for "irrational behavior" in extra-market operations is even greater than in market activities. Under stable conditions any continued internal inconsistency in market valuations or any recurring error of market judgment is likely to be shown up by extended repetition. It is frequently argued in economic treatises that, even though businessmen and consumers may make mistakes, they learn from experience. But operations designed to alter the data or the principles of behavior of the market are not repeated day after day. Either they succeed or they fail. If they succeed, they need not be undertaken again; if they fail, one is inclined to try something else. Consequently, in all extra-market operations designed to achieve these two intermediate objectives, errors can be made without ever being corrected. The same is true of market activities in periods of great instability; but in the case of extra-market operations the scope for uncorrected error is considerable even in periods of comparative stability. It should be noted, however, that, if the same operations are not repeated several times, the observer has less evidence of the alleged irrationality of the economic unit. Admittedly, the choice of extra-market operations in one set of circumstances may be inconsistent with the choice made in apparently similar circumstances on another occasion. But how can the observer be sure that the circumstances were substantially the same? In view of the heterogeneity of the motives behind extra-market operations, it is possible that the two situations differed in some important, but not obvious, respect, from the viewpoint of the economic unit. The difficulty of predicting behavior is the same, however, whether it be due to a lack of consistency of behavior in identical situations or to differences in the situation which are not discernible to the observer.

The importance of this problem should not, however, be exaggerated. Many extra-market operations may be observed in practice which are clearly related to what Marshall called "the steadiest motives in business life"[58] and are the result of "a close and careful watching of the advantages of different courses of conduct."[59] In all such cases the choice of extra-market operations turns on their relative productivity and the various controls still to be considered. The main thing is to be on our guard against the cases where this analysis is not adequate.

Apart from a general caution regarding the possibility of behavior departing from the apparently rational course, the only suggestion that can be offered is that a procedure be applied similar to that necessary in market theory, namely, a search for socially determined errors which might be predicted from social patterns if these latter can be determined.[60] The most flagrant instances of irrational behavior are likely to be those produced under the influence of mass emotion; and the general psychology of crowds may therefore give some indication of the errors of judgment which will be committed when mass emotion is active.

Social controls.—We now consider the social controls upon the activities which constitute extra-market operations. Were it not for the obstacles which organized society places in the way of certain extra-market operations, the market itself would not be sufficiently developed to be a worthy object of study. In particular, the use of violence and threats must be strictly controlled if buying and selling are to be conducted in peace; and the history of market activities shows them growing up under the shadow of the church, the town, and the state, as those authorities established some sort of law and order. On the other hand, the market cannot survive if a continued struggle for control of the state absorbs the energy of sectional groups, each desiring to use the authority of the state to circumvent the market or to alter its functioning. Similarly, a market requires for its proper functioning some restraints upon those "doubtful" practices which benefit the few so long as they do not become general.

It would be false to view the legal and other controls upon extra-market operations as measures designed purely for the defense of the market. Business interests are not the only ones that may be damaged by the prevalence of violence, and few political theorists have sought a complete explanation of the state in men's desire to trade with one

[58] *Principles of Economics*, p. 15.
[59] *Ibid.*, p. 21.
[60] See above, chap. v.

another. Nevertheless, confidence in the market as an institution and
satisfaction with its results on the part of those who are successful are
the natural allies of any system designed to limit the scope for violence
and other practices which can be made to serve as extra-market operations.

The state is the supreme organization, but not the only one, which
imposes controls upon extra-market operations. It is convenient to
distinguish four types of rules which prevent or, on the other hand,
favor recourse to particular extra-market operations: (*a*) laws enforced by the state; (*b*) rules of other formal organizations, such as labor unions and trade associations; (*c*) the moral code indorsed by religious doctrines and taught by religious organizations; and (*d*) the
social codes inforced by group approval and disapproval. The importance of laws enforced by the state is apparent from the history of
labor unions; the right to combine has at different times been expressly
forbidden and expressly guaranteed, and the same is true of certain
union practices. Enforcement of laws is, of course, the important
thing, not their enactment. This is abundantly illustrated by the attempts to control or prevent monopolies by legislation.[61] As to the
rules of other organizations, we may again refer to the trade practices
indorsed and forbidden by trade associations and illustrated by the
provisions of the N.R.A. codes.[62] The moral code indorsed by religion
and the social codes enforced by group pressure help to determine the
attitude toward violence, established property, coercion, and fraud.

All these controls vary from place to place and from time to time.
For instance, it is said (in Melbourne) that business morality is far
"lower" in Sydney than in other Australian cities. One finds, too,
significant differences in the attitude of different churches to economic
legislation. And the rules of the state and other organizations are subject to continuous revision in any country and vary from place to
place. We have already raised the question of extra-market operations designed to modify these controls, as distinct from operations designed to evade or alter the working of the market directly. We shall
later find a parallel in the case of certain market activities which are
designed not to maximize the immediate results obtainable in the
market but to produce changes in the data, so that better results can be
obtained in the future.[63] In attempting to predict the extra-market

[61] Cf. W. H. Hamilton, *Anti-trust in Action* ("Temporary National Economic Committee
Monographs," No. 16 [Washington, 1941]).

[62] Pearce, *op. cit.*, Appen. A.   [63] See below, chap. vii.

operations which will be undertaken in given circumstances, we must take account, therefore, not only of the canalizing effect of the various rules which are effective in the time and place under consideration, but also of the possibility that economic units may be dissatisfied with existing rules (as well as with the market) and seek to alter them through extra-market activities.

In addition to these positive rules, there are other elements in the "social climate" which affect the extent of extra-market operations.[64] One of the factors is the degree of popular education in economic matters—the degree of comprehension of the actual operations of the market and of the potentialities of extra-market operations. In this connection the academic doctrines of fifty years ago are of considerable importance today. Belief in the beneficent working of the laws of supply and demand is still a curb on the exploitation of extra-market operations. As the results of recent work on monopolistic competition permeate the popular mind (probably in distorted form), we may expect idealistic respect for the market as an institution to diminish and the severely practical view of it as an instrument which particular interests may exploit in various ways to become more common. Of course, the academic teaching of fifty years ago is not the only source of vulgar economic theory. The A-plus-B theorem of Major Douglas, for instance, has undoubtedly strengthened many a person's disposition toward extra-market operations which will alter the quantity of money.[65]

Another important element in the social climate is the general attitude toward experiment as against routine. The conventional view of the businessman, in economic theory, depicts him as continually ready to try out new ideas in the market. Professor Schumpeter, however, has emphasized that innovation is attractive to only a fraction of the business world. Many extra-market operations must be experimental. The problem has some affinities with that of uncertainty in market theory. Although extra-market operations often do not require a large investment of fixed capital, they do involve the diversion of resources away from other employment, particularly the time of business executives and sometimes the labor of hordes of minor employees.

---

[64] Cf. the views of Ohlin quoted below (chap. viii).

[65] For a suggestive treatment of the attractions of monetary reform as a political objective see V. F. Coe, "Monetary Theory and Politics," in H. A. Innes (ed.), *Essays in Political Economy* (Toronto, 1938).

The only asset thereby created is an organization or body of opinion, which is of little value except for the purpose of specific extra-market operations. The losses associated with failure in this field are as real as those resulting from unsuccessful experiments in the business world. But willingness to experiment does not turn only on the willingness to run risks, there is also the attitude toward unfamiliarity. We can assure that in extra-market operations as in market activities innovators will be followed by a host of imitators, even before the results of their experiments are beyond doubt. It is the exploratory operations, which may initiate a wave of new extra-market operations, that will always be difficult to predict.

CONCLUSION

This completes our review of the many factors which may influence the extent and form of market operations. It does not provide a set of simple propositions formulated as general laws or a series of two-dimensional diagrams. Those who think that theories must be of that form may contest our claim to have presented, in outline, a theory of extra-market operations. But the simplicity of a theory and the possibility of setting it out as a few general laws depend upon the degree of abstraction, as well as upon the complexities of the real world. Economic theory of the usual type can be presented as a few simple laws only as long as it is confined to a very high level of abstraction. As soon as we begin to make the categories substantial instead of formal, even market theory becomes primarily a classification of the various factors which may operate in a concrete case.[66]

It would not be impossible to construct a formal theory of extra-market operations, consisting of a few simple propositions, by abstracting from most of the complications reviewed in this chapter. For instance, we might construct a theory of the acquisition of goods by violence, as though that were the sole type of behavior. Any such theory, however, would be so remote from reality as to seem a mere caricature. We have chosen, therefore, to expound a theory at a somewhat lower level of abstraction, even though this involves giving the impression of a catalogue of possibilities rather than a simple model of a single process. And we have not depicted in any detail the actual mechanisms associated with each of the possible factors in extra-mar-

[66] See above, chap. iv.

ket operations, because these mechanisms are likely to vary so much according to time and place.

The only questions that remain are whether this theory is an improvement on plain horse sense, as a method of approaching concrete problems, and whether there is enough of it to provide a basis for a synthesis with market theory.

The first point can be finally demonstrated only by experiment. A priori, the case for a systematic review of the possibilities of extra-market operations before seeking to interpret a factual situation is the same as the case for a review of the possibilities of market behavior. Certainly there is no reason to expect that unaided common sense will find extra-market operations less complicated than market activities. But it is only in the study of practical problems that one can really test the value of an "engine for the discovery of concrete truth."

The second point raises logical issues which cannot be thoroughly examined here, as to what is involved in the synthesis of two abstract systems, each abstracting not only from some of the factors covered by the other but also from certain other factors of the real world. Synthesis is possible only if the *degree* of abstraction from these other factors is comparable in both theories. At a high level of abstraction we might consider the economic unit as confronted by a series of possible lines of action, some inside and some outside the market, and choosing among them according to what they promise in terms of the ends sought by the economic unit. This brings us very close to Professor Robbins' definition of economic theory, which imposes no limitation upon the *forms* that behavior may take, so long as it involves "disposing of scarce means which have alternative uses."[67] But between that definition of economic theory and its final application to concrete problems comes the process of theoretic construction, in which market behavior is considered in abstraction from extra-market operations. At the high level of abstraction implied in that definition, the synthesis of both forms of behavior has little interest.

The appropriate place to effect the synthesis anew would appear to be not in the construction of the theory, for here abstraction has its uses, but in the study of the concrete problem. There the economic unit is confronted with the choice of several lines of conduct, according to the actual conditions. Some of these lines of conduct are those covered by the theory of the market and the others by the theory of extra-

[67] *Op. cit.*, p. 16.

market operations. The two theories together cover the range of possibilities which are open in the specific instance under consideration; and the final decision will turn on their relative productivity, subject to the social controls already distinguished and the degree of rationality. By weighting all these elements in the situation, the economist can effect a synthesis of the two theories as applied to the particular case and attempt to judge which line of behavior is the most probable in the circumstances. Whether the quality of his judgment will be, on the whole, better after this procedure than if he took the findings of market theory alone and corrected them by the exercise of his unaided common sense must be tested by experience. At least the foregoing discussion suggests that the test is worth making.

CHAPTER VII

THE PROBLEM OF ECONOMIC CHANGE

I N THIS and the next two chapters we come face to face with one of the most fundamental difficulties in the way of realistic economics, namely, the impermanence of the conditions which form the premises of economic theory. "Economic situations," writes Mrs. Wootton, "appear to have a peculiar quality of uniqueness."[1] Marshall considered this an argument against the historical method: "In economic or other social problems no event has ever been an exact precedent for another."[2] But Mrs. Wootton regards this diversity of historical sequence as an argument against reliance upon theory; and it will be remembered that Professor Robbins gives it as a justification of "bigger and better realistic studies."[3] Earlier in the book, when we raised this problem, it was suggested that the economist who wishes to advise on policy must, like the "practical man," attempt to predict *changes* in the conditions of economic life, as well as the adjustments which will be made to given conditions. He cannot merely assume the continuation of conditions observed in the past, for they will often be out of date before the theory is applied. The question before us is whether the economist must rely entirely on his own personal judgment of how conditions are likely to develop or whether he can obtain some guidance from other sciences and from new developments in economic theory. If there is any hope of improving his judgment in this way, it is important that the point of liaison with other sciences be established and plans drawn, at least, for the necessary additions to economic theory.

In view of the rather pessimistic attitude of many economists toward this problem, it appears to be necessary to explore it fairly thoroughly, and the discussion will extend over three chapters. This chapter is confined to a consideration of the logical basis of prediction: questions of scope and method. In chapter viii we shall review some of the attempts made by other writers to work out a theory of economic development or to predict concrete changes in the conditions of economic

---

[1] B. Wootton, *Lament for Economics* (London, 1938), p. 76.

[2] A. C. Pigou (ed.), *Memorials of Alfred Marshall* (London, 1925), p. 166.

[3] See above, chap. iii.

activity. This will not provide a systematic history of theories of economic development. Our chief purpose is to stress the fact that such theories have a place in the tradition of economic science and to compare the logical structure of these earlier essays with that developed in the present chapter. Finally, in chapter ix, we undertake the task which arises from each of our discussions of the various deficiencies of present-day economic theory, namely, to indicate the points of liaison with other sciences and to sketch the extensions which must be made to existing theory, if economic science is to make the greatest possible contribution to the solution of the particular problems under consideration.

THE USE OF EXTRAPOLATION

Life would be unbearable, and a scientific view of the world impossible, if we could not assume some degree of stability in the conditions to which we must adjust ourselves. It is the usual practice of man to act on the assumption that the conditions of the past will continue into the future (or at least that part of it that immediately concerns him), unless there is good reason to the contrary. And what constitutes "good reason to the contrary"? The fundamental cause of uncertainty regarding the future is the observation of changes that have occurred in the past. The economist's fear of the probable impermanence of the conditions which constitute the data of economic theory rests upon the belief that the tendency to change is itself a permanent feature of the world in which we live. It is recognized that the risks involved in extrapolation are not uniform for all conditions. Economists have worried little over the possibility that a sudden change in human nature might invalidate predictions based on psychological postulates which were believed to be reasonably correct in the past.

We find, therefore, a natural tendency to extrapolate future data on the basis of past experience, including past experience of the changeability of conditions. From this it is but a short step to produce observed trends into the future, extrapolating the direction and rate of change as a continuation of past experience. "Something of inference respecting the economic changes of the future may be warranted from a study of the past."[4]

There are two reasons why simple extrapolation on the basis of past trends is often considered unjustified. The first is that the past trend may itself be insufficiently clear. If the only source of doubt is the ex-

[4] D. A. Wells, *Recent Economic Changes* (London, 1890), p. 459.

istence of fluctuations, we may be prepared to produce the "secular" trend into the future, as an indication of the probable "central tendency" of future fluctuations. Sometimes, too, a past trend may be analyzed into its component factors. For instance, no statistician would extrapolate on the basis of past trends of population, without a preliminary analysis of the trends of age and sex composition and of the distribution of past fertility and of mortality over the various age and sex groups. Following such an analysis, it is possible to estimate, on certain assumptions, how far the future trend of population will diverge from the trend indicated by crude extrapolation from past movements in population. Procedures such as these are designed to establish more clearly the "true" trend of the data in the past, before producing them into the future. If, when all this has been done, past changes do not yield an unambiguous trend, there is no satisfactory basis for extrapolation.

The determination of past trends and the extrapolation of future changes is more readily undertaken in the case of conditions subject to precise measurement, such as population, than in the case of changes usually conceived as qualitative rather than quantitative, such as industrial technique, human wants, and the institutional framework of economic life. Yet it is common to speak of an increasing tendency toward the mechanization of agriculture or a growing instability in the demand for luxury goods or a trend toward a stricter regulation of monopoly; and, in the absence of good reason to the contrary, we expect these past developments to continue, at least in the immediate future. If we set out with the intention of estimating future trends as accurately as possible, the use of various statistical measures to render somewhat more precise our knowledge of these past trends will receive a new impetus. While the susceptibility of changes to measurement varies for different types of conditions, extrapolation requires the fullest utilization of whatever indicators we can gain regarding the magnitude of past changes. This does not mean that we should substitute sets of figures for patterns of behavior or mental attitudes or that we should be uncritical of statistical totals and averages which hide significant qualitative differences. For purposes of extrapolation the determination of the general direction of past changes may be more valuable than the attainment of a spurious degree of precision in a statistical index which tells only part of the story.

The second reason why we sometimes cannot accept the results of pure extrapolation is that the study of the past may have suggested a causal law of change. If the causes which have produced changes in the past appear to be no longer present, extrapolation must be corrected according to the knowledge (or theory) at our disposal. Economists have often ventured to comment on the causes of past changes. For instance, Marshall gives a fairly full discussion of factors conditioning the health, strength, and skill of the population, which are among the factors likely to change in the course of time.[5] But his purpose appears to be to inform his reader of certain current tendencies rather than to establish a technique for the systematic correction of pure extrapolation. In any case it was just such excursions by Marshall into "amateur technology" that earned the reproach of Professor Robbins;[6] and many modern writers agree that this is "not economic theory." The real point at issue, however, is whether our beliefs regarding the causes of change, which must be taken into account in any prediction of future trends of the data, are based on the best available scientific evidence. This requires collaboration between the economist and other types of scientist, or at least the utilization of such findings of other sciences as are relevant. And, if the causes of change are to be found in the processes studied by economic science, the latter, too, has a part to play in the correction of results obtained by pure extrapolation.

We may distinguish three methods of predicting changes in the conditions of economic activity, all of which may be considered scientific.

1. Extrapolation of past trends, where the trend is unambiguous and there is no evidence of "disturbing" causes:

2. Extrapolation of past trends, "corrected" according to the findings of other sciences, regarding the causes of changes

3. Extrapolation of past trends, "corrected" according to the findings, if any, of economic science regarding the causes of changes

The third possibility depends upon the formulation of a satisfactory theory of economic development and upon its applicability to concrete cases. If a realistic theory cannot be constructed, economists will be limited to the use of the other two methods. To the extent that other sciences predict changes accurately, any economic theory of development is superfluous; and all the economist need do, if the other sciences exhaust the field, is to adopt the predictions of the other sciences as assumptions for his own analyses. For instance, if it is predicted by

[5] A. Marshall, *Principles of Economics* (8th ed.; London, 1922), Book IV, chaps. v and vi.

[6] L. Robbins, *Essay on the Nature and Significance of Economic Science* (1st ed.; London, 1932), p. 65.

soil scientists that erosion is going to reduce the cultivable area in certain districts, the economist adopts this finding as a datum. Or, if the plant pathologist predicts that the spread of a particular pest will be checked as the result of the introduction of a parasite, we take as a datum not the extrapolation of past experience of the spread of the pest, but its promised eradication. But, if other sciences do not predict changes in full and if there are ascertainable causes of changes within the field of economics, these causes should be made the subject of study by economists.

THE PURPOSE OF A THEORY OF DEVELOPMENT

It is necessary to be clear as to the scope and function of such a theory of economic development. We do not seek to "predict the complete course of an uncontrolled history";[7] theory is "not a body of concrete truth, but an engine for the discovery of concrete truth."[8] To unravel the implicit consequences of given concrete conditions, we need the assistance of a conceptual scheme. It is the complexity of the real world that makes economic theory necessary in any attempt to elucidate the consequences of given conditions; and it is evident that the forces making for changes in conditions are even more complex than those involved in adjustments to given conditions. How essential, therefore, is a conceptual map to guide us in our search for the *significant facts* in relation to changes in those conditions. A pure theory of economic development, like the pure theory of the market, would consist of a set of assumptions and a logical structure based on them, leading to significant conclusions and providing a basis for the classification of observed facts according to their significance. But there is this important difference. In the theory of the market the assumptions are chosen and the analyses directed so as to yield conclusions about behavior in the market under given conditions. But in a theory of economic development the assumptions and analyses must be designed to yield conclusions about changes in the conditions which form the data of present economic theory. Such a theory of development would not by itself provide a "formal outline of probable developments;"[9] the latter can be obtained only by applying the theory to the observed conditions. It will serve a purpose similar to that of existing theory in the investigation of a concrete problem, namely, it will classify the observed facts according to a significant scheme and tell us what facts to look for in a particular instance. But, whereas existing theory, taking

---

[7] *Ibid.*, p. 125.   [8] Pigou, *op. cit.*, p. 159.   [9] Robbins, *op. cit.*, p. 132.

its conditions as given, can be applied only to predict what will happen if conditions do not change, it is hoped that a theory of development can be applied to predict how conditions *will* change.

THE MEANING OF DEVELOPMENT

It must be recognized, however, that "development" is used in a number of different senses, which must be distinguished from that adopted here. For instance, the term "theory of economic development" is sometimes applied to a theory covering the adaptations of the market to changing economic conditions. Thus a contrast is drawn with the economics of stationary states. The term "development" has even been used without any assumption of changing conditions. Professor Lindahl gives as the aim of economic theory "to provide theoretical structures showing how certain initial conditions give rise to certain developments."[10] On this definition the establishment of equilibrium, as a result of certain initial conditions, might be called "development." Thus Professor Lindahl says that, "properly interpreted, static theory also [i.e., as well as dynamic theory] has for an object economic developments taking place in time, only the variables studied do not change their values with the lapse of time."[11] Dynamic theory, according to Professor Lindahl, takes for its data (*a*) the original plans of the economic subjects (which are "neither fully consistent with one another nor with the external conditions";[12] (*b*) the revisions which are likely to be made subsequently in these plans if the results and external conditions are different from those expected; and (*c*) "enough knowledge of external conditions to be able to make definite statements with regard to future changes in plans, and the results of actions undertaken." With these data "it should be possible to provide a theoretical construction of the developments that will be the outcome of the initial position."[13] There is as yet little agreement among economists as to the most useful meaning of the term "dynamics";[14] this and other analogies from mechanics are employed without sufficient examination of the extent to which the fundamental con-

---

[10] E. Lindahl, *Studies in the Theory of Money and Capital* (London, 1939), p. 23.

[11] *Ibid.*, pp. 31–32.   [12] *Ibid.*, p. 38.   [13] *Ibid.*, pp. 37–38.

[14] Cf. also J. M. Clark, *Preface to Social Economics* (New York, 1936), p. 196; C. F. Roos, *Dynamic Economics* (Bloomington, Ind., 1934), p. 7; F. H. Knight, *The Ethics of Competition* (London, 1935), p. 161; J. R. Hicks, *Value and Capital* (London, 1939), p. 115; R. F. Harrod, *The Trade Cycle* (London, 1936); J. A. Schumpeter, *Theory of Economic Development* (Cambridge, Mass., 1934); E. Barone, *Le Opere economiche* (Bologna, 1936), I, 79; M. Pantaleoni, *Erotemi di economia* (Bari, 1925), II, 75; etc.

cepts of mechanics are applicable to economic affairs. Admittedly, the term "development" is open to objection because it, too, is already used in several senses. But no other term suggests itself as equally convenient.

It must be made clear, therefore, that the developments which we are to study are the changes in the *data* of economic theory, and not merely the changes in the *dependent* variables or conclusions which may follow a change in the data. Our task is to construct a theory which will aid the economist to obtain "enough knowledge of external conditions" to permit prediction, even when those conditions change.

IS A THEORY OF DEVELOPMENT POSSIBLE?

It may not be immediately apparent that a useful theory of economic development can be constructed. Professor Robbins informs us that

the prospects are very doubtful. . . . . In the last analysis the study of Economics, while it shows us a region of economic laws, of necessities to which human action is subject, shows us, too, a region, in which no such necessities operate. This is not to say that within that region there is no law, no necessity. Into that question we make no enquiry. It is only to say that from its point of view at least there are certain things which must be taken as ultimate data.[15]

But, once this pronouncement is understood, it need deter nobody. All it means is that economics assumes certain conditions as given and explores their implications. Therefore, it does not explain those conditions. There may be an explanation, but economics does not seek it, in so far as economics studies only the implications of its data.

There still remains the problem of where explanation of these conditions can be found, if at all. Professor Robbins glances at some of the chief categories of data for economic theory, namely, population, technique, and the legal framework, and concludes that none of these is likely to change primarily, or even largely, through the processes which existing economic theory investigates. Of population changes he concludes: "We may all venture our guess. But surely economic analysis can have very little to do with it." Of changes in technique, his verdict is that "we need postulate no ultimate indeterminism, if we assume that, from the point of view of our system, such changes are unpredictable." Coming to the legal framework, he concedes that "there is an important sense in which the subject matter of political science can be conceived to come within the scope of our definition of economics." But the "manifest dependence" of change upon "the hetero-

[15] *Op. cit.*, pp. 131, 135.

geneous elements of contingency, persuasion, and blind force" renders prediction practically impossible. "There is no technique in economics which enables us to forecast these permutations of the spirit."[16]

THE DATA OF ECONOMIC THEORY

A more systematic investigation is required, however, before accepting this negative attitude. Professor Robbins does not examine all the data of economic theory, and his discussion of the three mentioned above is but cursory. We may adopt the same starting-point, but the matter must be carried further.

First, it is essential to have a clear idea of the conditions the constancy or variability of which is the objective of study. What are the data of economic theory? If it were customary to expound economic theory in strictly logical form, we might expect to find the data or assumptions listed in the books on "elements" or "principles" of economics. But such lists are rarely encountered, because the economist's preoccupation—despite all denials—with practical policy usually leads him to couch his exposition in substantial terms and to avoid an unduly formal arrangement of assumptions and deductions.

We shall make use of a well-known list, suggested by Professor F. H. Knight. It is intended to cover the "factors in regard to which change or the possibility of change must be studied" and is therefore particularly suited to our purpose. The list is as follows:

1. The population, numbers, and composition
2. The tastes and dispositions of the people
3. The amounts and kinds of productive capacities in existence, including
   a) Personal powers
   b) Material agents
4. The distribution of ownership of these, including all rights of control by persons over persons or things
5. Geographic distribution of people and things
6. The state of the arts; the whole situation as to science, education, technology, social organization, etc.[17]

In a later study of "Statics and Dynamics," Professor Knight gives a modified list of the "given conditions of the statically continuous economic life." This list is notable chiefly for the addition of two other factors to those quoted above. One is "public policy in its various phases," which, in discussing his earlier list, Professor Knight stated to be "indistinguishable from number 2, tastes and dispositions," although it seems to be also related to No. 6, "social organization." The

---

[16] *Ibid.*, p. 134.   [17] *Risk, Uncertainty, and Profit* (Boston, 1921), p. 147.

other is "monetary conditions," which might also conceivably be included in No. 6.

Each item on the list is, of course, a mere heading, under which various substantial conditions may be classed. For instance, the dispositions of the people might vary with respect to their preferences for work and leisure or their susceptibility to institutional norms, such as were considered in the previous chapter. Only certain of the conceivable assumptions under each head have hitherto been made the subject of theoretical constructions. On the other hand, certain particular assumptions have been common to almost all theoretical essays. For instance, Professor Knight, as we have already seen, considers it essential to the theory of exchange that, under No. 4, there should be *no* control by persons over other persons.[18] Similarly, a particular legal structure and a particular technology are assumed in most economic discussion.

As a general classification of the data of conventional economic theory, the list may be regarded as satisfactory, except for one serious omission, namely, the extent and nature of competition. The "market situation," with regard to the number of sellers and buyers, and the degree of standardization of the product are important conditioning factors in economic analysis, which do not fit so readily into No. 4 or any of the other classes listed as to render special mention superfluous. The possibility of changes in market situations is one of the problems for a theory of economic development; and it is convenient, therefore, to extend Professor Knight's list of the data of economic theory accordingly. For Professor Knight's own purpose (the study of free enterprise) it was more convenient to treat the question of monopoly elsewhere, its absence, like that of predatory activities, being treated as a necessary assumption for the free-enterprise economy. In considering the tendency toward monopoly from the latter viewpoint, Professor Knight does, in fact, enter the field of the theory of economic development, as here conceived.[19] His comments on predatory activities are also of importance in relation to our theory of extra-market operations. For the purpose of the theory of economic development, however, changes in attitude toward extra-market operations may be brought under *the tastes and dispositions of the people*, and *the state of the arts, including social organization*.

Allowing for the addition of "market situations," it may be asked

---

[18] See above, chap. v.

[19] Cf. *Risk, Uncertainty, and Profit*, chap. vi..

what phenomena, if any, are not covered by so comprehensive a list. For the purpose of an explanatory theory, however, a line must be drawn between *data* and *conclusions*, between independent variables and dependent variables. Professor Knight reduces the dependent variables to three:

1. The prices of final goods and services
2. The prices of productive services
3. The allocation of productive resources among enterprises within each industry[20]

These are considered to be the results of the operation of the economic system and vary according to the concrete content of the data.

Professor Knight remarks in parenthesis that "the distribution of final products among those who supply productive services is taken care of by the prices of the services and ownership," of which the former is a dependent variable and the latter one of the data. If we elevate the distribution of final products to the rank of a fourth dependent variable, we may say that the final positions of all four are implicit in the original conditions listed above.

This distinction between data and conclusions is not, however, so clear as at first appears. For instance, the third dependent variable, namely, "allocation of productive resources among enterprises within each industry," might be classed under No. 5 on the list of data—"geographical distribution of people and things"—and in some cases under No. 6—"the distribution of ownership." Certainly, the fourth dependent variable, namely, "the distribution of final products," could be classed under No. 6, in so far as the products can themselves be used in further production. In these cases the distinction between data and conclusions can be maintained only with respect to an agreed transaction or an agreed period of time. If no such limit is imposed, *the theory may include among its conclusions changes in the data.*

ENDOGENOUS DATA-CHANGES IN ECONOMIC THEORY

This point has been frequently stressed by Professor Knight:

Needless controversy and wasted effort have resulted from overlooking the fact that constants from one point of view may be variables from another.[21]

The means of want-satisfaction and the resources used to produce them, and the technology and business organisation according to which the process is carried out— all are *data*, causes, independent variables, in some regards and with reference to some time periods, and all are effects, dependent variables, in other regards and with refer-

[20] *The Ethics of Competition*, p. 174.

[21] "Ethics and the Economic Interpretation" (1922), reprinted in *The Ethics of Competition*, p. 20.

ence to other time periods. The only ultimately independent variables are those features of nature and human nature which are in fact outside the power of economic forces to change, and it would be hard to say what these are.[22]

Professor Robbins admits that "it is not always easy" to draw the distinction between endogenous changes (due to changes in the data) and exogenous changes (in the data themselves). "As Professor Knight has often pointed out, in some societies there exist definite financial incentives to certain individuals to produce changes in the data." Professor Robbins holds, however, that "over a large part of the field the classification (exogenous and endogenous changes) is intelligible enough and a positive aid to clear thinking. Until matters have been classified very much further its retention seems essential."[23]

It is, of course, only in practice that the problem of distinguishing between the two arises. In theoretical constructions there should be no difficulty in maintaining the distinction, if we desire to do so. All that it requires is an appropriate choice of assumptions. The same change may be exogenous to one set of assumptions but endogenous to another set. The difficulties encountered in the real world, in drawing the distinction between changes that can be regarded as endogenous to the economy and those that are exogenous, arise from doubt as to which set of assumptions is the more significant for the problem under consideration. A theory of economic development can easily be constructed by adopting assumptions which imply changes in the data, thereby making these changes endogenous instead of exogenous. Whether such a theory has any bearing on the course of economic development in the real world is another matter, which can be settled only by checking the theory against the facts.

If we approached the problem of constructing a realistic theory of economic development *ab initio*, the logical first step would be to consider each of the accepted categories of data and inquire as to the extent to which changes appeared to be the result of economic processes or of other influences outside the economic world. This we shall attempt, if only on a small scale. However, in view of the fact that we do not begin with a *tabula rasa* but with the whole of economic theory in the background and are considering the possibility of building a theory of development onto the existing body of doctrine, it is worth considering Professor Knight's problem a little further. We shall see

---

[22] "The Limitations of Scientific Method in Economics," in R. Tugwell (ed.), *The Trend of Economics* (New York, 1924), p. 263; reprinted in *The Ethics of Competition*, p. 142.

[23] *Op cit.*, pp. 127–29.

that, with the appearance of the same quantities as the results of one process and the conditions for another, economic development, as we have defined it, has already crept into economic theory, despite the economist's preoccupation with the study of "equilibrium" and of adjustments to given conditions.

Consider, for instance, the first two dependent variables in Professor Knight's list, namely, the prices of final goods and the prices of productive services. In any historical period certain prices have already been established as the result of preceding conditions. These existing prices constitute *data* for the individual economic agents, who adjust their behavior accordingly. If a succession of periods be studied, "a dependent variable in the system of to-day becomes an independent variable in that of to-morrow."[24] When we embark upon Marshallian "long-period analyses," we allow time for changes to "work themselves out" by influencing later short-period adjustments."[25] Indeed, Marshall allowed not only for changes in prices but also for such changes in technique as are consequent upon the long-period expansion or contraction of output which is taking place. So, too, in all "sequence analysis" or study of the phases of fluctuations the adjustments made in one arbitrarily chosen period help to determine the conditions to which adjustments are made in the next period.

When the final outcome is a state of equilibrium in the four dependent variables, it is permissible, of course, to conceive this as the consequence of an initial set of conditions, relating to the period before any prices had been established. Comparing this original situation with the final equilibrium, prices would then appear in the conclusions of the theory but not in the data. Such a conception ignores altogether the path by which equilibrium is achieved. Any attempt to show the *successive* adjustments to the original data reveals the fact that, if any prices have been established at an *intermediate* stage, before the *final* equilibrium is reached, those prices become data for the next stage in the process. In the same way, if the ownership of resources is changed or their geographical location, by way of adjustment to the data at one stage, this means that the data will be different for the next stage. For that matter, the allocation of resources may cause "the amounts, and kinds of productive capacities" to change from one period to the next; the results of the one adjustment become part of the data for the next.

[24] E. H. Phelps Brown, *Framework of the Pricing System* (London, 1936), p. 187.

[25] In short-period analysis, as Marshall notes, "we do treat variables *provisionally* as constants" (cf. *Principles of Economics*, p. 380 n.).

The complete separation of conditions from consequences, of data from conclusions, is possible, therefore, only if we confine our attention to the initial conditions and the final equilibrium, abstracting from the intermediate process. All the concrete problems that the economist is concerned with, however, arise in a community with a past history. Consequently, the "initial" conditions, which may lead to equilibrium, always include, in addition to factors which appear to be external, some factors which are themselves the result of a previous economic process. Here we have, in economic theory itself, one channel of economic development.

It may also be noted that abstraction from the *intermediate* adjustments derives most of its point from the assumption that the original conditions imply a state of equilibrium. It is appropriate, therefore, to stress the fact that the final destiny of these dependent variables may not be positions of equilibrium. Whether equilibrium is or is not implied in the original conditions depends simply on the substance which is given to the data. For instance, Professor Schumpeter's discussion of the "circular flow" of economic life establishes an equilibrium, by assuming conditions which imply such an equilibrium.[26] But, as Professor Robbins remarks, "it is easy to conceive of initial configurations of the data, which have no total tendency to equilibrium, but which rather tend to cumulative oscillation."[27] Indeed, this is the basis for several theories of fluctuation.

But we must go further and recognize that an appropriate "initial configuration of the data" might imply neither a "total tendency to equilibrium" nor "cumulative oscillation," but only continuous change, in one or more dependent variables, always in the same direction. For instance, if we assume a demand curve and supply curve, both negatively inclined, and if the slope of the latter exceeds that of the former, no position of stable equilibrium is implied, but only a continuous expansion of production and fall in price. If this conclusion be resisted as empirically improbable or as inconsistent with other propositions of economic theory, this constitutes a challenge to the acceptability of the original assumptions and shifts the discussion into the sphere of verification. But these assumptions and their conclusions are no less *conceivable* in pure theory than are assumptions which imply equilibrium.

Empirical observation suggests that equilibrium is rare in practice. The weight of equilibrium theory suggests that failure to achieve equi-

[26] *Op. cit.*, chap. i.   [27] *Op. cit.*, p. 102.

librium in practice *may* be due to continuous variation of the conditions of economic life; but it is equally conceivable a priori that there may be conditions which imply no tendency toward equilibrium. Since we are seeking a theory of economic development, such a possibility is not so distasteful as it may seem to the equilibrium theorist. If any set of conditions implies not equilibrium but continuous change—oscillatory or cumulative—there is no "final" position for the dependent variables; every successive position is "intermediate" to a subsequent one, and, though we may set out to construct a theory of market equilibrium, we finish up with a contribution (of sorts) to the theory of economic development.

A striking illustration of this is found in the implications of the assumption of "saving." If consumers are disposed to save a portion of their income and no investment is undertaken, incomes must fall to a level at which the disposition to save no longer operates. On the other hand, if some investment is undertaken and incomes are sustained at a level which makes continued saving possible, this investment involves a change in "the amount of productive capacities in existence," which is one of the conditions distinguished by Professor Knight. So long as there is any saving, equilibrium of all dependent variables cannot be reached, because saving itself implies a continuous change in one of the fundamental conditions of the economy. It should be noticed that the "disposition to save" is itself covered by the second condition of Professor Knight's list, "the tastes and dispositions of the people."

This is an example of economic development which is implied by the content given to the original conditions. In response to the latter, adjustments are made in the "dependent variables," including "the allocation of productive resources." The adjustment made in this variable involves an alteration of one of the original conditions. This process is already a commonplace of economic theory, though not usually recognized as a contribution to the theory of economic development.

A MORE REALISTIC VIEW OF DATA CHANGES

The foregoing discussion has shown that in the study of equilibrium and of adjustments to given conditions economic theory does make use of the concept of development and uses assumptions which imply changes in the conditions, as well as adjustments of market quantities to the original conditions. Our next task is to examine each of the chief classes of conditions (the *data* of economic theory) and to consider the changes to which they are subject in practice. Our objective is to determine the extent to which these changes can be brought within the scheme of economic theory, without doing violence to the facts, and the extent to which they must be regarded as due to independent causes. Professor Knight has made a somewhat similar review of the items in his own list on two occasions, but each time with a different purpose in view—in one case to investigate the extent to which individual economic subjects are uncertain regarding future changes and, in the other, to determine whether long-run changes in conditions are to be regarded as movements toward a position of stable equilibrium.[28] Professor Knight would probably be skeptical regarding the purpose we have in view,[29] but his own work provides considerable material which bears on our problem.

Two further preliminary points may be made. The first is that our interest is not confined to long-period changes. Indeed, it is short-period changes in conditions that are most likely to invalidate the economist's inferences from given data. As Professor Viner has pointed out, policy tends to be formulated with a view to the short period rather than the long period.[30] Our attitude toward the possibility of scientific prediction of short-period changes should not be unduly influenced by natural skepticism regarding the pretentious attempts sometimes made to interpret or predict the history of civilizations throughout the centuries. Not a philosophy of history on a grand scale but an interpretation of current history is what the economic practitioner needs most urgently. There may well be more hope of predicting the relatively small data changes that upset particular concrete analyses than of foreseeing the long-period evolution of the economic system.

The second point is that we may bring to the consideration of changes in the data not merely the theory of market adjustments, which constitutes the major part of conventional economic theory, but also the theory of extra-market operations, sketched in the preceding chapter. In working out this extension of economic theory we have

[28] See *Risk, Uncertainty, and Profit*, pp. 151 ff., and "Statics and Dynamics" in *The Ethics of Competition*, pp. 177 ff., respectively, for these two separate investigations.

[29] Prediction of long-period data changes "is a field for the exercise of informed judgment rather than for reasoning according to the canons of science. The movements of history are to be 'sensed' rather than plotted and projected into the future" (*The Ethics of Competition*, pp. 143–44).

[30] J. Viner, "Short and Long View in Economic Policy," *American Economic Review*, March, 1940.

already made abundant use of the concept of action directed toward the alteration of the data of the market and have considered conditions which imply the likelihood of such action. This means that we can approach the list of data, in which changes are to be investigated, with a much broader concept of economic processes than that obtained from conventional economic theory. It is only to be expected, therefore, that we shall be able to treat as endogenous many of the changes which have previously been considered exogenous to economic theory.[31]

We now proceed to consider each of the data included in the list given earlier (p. 149). A far more elaborate investigation than that made here might be undertaken, but only at the cost of covering much familiar ground. Even at the risk of seeming dogmatic, our conclusions under each head will be presented with a bare minimum of supporting argument.

1. POPULATION: NUMBERS AND COMPOSITION

Changes in the number of people in a community may come through "natural increase" (the excess of births over deaths) or decrease and through migration. There has been endless discussion of the extent to which natural increase may be affected through market adjustments. The survival rate at various ages obviously depends in part on the income of the individual or his "breadwinner" and on the prices of various foods and of medical attention; but it is also affected by wars, epidemics, climate fluctuations, public health organizations, and other factors outside the traditional economic scheme. Some wars and some public health measures might, at a stretch, be brought under extra-market operations; but there remain many factors which can be explained, if at all, only by sciences other than economics. The birth rate, too, is undoubtedly influenced by financial motives and by the provision of facilities for birth control and abortion at various prices. But the operation of these factors varies considerably according to income, occupation, and other factors. There are also powerful nonfinancial motives to be reckoned with, such as religion, social prestige, and family pride, which do not operate through the market at all. Altogether, the causes at work are so heterogeneous that it is ex-

---

[31] Those who prefer to regard our theory of extra-market operations as a branch of sociology rather than as an extension of economic theory may adhere to their narrower conception of economic processes. In that case the possibility of collaboration between economists and sociologists in the prediction of data changes remains, along with that of collaboration between economists and other scientists.

tremely difficult to isolate the economic processes involved in natural increase.

In migration, however, they are more easily distinguished. Three factors are involved: the attraction of the country to which migrants go, the unattractiveness of conditions in the country that they leave, and the facilities for the act of migration. All are influenced by the adjustments of prices and by the allocation of resources, in response to the previous constellation of the data. The economic analysis of the sources and destination of migration is well known; and attention may also be drawn to the role of commodity trade in stimulating both the provision of transport for human beings, as distinct from merchandise, and the commercial and other contacts which may make a change of home a less forbidding venture. Of course, there are other causes at work, particularly in periods of political upheaval; and the facilities for migration depend upon laws which often reflect motives outside the economic scheme. But it is nothing new to attempt to explain or predict the currents of migration; and economic factors can rarely be excluded from the argument, without doing violence to the facts.

Under the heading of population, Professor Knight mentions composition as well as numbers. Whether we consider age or race, the composition of the population is a compound of the factors mentioned above and the passage of time. The age composition today depends on the birth rate and the age incidence of deaths over a period as long as the life of the oldest inhabitant, and also on past migration, its spacing through time, and the ages of the migrants. These, however, are matters of arithmetic—a superstructure, as it were, upon the more fundamental factors already considered.

2. TASTES AND DISPOSITIONS OF THE PEOPLE

A thorough consideration of the data falling under this heading would involve a review of modern psychology. While some of the discussion in chapters v and vi would be relevant, it would touch only a fraction of the field. Of special importance, however, is the growing recognition that the individual personality is to a considerable degree the product of social influences, playing upon a very malleable native endowment. This means that many of our tastes and dispositions, far from being closely linked with organic needs or specific "instincts," are largely formed and modified by the society in which we live and the experiences which it brings us. Some of our tastes and dispositions appear to attain a high degree of stability; but those that are continuously subject to change must not be regarded as predominantly capricious. Their changes often reflect the disintegration of existing social norms and the evolution of new ones; they result from processes which we can investigate and attempt to understand.

Some of the processes are clearly "economic," in the everyday meaning of the term. Thus Professor Schumpeter considers it justifiable to "act on the assumption that consumers' initiative in changing their tastes is negligible and that all change in consumers' tastes is incident to, or brought about by producers' action."[32] At the same time, not all efforts in this direction yield the desired results, while others are more successful than they deserve to be: "The business of want creation, is of course, very uncertain and aleatory, or risky."[33] The economic process in this case may be upset, at any time, by "external disturbing causes." Professor Knight thinks that changes in attitudes toward productive activities are particularly subject to external causes and accordingly less amenable to economic analysis. This assumes, however, that economic theory covers only market adjustments. The theory of extra-market operations helps us to take account of such changes in opinion or attitudes to particular types of activity as are engineered by businessmen or others, with a view to making the market work more favorably *for them.* The cultivation of protectionist sentiment by manufacturers or of opposition to chain stores by groups of independents are obvious examples.

But, of course, the field is not exhausted by this type of analysis. Many of the changes in tastes and dispositions must be attributed to other social processes: the relaxation of moral taboos in wartime and in periods of religious revival, the changing attitude toward women workers, the liquor boom under prohibition, increased production from labor in wartime, the decline of Sabbath observance. Some light may be thrown on the causes of these changes by other social sciences —psychology, sociology, and anthropology; but there will long be doubt as to the validity of the various hypotheses offered.

3. THE AMOUNTS AND KINDS OF PRODUCTIVE CAPACITIES

a) Personal powers.—Although applied psychology has added much to our knowledge of innate ability and its relation to the acquisition of skill, there is still little scientific evidence about the changes that may take place in the distribution of the former throughout the community.

[32] J. A. Schumpeter, *Business Cycles* (New York, 1939), I, 73.

[33] Knight, *Risk, Uncertainty, and Profit,* p. 157.

Earlier generalizations regarding the supposed tendency toward differential reproduction of various income groups and the effects of this upon the average level of intelligence have been seriously undermined by later, more detailed statistical studies. Inequality of educational opportunity plays a much greater part in determining the intellectual (and economic) level attained by the individual than psychologists in the first flush of "mental testing" were willing to admit. Certainly, the channels into which general native ability is directed and the specific "personal powers" that emerge depend largely upon social and economic factors. The "allocation of resources" to general and vocational education is probably the most important source of change in the aptitudes of the population, though different results will be obtained, according to the type and quality of instruction and experience that is provided.

Almost as important, particularly if we start with a low level of physical health, are the changes which may be caused through the allocation of resources to preventive and curative medicine, sanitation, slum clearance, and the provision of the foodstuffs necessary for a balanced diet. Changes in working conditions may be another powerful factor in the modification of personal powers.

b) Material agents.—It is a commonplace of economics that, while the earth's surface is, for all practical purposes, fixed, the supply of natural resources is subject to change as a result of man's activity. On the one hand, there are activities tending progressively to exhaust existing resources; on the other, activities promoting their conservation, improvement, and transformation. Mining and soil erosion, irrigation and afforestation, illustrate these respective tendencies. The accumulation of capital equipment in various specific forms is, of course, one of the chief characteristics of modern economic systems and a prominent subject in economic theory. Apart from the physical destruction produced by such catastrophes as wars and earthquakes, changes in material agents must be regarded primarily as the outcome of economic processes—the allocation of resources to specific employments.

4. THE DISTRIBUTION OF OWNERSHIP OF THESE, AND RIGHTS OF CONTROL BY PERSONS OVER PERSONS AND THINGS

The data under this heading may, of course, be changed by authoritarian redistribution, directly through public appropriation of private property or indirectly through the effects of taxation policies. Systems of land tenure and customs of inheritance may bring about gradual changes in distribution through their own undisturbed functioning.

But the role of economic processes is very prominent in the growth of large fortunes, and the acquisition of controlling interests in great aggregations of capital.[34] Purchase and sale, the setting of prices for goods and services, the "distribution of final products"—all these market adjustments produce changes in the ownership of "productive capacities." "Ordinary economic forces tend toward a progressive concentration."[35]

5. GEOGRAPHIC DISTRIBUTION OF PEOPLE AND THINGS

Our discussion of migration applies equally to international and internal shifts of population; and natural increase also varies from district to district within a country. The drift to the towns, while it may be influenced by "nonfinancial" motives, too, is largely the result of economic processes and has been listed among the "implications of economic progress."[36] The geographic distribution of people and things depends largely upon the location of industry and partly on the relationship between dwellings and places of work. Changes in these factors have been largely explicable in the past by reference to market adjustments. In the unhappy present the prospect of aerial bombardment cuts across the ordinary economic calculations; and, in the future, authoritarian regulation of industrial and urban development—regional planning—may render the economic interpretation increasingly inappropriate.[37] But, apart from the nightmare of war and the dream of a "brave new world," changes in these data are produced chiefly through the processes studied by economic theory.

6. THE STATE OF THE ARTS: SCIENCE, EDUCATION, TECHNOLOGY, SOCIAL ORGANIZATION, ETC.

"This is one of the most treacherous concepts of all as a subject for scientific discourse."[38] The advance of technical knowledge has become increasingly a commercial enterprise, both because technology is a productive agent and also because it is a weapon in the struggle for monopoly power.[39] But these remain as incalculable elements in the progress of even the most systematic and determined attack upon any specific scientific problem, and the task of prediction cannot be lightly

---

[34] Cf. A. A. Berle and G. C. Means, *The Modern Corporation and Private Property* (New York 1933).

[35] Knight, *The Ethics of Competition*, p. 184.

[36] Cf. A. G. B. Fisher, *The Clash of Progress and Security* (London, 1935).

[37] Cf. Lewis Mumford, *The Culture of Cities* (London, 1938).

[38] Knight, *Risk, Uncertainty, and Profit*, p. 172.

[39] Cf. W. H. Hamilton, *Patents and Free Enterprise* ("Temporary National Economic Committee Monographs," No. 31 [Washington, 1941]).

undertaken. Later we shall review an interesting attempt to forecast inventions. At this stage it is sufficient to note that the commercialization of technical advance readers it necessary to take account of economic processes in any such essays in prediction.

Finally, we may notice the two classes of data which Professor Knight subsequently separated from his original list, which we have been considering, and our own addition to the list. *Monetary conditions* are likely to change through both public policy and private initiative. In the days when gold was the fundamental factor, the allocation of resources to mining, in response to price changes (of gold relatively to other things), was an important source of change in the monetary stock. The growth of credit institutions has made changes in the provision of means of payment still more of an economic process, while the public regulation of monetary conditions remains in an experimental stage. *Public policy*, which may be included under both Nos. 2 and 6, above, is likely to be modified, as we have already seen, by the judicious "allocation of resources" within and outside the market. *Market situations*, which we thought it necessary to add to Professor Knight's list, may be altered through the purchase of small firms by large ones or through the elimination of small firms in the course of competitive adjustments to market conditions.

From a purely formal viewpoint, therefore, it would seem that, although other factors are often prominent, many changes in the conditions of economic activity can be considered as being in large part the result of economic processes. That is to say, the original conditions, falling under the various classes of data, lead to changes in the dependent variables (prices, incomes, and the allocation of resources) which alter some of the conditions for the next period. And the possibility of extra-market operations extends the range of those developments in the data which may be regarded as economic responses to the original data.

The other changes which take place in the data must be ascribed to noneconomic causes. Some of them may be explained as due to the direct interaction of one class of data upon another. For instance, the state of the arts (No. 6) affects directly the natural increase of the population (No. 1); and the geographical distribution of people (No. 5) exercises a direct influence upon their tastes and dispositions (No. 2). In such cases a change in certain data produces a change in other data, not via the adjustment of the dependent variables of market analysis or the extra-market operations of people trying to make the

best of existing conditions, but through entirely different causal relationships. These other causal relationships are presumably objects of
study for other sciences; and the same is true of changes which may be
attributed to factors which could not be classified under any part of
this list of data. But the categories of the list are so broad that between
them they cover most of the phenomena of life and nature.

The task of prediction is difficult, however, not only because the
other sciences are not yet able to supply full information about the
changes that cannot be brought into the economic scheme but also
because perplexities arise over the substantial content of the data of
economic theory. For instance, the change in the geographical distribution of certain people and things can be predicted if changes in
the location of industry can be predicted: indeed, the problem is vir-
tually the same. We have a formal economic theory which represents
the location of industry as the result of market adjustments to "given"
data; but the substance of the data is rarely "given" to the economist
in sufficient detail for him to predict the location of a particular new
industry, even on the assumption that the data will not change. The
difficulties are essentially similar in the case of other data changes attributed to economic processes. If migration were due entirely to a
calculation of the economic advantages of residence in alternative
places and of the costs of moving, the economist would still find it
difficult to predict the results of the calculation. If family limitation is
considered an economic response to the costs of keeping children in
relation to the scales of preference for family life, the consumption
standards of the parents, and social status, we are still faced with the
difficulty of knowing what the relative valuations are for various
groups of people. In other words, there is still a considerable hiatus between the formal inclusion of data changes among the conclusions
which may be implicit in the general assumption of economic theory
and the prediction of economic development in concrete terms. "If
we are humble, we shall be modest in our pretensions."[40]

Nevertheless, the preceding discussion suggests that it would be premature to reject the possibility of correcting our extrapolation of past
trends in the light of economic theory as well as other sciences. Indeed, as will be seen in the next chapter, this practice has long had a
place in economic literature, though it has not always been explicitly
recognized as involving a contribution to the theory of economic development.

[40] Robbins, *op. cit.*, p. 135.

CHAPTER VIII

SOME THEORIES OF ECONOMIC DEVELOPMENT

I T IS not the purpose of this chapter to present a history of theories of economic development, although that might prove a fascinating task for a specialist in the history of doctrine.[1] It will be sufficient to illustrate the presence, especially in certain well-known works, of assumptions and logical constructions which belong to the theory of development rather than to the analysis of equilibrium under constant conditions. The attempt to enlarge modern economic theory so as to include a theory of changes in the data will then be seen not merely as a reaction against those modern trends which make economic theory less realistic but also as the perpetuation of a viewpoint which has always been present, if not always prominent, in economic thought.

We shall consider, not merely theories which claim to deal with economic development, but also the theories which are implicit in the predictions of future changes, which some economists have ventured to make. It is of some interest to compare the extent to which different writers use the three methods of prediction already distinguished in the preceding chapter, namely, (1) extrapolation from past trends, (2) extrapolation corrected by the findings of sciences other than economics, and (3) extrapolation corrected by considerations arising from economic theory.

MALTHUS AND HIS FOLLOWERS

The Malthusian theory of population immediately springs to mind as an attempt to explain the changes that take place in one of the most important data of economic theory. "The soundest economist," wrote Cannan, "will hesitate if asked directly, 'What is the Malthusian theory of population?' "[2] chiefly because Malthus modified his own views in successive editions of his *Essay on the Principle of Population* and his supporters found additional arguments to bolster up such of

[1] Professor E. Roll, almost alone among historians of theory, gives considerable space to the views of various writers on development, as well as on the traditional problems of economics. His *History of Economic Thought* (London, 1938) thereby achieves a degree of originality in an otherwise familiar field.

[2] E. Cannan, *A History of the Theories of Production and Distribution* (3d ed.; London, 1924), p. 134.

164

his views as they adopted. We may assume sufficient familiarity with his proposition that population tends to outrun the means of subsistence but is held in check by misery and vice or, in the second and subsequent editions, by prudential restraint. The question to be considered is: What methods of prediction are involved in this thesis?

Malthus originally argued that an increasing population, if unchecked, would increase in geometrical ratio and that food production could be increased only in an arithmetical ratio. Assuming a constant size for the typical family, the former postulate is a mathematical truism: If every pair of parents is to be replaced by a number in excess of two—say, four—who survive to become parents, the population will be equal to the product of the number of parents and a common ratio. In the absence of checks the size of the family would be constant, provided human fertility was constant. In effect, Malthus assumed constant fertility in the past and extrapolated this assumption into the future. But he considered the chief evidence for geometrical increase was the experience of North America, where the usual checks had not been operating. So the postulate may be regarded as based on extrapolation from population trends in that part of the world. His second postulate—no more than arithmetical increase of food production—was also a case of simple extrapolation on the basis of past trends in Great Britain. It was in flagrant contradiction with past trends in North America and, according to some contemporary authorities, conflicted with the opinions of agricultural experts.[3]

Much has been written on the question of where Malthus went wrong and why. It is clear from his own testimony that he thought there could be little doubt about these postulates. He wrote in the Appendix to his Third Edition:

It has been said that I have written a quarto volume to prove that population increases in a geometrical, and food in arithmetical ratio; but this is not quite true. The first of these propositions I considered as proved the moment the American increase was related, and the second proposition as soon as it was enunciated. The chief effect of my work was to inquire what effect these laws, which I considered as established in the first six pages, had produced and were likely to produce on society; a subject not very readily exhausted.[4]

The bulk of his theory, therefore, he conceived to be a theory not of changes in the data but of the adjustments which followed those changes.

The concrete conclusions of the theory stood or fell, however, by the

[3] *Ibid.*, p. 145.   [4] Cited by Cannan, *ibid.*, p. 143.

reliability of the method of extrapolation. The supporters of Malthus, who built still more elaborate theoretical structures upon these foundations, were evidently not satisfied to leave things where Malthus did. They accordingly attempted to support the results of simple extrapolation by appeal to contemporary theories of agriculture. The principle of diminishing returns from agriculture became the principal prop to the assumption that food production could not expand so rapidly as population would if unchecked. In its "static" form this principle suggested that additional food production could be obtained only by the extension of agriculture on inferior soils or the intensified cultivation of land already utilized; in either case production would not increase proportionately to the number of workers engaged. Taking a "dynamic" view, however, it was necessary to consider the possibility of technical improvements enabling increased production to be obtained from any given piece of land or providing access to "new" land superior to that already under cultivation. Even simple extrapolation from the past progress of agricultural science gave results inconsistent with the "dynamic" principle of diminishing returns; and attempts to retain the principle often took the form of assertions that future improvements could not be expected on the same scale as in the past. This "correction" of the results of simple extrapolation, however, was due to theoretic blight rather than to scientific evidence.

Into the subsequent debate on the alleged tendency of population to outrun subsistence we need not go. But, before leaving Malthus, attention may be drawn to his discussion of the possibility of influencing reproduction rates through social forces.

> In most countries, among the lower classes of people, there appears to be something like a standard of wretchedness, a point below which they will not continue to marry and propagate their species. This standard is different in different countries, and is formed by various concurring circumstances of soil, climate, government, degree of knowledge, and civilization, etc. The principal circumstances which contribute to raise it are liberty, security of property, the spread of knowledge, and a taste for the conveniences and comforts of life. Those which contribute principally to lower it are despotism and ignorance. In an attempt to better the condition of the lower classes of society, our object should be to raise this standard as high as possible, by cultivating a spirit of independence, a decent pride, and a taste for cleanliness and comfort among the poor.[5]

He also recommended a campaign to endow childlessness with greater social prestige: a curious precursor of more recent attempts to produce the opposite result. These observations of Malthus amount, in our

[5] T. R. Malthus, *Essay on the Principle of Population* (2d ed.; London, 1803), p. 557.

scheme, to the assertion that some of the data of economic activity react *directly* upon one another, e.g., knowledge upon the tendency toward childbearing. Accepting (without much scientific investigation) a direct causal relationship between them, Malthus is able to predict that, if part of the data can be altered, this will produce a change in another part of the data and so modify the incomes and prices which emerge from the data as a whole.

MODERN POPULATION THEORY

Without any pretense of reviewing the history of population theory, a few comments may be offered regarding the place of modern population theory in our scheme. The exploration of the effects of an increase or decrease in population, or of a stationary population, upon the level of production, the distribution of income, and the like is not, strictly speaking, part of the theory of economic development in our sense of the term. The "optimum" theory of population and similar but more sophisticated discussions of recent years[6] are essays in the theory of the adjustment of the market to "given" conditions. Although the "given" conditions may be assumed to be changing, it is the implications of these changes, not their causes, that are the subject of the theories.

Nevertheless, the theories have come into existence only because the future changes in population have been predicted by scientific workers, including some economists. As early as 1895, Cannan[7] forecast that the growth of population in England and Wales would be trifling by 1941–50. The population would then be about 37,300,000. It would increase very slowly to its maximum of 37,376,000, which would be reached about the year 1995. Cannan's estimate of the maximum was, of course, too low and was exceeded by 1921; but his conclusion that the decade 1941–50 would see the virtual cessation of growth was a remarkably good forecast. It was achieved by pure extrapolation, based on a more thorough analysis of past trends than contemporary statisticians were accustomed to make. "The generally accepted principle," he wrote, "is that of 'as the increase has been in the past so it will be in the future.' This is susceptible of more than one interpretation. . . . . A schoolboy whose arithmetic is described as

---

[6] E.g., W. B. Reddaway, *The Economics of a Declining Population* (London, 1939); also R. F. Harrod, *Modern Population Trends* ("Manchester School of Economic and Social Studies," Vol. X, No. 1 [1939]).

[7] E. Cannan, "The Probability of a Cessation in the Growth of Population in England and Wales during the Next Century," *Economic Journal*, V, 505.

V.G." might interpret it to mean the average annual increase over the period covered by the censuses for 1801 and 1891. "A person with a slight smattering of statistics" might interpert it to mean the rate of increase, assuming the multiplication of population by a constant factor. (Shades of Malthus!) But "a very able mathematician to whom I gave the figures of the ten censuses tells me that they are so irregular that no law of increase of the smallest value can be deduced from them." Even the lowest decennial rate of increase gives absurd results if produced into the future.

"The truth is that every estimate of population, past, present and to come, ought to be founded on a consideration of the factors on which the growth or decline of population is dependent—births, deaths and migration and emigration." Cannan assumed that the loss by mortality and emigration in each age group would remain at the same proportion as in the period 1881–90 and that the absolute number of births would remain the same as in 1881–90. The latter assumption was justified by the observation that "the effect of the births having been practically stationary for twenty years (in the past) will be to change considerably the age distribution of the group of people between twenty and forty"; consequently, the birth rate could be expected to fall to about 8 per cent of the number of persons in this age group by 1911. On these assumptions, Cannan, starting with the age distribution at the 1891 census, worked out "by proportion sums" the number there would be in each age group in successive census years and added up the result to get the total population.

In more recent years, statisticians, led by Kuczynski, have refined the methods of estimating future population even further and have introduced various assumptions regarding the permanence or impermanence of present fertility rates and mortality rates in various age groups. Professor Carr-Saunders says that the calculation, on the basis of these given assumptions, "hardly deserves the description of an estimate"; this term he would reserve for calculations based on an opinion regarding the future trend of fertility and mortality.[8] As already indicated, these statistical refinements, such as the specific fertility rate, may be regarded primarily as methods of determining the true past trend on the basis of which extrapolation may be undertaken. They also provide more sophisticated methods of extrapolation than, say, producing a straight line drawn through a series of past ob-

[8] A. M. Carr-Saunders, *World Population* (London, 1934), p. 128.

servations, and they demonstrate the period within which any change in fertility or mortality will affect the movement of total population.

The investigation of the causes of changes in fertility and mortality in various age groups, with a view to predicting future changes in these factors, arises from the need to correct even the most refined methods of pure extrapolation, according to the changes which appear probable. In the case of fertility, in particular, these investigations are still at an elementary stage, but it is clear that the growth of the practice of family limitation cannot be explained primarily in economic terms. Professor Carr-Saunders argues that the practice spread through countries, which had reached a similar stage of civilization, "much as so many other novel habits and new ideas spread."[9] But attempts have been made to discourage the practice in particular countries, on the assumption that local factors can be influential; and financial inducements figure prominently in such measures.[10] But considerable difficulties are encountered in the attempt to make it advantageous, on individualistic grounds, for persons to have larger families.[11]

So far as population is concerned, the theory of economic development (in the sense of the explanation of changes rather than their implications) has already become a specialty, drawing on sociology, medicine, and economics. In the discussion of the economic effects of future population changes the economist must use the best information that the population theorists can offer. He will not seek to bring their field into the framework of economic theory; but he must press for its rapid cultivation in certain directions, because the results may be so important for economic organizations; and he will be eager to furnish any new economic analyses for which the population theorists may feel the need.

RICARDO: THE DECLINE OF PROFIT

We return to the period in which Malthus wrote to consider another instructive example of an economist attempting to predict the future development of the data. Ricardo conceived the principal problem of political economy to be the determination of the laws which regulate the distribution of the produce of the earth among the three classes of the community—a problem which derived much of its inter-

[9] *Ibid.*, p. 113.

[10] D. V. Glass, *Population Movements and Policies in Europe* (London, 1940).

[11] G. Myrdal, *Population: A Problem for Democracy* (Cambridge, Mass., 1940).

est from the fact that different proportions of the whole produce will be allotted to each class in different stages of society.[12] In seeking to establish the laws of distribution he came upon certain historical tendencies, which he combined with his theory of exchange and distribution into a theory of economic development.

Adam Smith had already observed a tendency for profits to fall, on the average, with economic progress. The same notion of a falling rate of profit is found in the work of both Ricardo and Marx, although the explanations which they offer are different from that offered by Smith. The starting-point of Ricardo's theory is the principle of "rent": every increase in population is supposed to drive cultivation out onto inferior land, thus raising the rent on the better land which was already in cultivation. On inferior soils an additional amount of labor will be required to produce a given quantity of food, and the price of foodstuffs is consequently increased. Money wages rise accordingly, because wages must cover the subsistence of the worker. Thus two of the three shares into which the produce is divided increase, and the share going to "the farmer" as profits decreases.

The natural tendency of profits is to fall. . . . . This tendency, this gravitation, as it were of profits, is happily checked at repeated intervals by the improvements in machinery, connected with the production of necessaries as well as by discoveries in the science of agriculture, which enable us to relinquish a portion of labour before required and therefore to lower the price of the prime necessary of the labourer. The rise in the price of necessaries and in the wages of labour is, however, limited; for as soon as wages should be equal to . . . . the whole receipts of the farmer, there must be an end of accumulation; for no capital can then yield any profit whatever, and no additional labour can be demanded, and consequently population will have reached its highest point. Long indeed before this period, the very low rate of profits will have arrested all accumulation, and almost the whole produce of the country, after paying the labourers, will be the property of the owners of land and the receivers of tithes and taxes.[13]

Ricardo's theory of rent, wages, and profits has been sufficiently discussed, and we may assume familiarity with the criticisms to which it is subjected. Our concern is with the logical basis of his theory of development. This involves not only his theory of distribution, errors and all, but also certain assumptions about the future behavior of economic conditions. In particular, there is the assumption of continued expansion of population—a definite supply curve of labor in exchange for wages. This Malthusian assumption has already been considered

[12] D. Ricardo, *Principles of Profits and Taxation* (London, 1817), Preface to the first edition.

[13] *Ibid.*, chap. vi (McCulloch's ed. [1852], pp. 66–67).

(p. 165). Ricardo also assumes that the rate of scientific progress will not be sufficient to stave off indefinitely the developments which he envisages. Finally, he assumes that market forces will be permitted to work themselves out, without the intrusion of extra-market operations which alter the conditions of economic activity.

Abstraction of this type is necessary, when one's purpose is to show the nature of market forces; but a theory of economic development should not abstract from factors which are prima facie relevant. This point was stated clearly in Mallet's diary, recording a Political Economy Club discussion on Ricardo in 1831. His comment is of interest, even though his account of Ricardo's views may not be quite accurate.

He [Ricardo] always reasons out his propositions, whether true or false, with great logical precision to their utmost consequences; but without regard to the many modifications which are invariably found to arise in the progress of society. One of the errors of Ricardo seems to have been to have followed up Malthus' principles of population to unwarrantable conclusions. For, in the first place, it is clear from the progress of social improvement and the bettering of the condition of the people in the greater part of the civilised world, that Capital, or the means of Employment—the fund for labour—increases in greater ratio than the population, and the interest of the capital besides, which surplus goes to increase the fund for labour. Then he looks forward from the gradual demand for food and the use of land, to the gradual lowering of wages and profits until nothing remains but rent to the Landlords. *But long before that, modification would take place in the state of society which would make such conclusions all wrong.*[14]

For a concrete illustration, Mallet turns to Ireland, "where rent absorbs everything, in consequence of the immense competition for land," and predicts that "a system of Poor Laws is likely soon to equalise the division."

It is, however, easier to point out the inadequacy of a theory of development which abstracts from essential factors than to construct a systematic theory which takes full account of them. The latter was not undertaken by Ricardo's friendly critics of the Political Economy Club. For the first systematic attempt in this direction we must go to the writings of Marx.

MARX: THE EVOLUTION OF CAPITALISM

Until recently it was customary among economists to discount the value of Marx's work, except, perhaps, for a couple of hundred pages of vivid, though biased, industrial history. In the realm of economic theory he was noted primarily for his adherence to the long-exploded Ricardian theory of value and for the intellectual contortions of his attempt to solve his own conundrum regarding the different proportions

[14] *Political Economy Club of London*, VI (London, 1921), 225.

of constant and variable capital in different industries. And his essays in economic prophecy were considered to have been vitiated, not, as in the case of his static analysis, by theoretical criticism, but by historical fact. Since the depression of 1930, however, several non-Communist writers have conceded that Marx was a better prophet than the "bourgeois" economists of the nineteenth century. "If people want to anticipate the development of Capitalism over a long period," writes Professor Lange, "a knowledge of Marx is a much more effective starting point than a knowledge of Wieser, Boehm-Bawerk, Pareto or even Marshall (though the last-named is in this respect much superior)."[15]

Among the developments predicted by Marx, Professor Lange points to the concentration of capital, the growth of protectionism, and the increasing severity of crises.

> The first of these was denied by "bourgeois" economists or if admitted, was regarded as of minor significance for the nature of the economic system, until the monopolistic (or oligopolistic) character of the basic industries became so obvious that a special theory of limited competition had to be developed to supplement orthodox economic theory. The transition from free trade to protectionism was mainly interpreted as an act of economic folly; its close connection with the transition from free competition to monopolistic control has as yet scarcely been realised by "bourgeois" economists. . . . . It was very generally held among "bourgeois" economists both at the beginning of the twentieth century and in the years preceding 1929 that the economic stability of capitalism was increasing and that business fluctuations were becoming less and less intense. Thus the Marxian claim that "bourgeois" economists failed to grasp the fundamental tendencies of the capitalist system proved to be true.[16]

These matters may be contentious. And, even if Marx was right in his predictions, this may have been due to luck rather than to the quality of his analysis. Professor Lange, however, attributes Marx's success as an economic prophet to his formulation of a *theory* of economic development, based on the "definite specification of the institutional framework in which the economic process goes on in capitalist society."[17]

Equilibrium theory is a theory of exchange relationships under given conditions; and abstracts from all personal relationships and social status. Its only institutional assumptions are those which are strictly necessary to facilitate exchange. This is as true of Marx's ex-

[15] O. Lange, "Marxian Economics and Modern Economic Theory," *Review of Economic Studies*, II, 191.

[16] *Ibid.*, p. 190; see also W. Leontief, "The Significance of Marxian Economics for Present Day Economic Theory," *American Economic Review*, Suppl., March, 1938, p. 1.

[17] *Op. cit.*, p. 194.

position of the labor theory of value in a simple commodity economy as it is of the modern theory of equilibrium. But, when Marx moves on to consider capitalistic production, he introduces at once the division of society into those who own capital and those who have only their labor to exchange.

As we quit the sphere of simple circulation or the exchange of commodities, which provides the common or garden free trader with his views and ideas, and with the standard by which he judges a society based upon capital and wage labour, we seem to note a change in the physiognomy of our persons of the drama. The one who came into the market as the owner of money, leaves it striding forward as a capitalist; the one who came to the market as the owner of labour power, brings up the rear as a worker. One of them, self-important, self-satisfied, with a keen eye to business; the other timid, reluctant, like a man who is bringing his own skin to the market, and has nothing to expect but a tanning."[18]

In Marx's hands the economic system becomes an institutional framework, not only for the exchange of goods and services, but also, and principally, for the "exploitation" of labor by the owners of capital. The increased use of machinery increases the scope for exploitation in Marx's sense; it also creates a reserve of technological unemployment which effectively prevents wages from rising; hence the "necessity" for technical progress and the accumulation (and concentration) of capital. Then it is argued that with the growth of aggregate capital the *rate* of profit tends to fall. But instead of this discouraging accumulation, as in Ricardo's scheme, it constitutes a continuous urge to greater accumulation, in order to facilitate further exploitation of labor and to check the fall in the rate of profit.

Despite the affinity between Marx's law of falling profit and Mr. J. M. Keynes's doctrine of the diminishing marginal efficiency of capital,[19] there are apparent inconsistencies in Marx's theory which stand in the way of its acceptance. In particular his analysis of the falling rate of profit seems to exclude the possibility that technical progress may increase the rate of exploitation sufficiently to keep profits in a fixed proportion to capital. Marx's theory of development rests, in fact, upon certain assumptions regarding the future rate of technical progress and the empirical relation of machinery to the productivity of labor, as well as upon his labor theory of value and the assumption of a specific institutional framework.

Nevertheless, the general *method* of Marxian analysis (as distinct from the content of his assumptions) follows the lines that are essential

---

[18] Marx, *Capital*, trans. Paul (London, 1928), p. 165.

[19] *General Theory of Employment, Money and Interest* (London, 1936), p. 315.

to a theory of development. It sets out to construct a theory with *change*, rather than equilibrium, as its goal. Accordingly, it selects assumptions which imply development of the data rather than an immediate equilibrium. Thus the assumption of two classes, the capitalist and the worker, leads not merely to the terms of exchange between wages and labor but also to the concentration of additional capital in the hands of the propertied class and further mechanization of industry. In other words, the market operations which take place within these assumptions bring about a change in the institutional framework. Nor is the capitalist or the worker confined to market operations. In Marx's scheme both seek their ends by extra-market operations whenever these appear to promise greater advantage than market operations.

It is this method rather than the concrete propositions of Marx's theory which is important for our present purpose. It even provides a basis for the criticism of his conclusions. In the period since he wrote, there have been changes in the data which were not allowed for in his original assumptions but which are even now influencing the trend of economic development. One may instance the decline in the rate of population growth, which many believe to be an important factor in the increased intensity of recent fluctuations, or the growth of product differentiation and advertising, which may check the concentration of capital, while menacing the stability of capitalism from another direction, namely, the increased rigidity of the system in the face of changing conditions. Thus some of Marx's conclusions, though right, may be based on false reasons; and in some cases his conclusions, as well as his reasons, may turn out to be wrong.

On the other hand, we may agree, with Professor Lange that, if the problem of economic development be approached along similar lines, that is, by enlarging our data to include those institutional factors which are relevant to development, as well as those relevant to the exchange process, "modern economic theory makes it possible to construct a far more satisfactory theory of economic evolution."[20] It was Marx's correct conception of the logical structure of such a theory and not, as Marxists frequently argue, his labor theory of value which helped Marx to predict the future more accurately than other economists. (Ricardo, it will be noted, held substantially the same theory of value.) Only Marxists will deny Professor Lange's further observation that modern economic theory is a better guide to short-run predictions:

[20] *Op. cit.*, p. 200.

"Marxian economics would be a poor basis for running a central bank or anticipating the effects of a change in the rate of discount."[21]   In other words, provided we take a period so short that there are no significant institutional changes, the failure of modern economic theory to cover institutional changes is a less important defect than the failure of Marxian theory to deal adequately with the principles of exchange. Nevertheless, modern theory is often an unreliable guide to practice, because the time period involved in many concrete problems is long enough to permit *some* development in the institutional and other data. This is particularly the case when conditions are "unstable" and the tempo of development is accelerated. The practical utility of economic theory should therefore be increased by enlarging its assumptions and pressing its implications in the direction necessary to produce a theory of development. A theory of "economic evolution," in the grand manner attempted by Marx, will always be subject to error, because its assumptions require a dangerous degree of extrapolation. In the shorter period which public policy is expected to cover, however, the risks are not so great.

SCHUMPETER: THE EMERGENCE OF INNOVATIONS

The nearest approach to a theory of economic development based on modern equilibrium theory is Professor J. A. Schumpeter's *Theorie der wirtschaftlichen Entwicklung*.[22] This is, however, not a complete theory of data changes, such as appears to be necessary for the handling of many concrete problems; it is concerned only with "the problem of economic development in a very narrow and formal sense."[23] Nevertheless, it is instructive to examine the principle on which Professor Schumpeter distinguishes between economic development in this narrow sense and economic development in the broader sense and also to examine the logical structure which enables him to build his theory onto the "static analysis." It may also be noted that the impulse to extend economic theory to cover development in Professor Schumpeter's narrow sense arises from the inability of "static" analysis to deal adequately with *certain* concrete problems, particularly those arising from economic fluctuations. He writes:

By development we shall understand only such changes in economic life as are not forced upon it from without but arise by its own initiative from within. Should it

[21] *Ibid.*, p. 192.

[22] 3d ed.; Munich, 1931. References are to the English translation: *The Theory of Economic Development* (Cambridge, Mass., 1934).

[23] *The Theory of Economic Development*, p. 63.

turn out there are no changes arising in the economic sphere itself, and that the phenomenon that we call economic development is in practice simply founded upon the fact that the data change and that the economy continuously adapts itself to them, then we should say that there is *no* economic development. By this we should mean that economic development is not a phenomenon to be explained economically, but that the economy, in itself without development, is dragged along by the changes in the surrounding world, that the causes and hence the explanation of the development must be sought outside the group of facts which are described by economic theory.[24]

This statement assumes a clear definition of "economic life," a clear distinction between "the economic sphere" and "the surrounding world." Professor Schumpeter is content to define "economic conduct" as "conduct directed towards the acquisition of goods."[25] But economic investigation comes to an end when

we ground upon a non-economic bottom. . . . . We have then accomplished what we, as economists, are capable of in the case in question, and we must give place to other disciplines. This is true for general theory as well as for concrete cases. If I could say, for example, that the phenomenon of ground-rent is founded upon differences in the qualities of land, the economic explanation would be completed. If I can trace particular price movements to political regulations of commerce, then I have done what I can as an economic theorist, because *political regulations of commerce do not aim immediately at the acquisition of goods through exchange or production, and hence do not fall within our concept of purely economic facts.*[26]

"Economic life" is also defined, for practical purposes, as "a special group of people whose chief activity is economic conduct or business" and who may be distinguished "from other classes in which the economic aspect of conduct is overshadowed by other aspects."[27]

Professor Schumpeter gives specific examples of "changes in the surrounding world" which do not constitute economic development in his "very narrow and formal sense." His examples include "the mere growth of the economy, as shown by the growth of population and wealth,"[28] "spontaneous and discontinuous changes in consumers' tastes,"[29] "non-social data [natural conditions]" and "non-economic social data [here belong the effects of war, changes in commercial, social, or economic policy]."[30] J. S. Mill had considered how the economy adjusts itself to some of these causes of disturbance; but he

[24] *Ibid.*, p. 63.

[25] *Ibid.*, p. 1. References to the position adopted by a living author always run the risk of being falsified by a subsequent change of view. Our account, in every case, relates to views expressed in a particular work; and the Professor Schumpeter here referred to is the one who wrote *The Theory of Economic Development*, except where special reference is made to *Business Cycles*. As Professor Schumpeter says, books "lead their own lives, while the authors lead their own also" (Preface to the English ed.).

[26] *Ibid.*, p. 5; my italics.   [28] *Ibid.*, p. 63.

[27] *Ibid.*, p. 4.   [29] *Ibid.*, p. 65.   [30] *Ibid.*, p. 62.

had also included some changes (namely, changes in technique and productive organization) which, according to Professor Schumpeter, "require special analysis and evoke something different again from disturbances in the theoretical sense."[31] This "special analysis" is his theory of economic development: it deals not with exogenous changes in the data or with the internal adaptation to them but with the "new combinations" of materials and forces which are initiated spontaneously by businessmen. In practice it may be difficult to distinguish between new combinations which are themselves responses to the data and those which are spontaneous. Perhaps in a desire to meet this difficulty Professor Schumpeter decided to exclude new combinations which "in time grow out of the old by continuous adjustment in small steps"; economic development is finally taken to mean only those new combinations which appear discontinuously[32]—"that kind of change arising from within the system which so displaces the equilibrium point that the new one cannot be reached from the old one by infinitesimal steps."[33]

Five specific examples of economic development in this sense are given: (1) The introduction of a new good—that is one with which consumers are not yet familiar—or of a new quality of a good. (2) The introduction of a new method of production, that is one not yet tested by experience in the branch of manufacture concerned, which need by no means be founded upon a discovery scientifically new, and can also exist in a new way of handling a commodity commercially. (3) The opening of a new market, that is a market into which the particular branch of manufacture of the country in question has not previously entered, whether or not this market has existed before. (4) The conquest of a new source of supply of raw materials or half-manufactured goods, again irrespective of whether this source already exists or whether it has first to be created. (5) The carrying out of the new organization of any industry, like the creation of a monopoly position (for example through trustification) or the breaking up of a monopoly position.[34]

Three further points may be mentioned. Of these, the first is that Professor Schumpeter thinks that "spontaneous changes in tastes" are rare,[35] as we noted in chapter vii. In his more recent work, *Business Cycles*, he prefers to "act on the assumption that consumers' initiative in changing their tastes is negligible and that all change in consumers' tastes is incident to, and brought about by producers' action."[36] Presumably this action would fall under points 1 and 3 above. The second point is the status of inventions. These are treated as development when they are adopted; "as soon as an invention is put into business practice, we have a process which arises from, and is an ele-

---

[31] *Ibid.*, p. 60 n.

[32] *Ibid.*, p. 65.

[33] *Ibid.*, p. 64 n.

[34] *Ibid.*, p. 66.

[35] *Ibid.*, p. 65.

[36] (New York, 1939), I, 73.

ment of, the economic life of its time, and not something that acts on it from without." Until it is adopted it has no influence upon economic life. "In no case, therefore, is invention an external factor. This may sound stange."[37] Finally, it may be noted that Professor Schumpeter, in his later work, recognizes the increasing difficulty of determining whether a change in the institutional framework is an "external" factor or "an act of business behaviour." The frequency of difficult cases "is but a consequence of the fact that our economic system is not a pure one but in full transition toward something else, and, therefore, not always describable in terms of a logically consistent analytic model."[38] Whether there ever was a pure economic system may, however, be open to doubt. Nor would the impurity of the system, whether a transitional phase or a chronic state, prevent it from being described in "terms of a logically consistent analytic model," provided that the assumptions of the analysis are sufficient to cover all the forms of behavior which are, in fact, encountered. The theory of "extra-market operations," sketched in chapter vi, is an essential part of such a comprehensive analytical model.

Professor Schumpeter's theory of "development in a very narrow and formal sense" amounts, then, to an explanation of how new combinations of resources can arise from within the "circular flow" of an otherwise "static" system. The assumptions of the static system are a given constellation of wants and resources, including certain familiar and well-tried productive methods (or combinations).[39] Such a system can adjust itself to changes in the data but cannot produce such changes (except presumably such small changes in wants, resources, and methods as arise in the course of adjustment to given data). In order that discontinuous new combinations should arise, it is necessary to introduce new assumptions which were not necessary for the analysis of the circular flow.

The first new factor is the activity of "entrepreneurs" who are not content to apply familiar and well-tried combinations of resources but seek the greater profits which may be obtained by the successful exploitation of known but untried combinations. It is also assumed that there *are* such combinations which promise to be more advantageous than the old ones but that the mass of businessmen are not willing to make such experiments, even if they need supply only "will and action," thereby risking only their reputation, for, although the entre-

---

[37] *Ibid.*, p. 9.   [38] *Ibid.*, p. 11.
[39] The static system is sketched in chap. i of *The Theory of Economic Development*.

preneur may also, in the capacity of capitalist, use some of his own resources, this is not essential. The greater part of innovations are carried through, not by existing firms, but by new enterprises and are
financed by bank credit. Thus Professor Schumpeter introduces credit
creation as a necessary factor in economic development.

The essential assumptions of his theory, therefore, are the uneven
distribution of entrepreneurial conduct throughout the community,
the availability of more advantageous but untried combinations, and
a credit system which enables the entrepreneur to obtain control over
additional resources. On these assumptions, together with those essential to the circular flow of a static economy, Professor Schumpeter
builds a logical construction, indicating the process by which innovations are adopted in the economy and tracing their consequences in
cyclical fluctuations.

Although some commentators have suggested an affinity between
this theory and that of Marx,[40] we must agree with Professor Schumpeter when he says "my structure covers only a small part of his
[Marx's] ground."[41] Similarly, it covers only a part of the ground
mapped out for the theory of economic development in the preceding
chapter. Our method has something in common with Professor
Schumpeter's. We, too, seek to build development onto conventional
economic theory by enlarging its assumptions. We, too, recognize the
possibility of endogenous developments in wants, technique, and the
institutional framework. But we desire a logical structure which
might be used to account for concrete changes in these data. His theory "is not at all concerned with the concrete factors of change, but
with the method by which these work, *with the mechanism of change.*"[42]
Consequently, our assumptions must be still broader than his, and our
logical construction more comprehensive.

ROBBINS: ECONOMICS AND POLITICS

In view of Professor Robbins' skepticism regarding the possibility of
a scientific theory of economic development, inclusion of his work in
this chapter may cause surprise. Nevertheless, he has written articles
and books which involve an incursion into this field, whether it be in
the capacity of a professional economist or as an amateur sociologist,
and it is instructive to examine the logical structure of some of these
contributions.

[40] Cf. Lange, *op. cit.*, p. 197.

[41] *Theory of Economic Development*, p. 60 n.   [42] *Ibid.*, p. 61 n.

His *Economic Planning and International Order*[43] is

essentially an essay in what may be called Political Economy, as distinct from Economics in the stricter sense of the word. It depends upon the technical apparatus of analytical Economics; but it applies this apparatus to the examination of schemes for the realisation of aims whose formulation lies outside Economics; and it does not abstain from appeal to the probabilities of political practice when such an appeal has seemed relevant.[44]

The thesis of the book may be briefly summarized: "The various kinds of national planning now in vogue . . . . involve at once a shrinkage of international division of labour and an increase of international instability. We have also seen that they involve an increase of the danger of war."[45] In the wider international field, liberalism, "with all its deficiencies . . . . would still provide a safeguard for happiness and spontaneity more efficient than any other which has yet been suggested."[46] Propositions such as these belong to the theory of economic development because they suggest that one set of conditions, e.g., planning or liberalism, implies the emergence of other conditions, which are treated as data by economic theory in the usual sense. Unless they are mere dogma they should be capable of presentation as the conclusions of a theoretical structure, which differs from the constructions of economic theory in the range and content of its assumptions but not in logical precision.

The book abounds in propositions which are formally similar to those of economic theory and presumably subject to the same tests of internal consistency and correspondence with experience. One difference, however, may be noted. Professor Robbins' propositions regarding political and other changes are usually, and justifiably, qualified by some such term as "probably." The analytical significance of this literary device will be considered later.

One of the earliest examples is incidental to a contrast between tariffs and quotas. With a tariff,

if there are new changes in the conditions of supply and demand the volume of trade is automatically adapted. . . . . With the quota, however, it is different. So long as the quota is not changed, the volume of trade is definitely limited. But cannot the quota be shifted? Quite obviously it can and often is. But the shifts are a cumbersome business. . . . . *Moreover the probabilities are against the shifts being made in what, from the international point of view can be called the equilibrium direction. A quota is not likely to be enlarged if a change in productive conditions elsewhere makes it possible for the foreigner to offer his goods on cheaper terms.*[47]

[43] London, 1937.   [45] *Ibid.*, p. 99.

[44] *Ibid.*, p. vii.   [46] *Ibid.*, p. 268.   [47] *Ibid.*, p. 57; my italics.

Steps are omitted from the logical argument because they can be taken for granted. But the form of the argument is clearly that, on certain assumptions, quotas will be administered in a particular way.

The next obvious example is the argument that "the organization of the world on national socialist lines . . . . is *almost certain* to make the achievement of international socialism much more difficult than ever before." This turns out to rest on the assumption that "the citizens of the wealthier areas" will (probably) not be prepared to share the sources of their incomes with the citizens of the poorer areas.[48] Further exploring the implications of national planning, Professor Robbins observes that "the absence of freedom to migrate *reinforces protectionist tendencies and produces a situation* which will aggravate the political and economic instability of the world for many years to come."[49] Here we have one item in the data influencing another—a clear case of economic development. After such comment on "the economic consequences of independent national planning," Professor Robbins continues: "Even more important and even more disturbing are its probable political consequences. There is reason to believe it is likely considerably to enhance international political friction."[50]

These fragments of development theory freely combine deduction from assumptions about human nature with extrapolation from past historical trends. "The whole history of government dealing *proves* this" (that "the actions of boards are likely to be much more the instruments of political strategy, much less dictated by considerations of profit, than the actions of private dealers"[51]). But usually the qualification, "probably," robs the proposition of the precision and complete conviction of the propositions of pure theory. What does "probably" really mean in this connection? Only that the analysis is not complete. While it takes account of the factors which are believed to be significant, it is admitted that on some occasions, at least, other factors may interfere and vitiate the conclusion. In other words, "probably" plays much the same role in Professor Robbins' theory of development as *ceteris paribus* does in empirical propositions of general economics.

We may leave the reader to seek further fragments of development theory in other essays by Professor Robbins, such as those collected in *The Economic Basis of Class Conflict* and *The Economic Causes of War*,[52] and

[48] *Ibid.*, p. 66; my italics.

[49] *Ibid.*, p. 90; my italics.

[50] *Ibid.*

[51] *Ibid.*, p. 78; my italics.

[52] London, 1939 and 1940, respectively.

to test our observations regarding his method. No appraisal of his conclusions will be attempted here.

FISHER: PROGRESS AND INSECURITY

Professor A. G. B. Fisher's book on *The Clash between Progress and Security*[53] contains some material which is necessary to the theory of economic development, although it is primarily concerned with the adaptation of economic life to changing conditions rather than to the explanation of these changes.

> The rate of material progress which we are able to maintain is seriously diminished by widespread ignorance of the character of the changes and adjustments which it demands, and the disappointingly slow rate of recovery from the depression is in no small measure to be explained by this fact. . . . . In these circumstances it is an important part of the economist's task to depict as simply and as clearly as he can the nature of the changes, the adjustments and adaptations, which are needed for the realisation of the community's desires for further progress.[54]

Professor Fisher inclines to the belief that changes in tastes and technique are unpredictable but claims that "we can predict in general terms the consequences for the general structure of our economy" when "improvements make possible higher average income levels."[55] What basis can we take for such forecasts?

> Though we cannot predict in detail the nature of the new goods and services which a community with rising income-standards will wish to purchase, observation of the expenditure habits of people who are already wealthy, aided by general reasoning, enables us to make some safe generalisations about what is likely to occur when poor communities find that they can spend more than they have been in the habit of spending in the past.[56]

From this emerges the thesis that progress implies a continual transfer of labor and other resources from "primary" to "secondary" industries and, in really prosperous countries, to "tertiary" industries. "So long as the objective conditions for material progress are present, there will always be a tendency for the relative importance of primary products to diminish, and the relative importance of tertiary industry to increase."[57]

If this were all, Professor Fisher's work, though important in itself, would fall hardly at all within the field of the theory of economic development as here defined. His assumption that technical improvements will continue is a proposition about development—arrived at by the extrapolation from observed past trends. He also assumes the constancy of a hierarchy of wants for the products of primary, second-

[53] London, 1935.
[54] *Ibid.*, pp. 1 and 2.
[55] *Ibid.*, p. 10.
[56] *Ibid.*, p. 25.
[57] *Ibid.*, p. 33.

ary, and tertiary industries. But the analysis of the implications of the continuance of improvements, in terms of the re-allocation of resources between different employments, is an exercise in market theory. The principal contributions of Professor Fisher to the theory of economic development, however, consist in his study of the resistances which the transfer of resources encounters and his observation that, when these resistances are effective, market adjustments are not completed and available improvements are not utilized.

Resistance may take many forms. *Passive* resistance in the form of a refusal to move to places of higher remuneration is a common feature in discussion of "factor mobility"; economists have found this concept essential to explain persistent inequalities in remuneration or in employment opportunities. But resistance may be active, through politics and other channels outside the market. Any analysis of the conditions which imply active resistance of this type is an essay in the theory of what we have called "extra-market operations." In our own development of the theory we have made use of points stressed by Professor Fisher, particularly the strength of the motive of security and the various institutional and other factors which may determine the form which resistance takes. Indeed, we found that much of this has wider application than Professor Fisher gives it; for, while material progress is not the only menace to the security of particular groups and security is obviously not the only motive to extra-market operations, the factors which influence resistances to the implications of progress may also affect the general preference of individuals and groups for extra-market operations as against market activities.

We have seen that Professor Schumpeter treats inventions as economically irrelevant until they are given practical application as a "new combination" of resources. Professor Fisher's analysis reveals incidentally an important factor among those which determine when an invention will become economically relevant in this sense. "In general the material progress, which growth of knowledge makes possible, necessitates the transfer of labour and of capital from such industries as the advance of knowledge has made more efficient, into other, and, in many instances entirely new industries."[58] Resistances to transfer not only cause overproduction and depression in the former industries but also prevent the emergence of the new industries. Professor Fisher does not altogether solve the problem of the hen and the egg; resources must be transferred to new industries if we are to have

[58] *Ibid.*, p. 32.

increasing real incomes, yet there will be no demand for the new products unless incomes are, in fact, increased. But at least he makes it clear that there will be fewer eggs if resistances to transfer are strong, despite the presence of demand for new or additional goods, e.g., if professional restrictions hamper an expansion of the medical profession when the demand for increased services is expanding.

Professor Fisher is not concerned to present a coherent theory of economic development in our sense; but, as is the case with other writers, fragments of such a theory may be discovered in his analysis of his own chosen problem. This really means that those problems lie partly in a field, which, it is suggested, should be systematically cultivated by the theory of economic development.

OHLIN: FUTURE ECONOMIC ORGANIZATION

We now consider an explicit essay on the prediction of future economic development which Professor Ohlin contributed in 1937 to a symposium on *The World's Economic Future*.[59] Although couched in the modest form of a popular lecture, this short essay is of particular interest as an illustration of the three methods of prediction distinguished above.

It is interesting to note the extreme caution of all the contributors to this symposium and their modesty regarding their capacity to forecast the future. "The difficulty of interpreting the past or of understanding what is happening around us to-day in this world that seems to be dominated by everything but reason," writes Mr. Loveday, "is so great that no prudent person would commit himself willingly or wittingly to prophecies about the future." He even feels that he "is perhaps unduly venturesome" in considering "some of the forces which have driven recent events into the course along which they have flowed, and to endeavour to estimate their probable strength in the future."[60] This amounts to pure extrapolation, modified by personal judgment. Similarly, Professor Condliffe begins by saying: "I, for one, am no prophet and cannot pretend to foretell even the immediate future. All that one can do is to draw attention to significant trends of development in the recent past which seem likely to project themselves into the future. Even this limited objective presents a task in which past observers have not been conspicuously successful."[61] Ac-

---

[59] Loveday and Others, *The World's Economic Future* (Sir Halley Stewart Lectures [London, 1937]).

[60] *Ibid.*, p. 17.   [61] *Ibid.*, p. 43.

cording to Professor Heckscher: "There is only one thing certain with regard to the future, and that is its uncertainty."[62] He, too, is chiefly concerned with observed "tendencies already afoot," although we may note one proposition with an analytical flavor: "Whereas *laissez-faire* did and does nothing to prevent a development opposed to itself, the belief in interference and monopolistic organisation consciously counteracts tendencies to change."[63]

Professor Ohlin himself regards his essay as a departure from the rule that it is wise from the scientific viewpoint for economists "to confine themselves to a study of what has already happened"; but he recognizes that practical policy requires the formation of opinions about the future, "for our actions are concerned with the future."[64] Having undertaken to "speculate a little about some future economic tendencies," particularly in the field of organization, Professor Ohlin begins with "some observations about the tendencies which have characterised the past decades. If there are no special reasons for expecting a change, one can assume a certain probability of a further movement in the same direction. Hence, one has to establish what this direction has been, and then to analyse carefully all possible reasons for a change in movement."[65] This position is similar to that adopted in the present work. As compared with other contributions to this symposium on *The World's Economic Future*, Professor Ohlin's essay is distinguished by a more systematic approach to the problem of correcting extrapolated trends by the analysis of "possible *reasons* for a change in movement."

Professor Ohlin suggests that "the chief characteristic of change in the organisation of society in the last half-century has been the growth of central organisation and control"[66] by trusts, trading associations, large firms, and public authorities. Some of the causes of the change can be determined. This development has been "called forth" by certain other changes: the growth of large-scale production and monopoly, the growth of trade-unions and the rigidity of wage rates, the reduced facilities for international migration, and the severity of recent economic depressions. "As one piece of relatively automatic machinery breaks down so it becomes necessary more completely than before to manage also the rest of the system."[67] The development of control is explained, however, only in part by *the greater need for organization;* other factors are *"our growing ability to organise"* and "a slow but none

---

[62] *Ibid.*, p. 81.   [64] *Ibid.*, p. 65.   [66] *Ibid.*, p. 66.

[63] *Ibid.*, p. 94.   [65] *Ibid.*, p. 66.   [67] *Ibid.*, p. 71.

the less radical change *in the attitude and mentality of business men.*" The latter amounts to a decline in the belief in the inevitability of progress and an increased willingness to co-operate and accept control. With it goes the assumption of a right to state assistance in various forms. Professor Ohlin writes:

> The impression one gains from a review of the kind I have attempted is that the change in organisation of our society in the last half-century can be regarded as a double adaptation to new technical and international conditions and to variations in the social outlook of man. There is of course a mutual inter-dependence between the new forms of organisations and the attitude and outlook which has led to them. The changed milieu and the changed psychology are parts of the same process, and *it is largely arbitrary which one wishes to regard as cause and which one wishes to regard as effect.* That there is a certain inherent necessity in this development can hardly be doubted.[68]

So much for the past. But Professor Ohlin's problem is "whether these tendencies towards a more highly organised society are likely to continue or not. To form an opinion on this question it is necessary first of all to remember that many of the basic circumstances which have hitherto led to growth of organisation remain" and "will in the future also call for central direction and control in many ways."[69] It is doubtful whether present conditions favor a growth of large-scale production or a trend toward smaller units; factors operating in the latter direction include automatic machinery, electric motors, and the automobile. "But one thing seems certain: that to interpret recent developments simply as a movement back to the nineteenth-century type of small, entirely independent units is unjustifiable."[70] Professor Ohlin sees the need for an economic system "which combines flexibility with the possibility of centralised direction in certain special respects. If I am right in saying that there exists a need for something like this, then I think one may also expect that an actual movement in this direction will come."[71]

From this outline it will be apparent that Professor Ohlin treats these changes in economic organization as *adjustments* to given conditions. The data are similar to those of economic theory—methods of production, the distribution of ownership of resources, and the wants of consumers and producers. But, instead of assuming that buying and selling are the only possible adjustments to these data, Professor Ohlin admits and explores the possibility of other adjustments which are expected, by the economic subject, to give greater satisfaction than mere buying and selling under existing conditions. In the light of the causal

[68] *Ibid.*, p. 74; my italics.   [70] *Ibid.*, p. 80.
[69] *Ibid.*, p. 76.   [71] *Ibid.*, p. 84.

relations which appear to be established by such studies, he then modifies the results obtained by simple extrapolation from past trends.

GILFILLAN: THE PREDICTION OF INVENTIONS

In view of the reluctance of economists to claim any competence to forecast changes in productive technique, special interest attaches to a sociological approach to the problem of prediction. In an attempt to improve on the simple extrapolation from past trends or flights of sheer imagination, which form the basis of predictions made by some writers on "popular science," S. C. Gilfillan has drawn on both sociology and economic theory.[72]

Mr. Gilfillan refers to an article in the *Scientific American* magazine of October, 1920, which, although "it was aimed not more than 75 years in the future, reads to-day as a very reasonable, clear-sighted pre-view of the developments of the past 16 years, and those that we would predict to-day . . . . 3 per cent have been proved wrong; 3 per cent will be proved wrong in the writer's opinion; and 22 per cent are doubtful." It is suggested that "the proportion right is much larger than one would expect from mere luck" (although "we do not know how to estimate the number of hits that could have been obtained by sheer luck").[73] The article in question, however, omitted two important inventions—radio broadcasting and the talking picture. In both cases the fundamental inventions were already known; but their practical applications and commercial development were not foreseen. This is an interesting commentary on Professor Schumpeter's view that inventions are not data until they are applied. It would be a great aid to the formulation of economic policy if we could predict which of the inventions at present known to scientists will be developed and exploited, even though we might not foresee *new* inventions.

Other examples of moderately successful forecasting are quoted, including Mr. Gilfillan's own essays in this field over the last twenty-five years. The best seers of all, in his opinion, are

distinguished technical and scientific men, who choose to predict in their own general field. . . . . Yet they are liable to upsets from developments in outside lines, and from the tendency of the ordinary scientific or technical man to see little change ahead. For these are usually much impressed with the failures of all past inventors to achieve this and that, because of supposed scientific principles that bar the path. . . . . There

[72] National Resources Committee, *Technological Trends and National Policy* (Washington, 1937), pp. 15–38; also S. C. Gilfillan, *The Sociology of Invention* (Chicago, 1935).

[73] National Resources Committee, *op. cit.*, p. 15.

seems to be a clear case for a committee of technical men uniting their labours, together with those of social scientists and students of prediction.[74]

Extrapolation from past trends "appears to give the best results for short prognostication." Most great inventions are not single inventive acts but represent

an agglomeration of a vast number of detail inventions. . . . . Just as a merchant whose figures show a steady growth of his business expects still more business in the future, so when we see patents piled ever thicker upon food syntheses, or see aircraft capable of landing in less and less space, or television screens growing larger and finer, we readily, confidently and justifiably project these trends a short way into the future.[75]

Moreover, there is a considerable period of time between the first conception of an invention and its embodiment in a working model and a further period before it receives commercial exploitation. "Here is, then, an excellent rule of prediction—to predict only inventions already born, whose physical possibility has therefore been demonstrated, but which are usually not yet practical, and whose future significance is not commonly appreciated."[76]

"The second reason why inventions can be predicted is that they have causes. They are not just accidents, nor the inscrutable products of sporadic genius, but have abundant and clear causes in prior scientific and technological development. And they have social causes and retarding factors."[77] Evidence of this is found in the remarkable frequency of simultaneous discovery by independent workers. Mr. Gilfillan admits that "we have not yet learned" to use "this wide causative base" *scientifically* to predict specific inventions; but he claims that we do "reason from such bases." This is illustrated by an analysis of the factors affecting the development of stereoscopic sound production. Several developments in diverse fields have created a need for this invention, and acoustic devices generally are improving. Methods are known for producing stereoscopic sound effects (and have been demonstrated in Australia since Mr. Gilfillan wrote). On the other hand, the resistances are such as will be overcome in time: cost, by rising incomes; unfamiliarity, by the growth of popular knowledge; and so on.

This method involves the modification of an extrapolated trend to take account of all the possible complicating factors. Mr. Gilfillan suggests that it may give good results over a longer range than the method of simple extrapolation.

[74] *Ibid.*, p. 16.

[75] *Ibid.*, p. 18.

[76] *Ibid.*, p. 19.

[77] *Ibid.*

For predicting the broad social consequences of inventions, Mr. Gilfillan uses the concept of equivalent invention, arguing that, though a prediction may be wrong as regards the particular technical device, some other device meets the same needs and produces much the same effects upon the general life of society. For economic policy it is usually important to estimate future trends with greater accuracy, since we are often concerned with particular industries or groups rather than social life as a whole. Nevertheless, in considering the development of other economic data, such as the sociolegal framework of society, the concept of "equivalent invention" or —shall we say?— "equivalent change in data" may prove of value.

This review of Mr. Gilfillan's "theories" is not intended to show that economists should add to their present field the prediction of the future course of scientific discovery. But an economist who would advise on the problems of a particular industry may well have to modify and supplement the engineer's forecast of future technical developments in the light of his own special economic knowledge. And he will accomplish this task better if he has studied the interplay of economic behavior and other factors in the production of data changes, instead of confining his attention to the response of the market to a given set of data.

BUSINESS-CYCLE THEORY

Professor Schumpeter's theory of economic development appears to have its origin in the recognition that, under the assumptions of "static" theory, the cyclical fluctuations which are a feature of the real world, are impossible. Other writers, in developing a theory of business cycles, have been forced to introduce assumptions which convert economic theory into a theory of economic development. Even those who have attributed the recurrence of crises to "external" causes, such as harvest fluctuations and sun-spot cycles, have usually found it necessary to add some process of internal development, through which the repercussions of the external disturbance were propagated throughout the whole economy.

The usual type of business-cycle theory consists of a series of demonstrations of the way in which one "phase" grows out of the preceding one and contains the tendencies which finally produce the following one. "The boom sows the seeds of depression." But the process by which one phase grows out of its predecessor is found in the market adjustments which the individual economic subjects make to the data and the new form of the data ushers in the next phase of the cycle. This general pattern of development in the data through market adjustments to the data will be found to be common to all theories of the business cycle, though the theories differ considerably in their choice of assumptions and, consequently, in the processes which are supposed to produce one phase out of another.

In the sequence analysis favored by Professor D. H. Robertson[78] and Dr. Erik Lundberg[79] this modification of the data through market adjustments in each time interval is still more explicit. Indeed, this is the essence of sequence analysis; instead of merely seeking assumptions which imply continuous oscillation of the dependent variables, it seeks to trace the process at work in successive stages of the fluctuation.

Beyond the suggestion that the problem of fluctuations may be seen a little more clearly if it is thought of as a particular case of economic development, the subject need not be pursued further. The reader will not expect, at this stage, any detailed account of particular essays in business-cycle theory from this point of view.

CONCLUSION

We have not attempted to expose every trace of development theory that can be discovered in economic literature. Some of the more important analyses to be found in present-day economic theory will be utilized in the following chapter. The purpose of the foregoing fragments, it will be remembered, is to show the honorable place which the theory of economic development occupies in the tradition of economics and to observe the extent to which various writers have relied upon the three methods of prediction previously noted. Our next task is to indicate the main lines of a theory of economic development which may be used to help out existing economic theory in the interpretation and prediction of events.

[78] *Essays in Monetary Theory* (London, 1940).
[79] *Economic Expansion* (London, 1937).

CHAPTER IX

NEXT STEPS IN THE THEORY OF ECONOMIC DEVELOPMENT

THE position we have reached may now be summarized. The economist who advises on practical problems is concerned with the prediction of events. If he bases his predictions upon the assumption that the conditions of economic activity will remain unchanged while prices, production, and incomes adjust themselves to the initial conditions, these predictions are likely to be wrong. The conditions themselves are continually changing, partly because some conditions react upon the others directly (e.g., geographical distribution of persons reacts upon their tastes); partly because the best adjustment some people can make to the given conditions is to try to alter them; and partly for no reason at all, so far as we can see with our limited comprehension of the world about us. The economist is forced to estimate how these conditions are likely to develop in the period under consideration—or to adopt somebody else's estimate—and must base his analysis of market or extra-market behavior on the assumption that the data will change according to the estimate.

When past experience includes changes for which no explanation can be offered, the only practical method of predicting future changes is pure extrapolation. The chief problem encountered in this method is the determination of the "true" past trends. Any advance in the technique of observation, of isolating the "central tendency" of diffused movements and analyzing a total into its component parts (as in population forecasts) will improve the chances of accurate extrapolation. Some enterprising economists have contributed to the art of extrapolation in the past; and others may be led, by interest in a concrete problem, to attempt to improve existing methods. There is no reason to consider this work to be outside the sphere of the economist, any more than the empirical studies which are necessary to verify the assumptions of market theory or to "discover new types of configuration of the data suitable for further analytical study."[1] But when (as in the case of population forecasts) a band of workers makes a new specialty of the determination of past trends and the calculation of ex-

[1] L. Robbins, *Essay on the Nature and Significance of Economic Science* (2d ed.; London, 1937), p. 118.

trapolated trends, most of us general practitioners will be glad to consult the specialist on all cases where pure, but far from simple, extrapolation is required. Even where science throws some light on the causes of change, it will often be safer to use our scientific knowledge to modify the results of pure extrapolation than to attempt a forecast based entirely on a causal hypothesis. In most economic problems some use of extrapolation is essential, because science can give only an incomplete causal analysis of the changes observed in the past.

But to rely on pure extrapolation alone, when our knowledge of the causes of changes suggests that such a procedure would give inaccurate results, is out of the question. The economist concerned with practical affairs must take a lively interest in the extension of knowledge regarding the causes of development; and, in so far as the causes are to be found within the field of economics, it is for economists themselves to discover them.

The essays in prediction and the theories of development noted in the preceding chapter employed pure extrapolation—and extrapolation corrected according to the findings (not always correct ones) of economics and other sciences. But there has been the greatest variation in the use made of these three methods of prediction; and it may be hoped that a systematic examination of their respective possibilities and a consideration of the relations between them will assist their better utilization in the future.

LIAISON WITH OTHER SCIENCES

The economist has worries enough of his own without extending his investigations into fields already tilled by other sciences. But it is necessary to establish points of liaison with these other sciences so that their findings can be utilized in the prediction of economic development. In particular, the economist needs to know whether other sciences have determined unambiguously the past trend of the conditions of economic activity and whether they have discovered the causes of changes in these conditions. If other scientists, working in the fields to which these questions are appropriate, tend, under the pressure of other interests, to neglect or postpone the investigations which might provide answers for the economist, he must take the initiative himself and press for the recognition of his problems by the other sciences. As was indicated in our discussion of the need for collaboration among the sciences in the study of human behavior, the economist's request for assistance is more likely to yield results if he can pose his questions in such a way that they will be recognized as problems of interest to the other sciences. This requires some appreciation of the scope and methods of the other sciences. On the other hand, the economist must be able to reciprocate with a similar service when it is needed. If, as in the case of population forecasting, specialization has developed and the specialists are combining the three methods of prediction already distinguished, the economist must be ready to contribute the best possible analysis of the economic factors concerned. The implications of this for the general development of economic theory will be considered later in this chapter.

A very brief re-examination of the various classes of economic data, using the list already discussed (p. 149), will serve to indicate some of the other sciences with which liaison is necessary and also those changes in conditions which have not yet been sufficiently investigated in the way that is required for our present purpose.

In relation to the prediction of *population* changes, little more need be said. From the ranks of the statisticians, the sociologists, the psychologists, the medical scientists, and others, as well as economists, an increasing number of workers has felt the attraction of this field of research and, once initiated to its mysteries, has had to enlarge their inquiries beyond the usual limits of the science for which they were originally trained. Population studies have already developed, as we have noted, into a specialty, requiring the employment of several different techniques. The study of past changes, with a view to extrapolation, is systematically undertaken; and the limitations of existing records will be gradually removed, as governments become increasingly "population conscious." The problem of causes, too, is being attacked from many angles. In the future the population specialist rather than the economist may assume the initiative in seeking collaboration; as the interaction of economic and other processes in this field comes to be better understood, there will be need for the economist to work out more fully the particular economic problems which emerge from the study of the population question as a whole. For instance, we know relatively little, yet, about the cost of successive children and the particular readjustments of consumption which an increasing family imposes on people of different income grades. Again, the future movement in other costs, such as those for houses, domestic service, and medical attention, will react in turn upon the economic problems of the increasing family. It is likely that the economist can contribute to the general problem by the study of such specific economic questions as these. But we cannot expect to anticipate, a priori, all the particular matters which will require his attention from the viewpoint of population forecasts.

Population stands alone among the data in having been made the subject of a special branch of science, concerned primarily with the prediction of its future changes and resting on an appreciation of the economic and political importance which these changes are likely to assume. Most items in the list of data have found a place in studies of a more or less scientific nature, but the objective has rarely been the prediction of data changes for purposes of economic analysis. The development of specialist studies, each centered in one of the main classes of economic data but drawing on the methods and findings of other sciences, as well as on those of economics when they are relevant, would undoubtedly facilitate the improvement of the technique of pure extrapolation, as well as its correction for causes of change. Available statistical records would be ransacked, and new statistical material might be collected, as the political and economic importance of changes in particular types of data came to be more widely understood. And the workers in any one of these specialized sciences of prediction would, like the students of population changes, see the interplay of the different causal processes more clearly than the workers who confine their attention to one of the general fields of research in which these processes are revealed.

It may be that the foundations for such specialties must be laid by economists or other social scientists, who, driven by the desire to predict changes in their own data, draw from other fields the material for extrapolation. Thus Cannan laid foundations for the modern technique of population forecasts, though he did not devote himself to its further elaboration. In the prediction of inventions the initiative has come from a sociologist. It is to be hoped that a number of workers will be attracted to specialize in this field and that there will not be so long an interval between the pioneering work of Mr. Gilfillan and the development of the specialty as there was between the work of Cannan and Kuczynski on population changes.

There is no group of specialists busy on the prediction of changes in the second class of economic data, namely, *the tastes and dispositions of the people* but relevant material will be found in a number of sciences other than economics. Psychology, sociology, and political science have sought to reveal the springs of human action and the channels into which individual and group behavior flows. History has recorded many of the changes in tastes and dispositions that have attracted attention in the past; and social and political theorists, as well as businessmen, have speculated on the course of future changes in the particular field which held their interests. But of systematic extrapolation, corrected according to theories of the causes of change, the economist will find little in a form immediately useful for his purposes, until he presses for work along these lines. Moreover, the various related fields have not been exhaustively studied by scientific methods. For instance, changes in consumers' tastes have been described by some writers, but inadequately. One method of arousing the interest of other scientists in these problems of extrapolation is for some economists to rush in where their colleagues fear to tread and, by their own amateurish essays in these related fields, stimulate the appropriate specialists to draw on their superior knowledge and technique in order to set the "intruders" right. This method may yield more results than grandiose projects for organized collaboration between scientists who have not yet learned one another's languages.

Turning to *the amounts and kinds of productive capacities*, we find an even larger array of specialized sciences which should be able to provide a basis for extrapolation. On the side of *personal powers*, individual psychology, educational records, statistics of sickness (from hospitals or health insurance), and results of periodical physical examinations contribute to our knowledge of past changes; and investigation of the causes of change has proceeded along various lines. On the side of *material agents*, there are scientific studies of soil erosion, evaporation, forestry, mineralogy, and similar factors affecting the supply of natural resources; while industrial history and statistics of building, machine production, and transport facilities reveal past trends in the accumulation of capital equipment.

Many of these factors are already the subject of public policy, designed to influence future development. Pure extrapolation, on the basis of past experience, will be a poor guide to future changes in these cases, unless the effects of policy are merely to confirm and continue past trends. The prediction of "planned development" must be based, in the first instance, on a knowledge of the plans and should proceed by estimating the capacity of the executive authorities to achieve them. This may depend upon economic considerations, because the plans of various authorities sometimes react upon one another through their demands on the market for labor, materials, and capital. Consequently, the economist must apply his own technique in the case of those material agents which are produced as a result of business decisions.

For material on which to base pure extrapolation of changes in *the distribution of ownership* we must rely on "economic" statistics; and it is largely to economic science that we must look for the correction of pure extrapolation according to the operation of discernible causes of change. It is much the same in the case of *the geographic distribution of people and things*, though here again we must also reckon with the effects of public policy, and particularly of "planned development."

In *the state of the arts* we reach another class of data, changes which are the subject of study by other sciences. The history of science and technology should provide some basis for pure extrapolation of future developments; and, as we have seen, the correction of such extrapolation according to knowledge of causes (including those that work through economic processes) has already been essayed in the special case of inventions.

Turning to the three special additions to Professor Knight's original list, we find special sciences concerned with various aspects of *public policy:* political science, law, public administration, and such particular sciences as are drawn upon in planned development. While forecasts of public policy are important for many people, the difficulties are such as to discourage the emergence of a specialized science of prediction. *Monetary conditions* have been traditionally within the field of economics, and the necessary contacts with the technology of banking, coinage, exchange, and the like have long been established. *Market situations* have not been made the subject of a special science of prediction, but study of the causes of changes has been shared by law and economics.

To sum up, we have a special science of population prediction and the beginnings of one for the prediction of inventions. But for all changes in the other data of economics it is necessary to draw on a number of unrelated sciences and to effect a synthesis of their independent contributions. In some cases, such as the tastes and dispositions of the people, when all the other existing sciences have been tapped, there will still remain considerable gaps in our knowledge. Pending the development of new special sciences concerned with the prediction of changes in particular classes of data, the preparation of forecasts by the method of extrapolation and the necessary synthesis of available knowledge from various fields to correct the results of pure extrapolation will not be undertaken by anybody, unless by the economist himself. The initiative in collaboration among the sciences must come from those who require, for their own work, information which their own specialized techniques do not provide; and this is the position of the economist, who, in the interests of realism, must work with estimates of future development in the conditions of economic activity.

As in other sections of this book, our discussion points the way to a field for research rather than providing at once the additional knowledge which is suggested as necessary for realistic economics. But it must be pointed out that, beyond a certain point, the cultivation of this field, in only general terms, will yield decreasing returns. Just as the conditions of economic activity vary from place to place and from time to time, so, too, the rate and direction of change, and even its causes, will vary. It is this that renders so difficult any attempt to predict "economic evolution" for the world as a whole. But, as already pointed out, the economist is more likely to be asked for advice on limited, local problems; and the field of research can therefore be subdivided into more manageable allotments. And, even though the backwardness of some sciences may leave considerable gaps in any attempt to present a synthetic estimate of future changes in the data of a particular economic problem, it is suggested that the capacity to make the most of the available facts in such estimates should form part of the equipment of the economist. This capacity is more likely to be developed by the systematic exploration of the problems of economic development by the three methods already distinguished and by the cultivation of the necessary contacts with other sciences than by concentrating on the study of equilibrium theory and trusting to common sense for the rest.

Moreover, it is necessary to pose the general problems involved in the prediction of economic development, in order to stimulate the analysis of those economic processes which are partly responsible for the data changes. This is the specific contribution which the economist might be expected to make to the theory of economic development, as distinct from the synthesis of the contributions of various sciences.

ECONOMIC PROCESSES IN DEVELOPMENT

We turn, therefore, to the economic theorist's special contribution and consider the implications for economic theory of the observation that economic processes play an important part in the production of some of the changes which constitute economic development. If the results of pure extrapolation are to be corrected according to our knowledge of the causes of change, we must make our knowledge of the economic factors as full as possible. This involves the exploitation of those existing economic theories which do throw light on development and the construction of new ones to fill the gaps in our analytic technique.

Does this mean that we should add to our science a special department, like the production, exchange, and distribution of the old-fashioned economists and the statics and dynamics of the most modern? To Professor Roll belongs the distinction of having set aside a whole part, in an elementary textbook, for a discussion of "Problems of Change."[2] He does not, however, venture upon a systematic exploration of economic development. "Modern economics can say little" about the causes of change in the data. "It may be possibe to enunciate general laws of change, but it is beyond the competence of the economist of today to do so; the knowledge of the historian, sociologist and philosopher is required as well." Admittedly, "the economist can make some contribution towards answering inquiries into the causes of change, for some of the causes lie within the economic system. . . . . But there are other causes to be taken into account."[3] Professor Roll sets out, therefore, to consider only "what changes in economic relations will be necessary in order that a change of data may be, so to speak, 'absorbed' into the system." This position is similar to that adopted in Professor Fisher's *The Clash of Progress and Security*, discussed earlier.

But, in dealing with population, tastes, and technique, Professor Roll does, in fact, consider the *causes* of changes, if only in summary fashion. For instance, he distinguishes "three types of changes in tastes."

> There are, first of all, changes the causes of which cannot be easily traced; these we might call *autonomous*. Then there are others which are themselves the results of changes in population, capital, productivity, etc.; these, for want of a better word, we might call *repercussive* changes in consumers' demands. And finally, there are changes in tastes which are deliberately brought about; they are induced.[4]

As it turns out, Professor Roll gives more space to illustrating and discussing these causes of change than he does to "the reactions of the economic system" to the changes themselves. The content of his discussion suggests that "repercussive changes" fall under, but do not ex-

---

[2] E. Roll, *Elements of Economic Theory* (London, 1937), Part III.

[3] *Ibid.*, pp. 205–6.   [4] *Ibid.*, pp. 217–18.

haust, our category of changes which can be traced to the direct influence of other data.

There is no reason to be dogmatic about the arrangement of the body of economic theory for purposes of exposition; and a concluding division on "economic change" provides a convenient home for the problem of fluctuations. But such a division will tend to be scrappy and ill-furnished, until such time as the possibility of analyzing data changes is systematically investigated throughout all the divisions of theory. It seems preferable, therefore, to place the problem of economic development among the central problems of economic theory, on an equal footing with the adjustment of the market to given conditions, and to bring it to the notice of students early. Then the two types of analysis can be elaborated in close relation to each other; and in many of the theories of which the establishment of equilibrium at present appears to be the climax the analysis can be pushed on into the realm of data changes. If, after the exploration of market activities, extra-market operations are analyzed, their role in the development of the data will be too obvious to be ignored.

The present problem, however, is not that of exposition but that of theoretical construction. The goal of development theory has already been indicated as the discovery of those economic processes which contribute to the production of change; and the relation of this type of theory to the task of concrete prediction has been set out. But the material for a "Principles," in which development will figure as prominently as equilibrium, has not yet been assembled. That task, like others indicated in this book, is large enough to keep many workers busy for some time. All that can be attempted here is to turn out for inspection some of the material which is already to hand, although its suitability for this purpose has not been previously recognized, and to suggest some further lines of exploration.

We must, of course, be on our guard against theoretic blight in this field, as in others. Examples of theoretic blight in development theory are, indeed, not uncommon. For instance, economists have argued that, because one set of economic conditions could be the logical consequence of certain practices, the latter are in practice the cause of the former. Even Professor Roll uses language which suggests this type of bogus theory of development. "Division of labour and the use of machinery *give rise* to two important social institutions, private property and exchange."[5] All the historical and anthropological evidence

[5] *Ibid.*, p. 23.

points to private property and exchange being older than both division of labor and machinery. But, while this may serve as a warning, it need not discourage us from seeking less questionable fragments of development theory in general economics.

Some examples have already been referred to in the preceding two chapters, notably Marshall's long-period analysis, the theory of saving, and business-cycle theory in general. Some scraps of straight economic theory will also have been noticed in Professor Ohlin's essay on future development, summarized in chapter viii. It is not proposed to go back over this ground. Although each of the examples already mentioned would bear considerable elaboration, that should not present great difficulty for any economist who has grasped the general method involved, namely, to search for assumptions pregnant with inferences about data changes rather than mere adjustments to given data and to ignore the self-denying ordinance which has confined economic analysis to the latter. The possibilities of the method may be illustrated by a short review of some constructions of modern theory which, while not explicitly designed as part of the theory of economic development, nevertheless contribute to it.

INCREASING RETURNS AND THE TREND TOWARD MONOPOLY

Perhaps the most famous example of developmental implications in market theory is Marshall's observation of the difficulties inherent in the assumption of increasing returns in a competitively organized industry. Cournot, who anticipated so much of modern monopoly theory, had drawn up a curve of competitive supply price, by adding the output of each competitor at each given price and assuming a decreasing cost curve for each competitor. Writers such as Cournot, says Marshall, apparently did not notice that "their premises lead inevitably to the conclusion that, whatever firm first gets a good start will obtain a monopoly of the whole business of its trade in its district."[6] For equilibrium theory this raised the problem of the inconsistency of the assumptions of decreasing supply price and pure competition. This inconsistency could be removed only by introducing the assumption of "external" economies, which were associated with the growth of a particular industry and served to lower the individual cost curves of all the firms in the industry, while still permitting each individual firm to operate under conditions of constant or increasing average cost.

[6] A. Marshall, *Principles of Economics* (8th ed.; London, 1922), p. 459 n.

Doubts as to the frequency, in practice, of economies which were "external" to the firms but "internal" to a single industry gave added interest to the development of the theory of "imperfect competition." Marshall himself had given the clue. "Manufactures, which are adapted to special tastes" are likely to be produced on a small scale

under conditions of decreasing cost. . . . . But these are the very industries where each firm is likely to be confined more or less to its own particular market; and, if it is so confined, any hasty increase in its production is likely to lower the demand price in that market out of all proportion to the increased economies that it will gain, even though its production is but small relatively to the broad market for which in a more general sense it may be said to produce.[7]

With the systematic development of the theory of the particular market,[8] the issue in equilibrium theory was cleared up.

But Marshall's observation of the conflict between pure competition and decreasing costs was also adopted to explain the growth of monopoly. Both Professor Taussig and Professor Clay in their general textbooks ascribe the prevalence of monopoly in public utility industries to the fact that these industries, with their huge overhead costs, yielded decreasing average cost as output increased.[9] The common observation that monopoly is more probable in industries where large-scale production is economical is another statement of the same principle. This is really a proposition in the theory of economic development. If we assume competition to begin with and a standardized product and add the assumption that average costs will decrease as long as any firm increases, we can predict that competition will give way to monopoly, for this is implicit in our premises.

It should be noted, however, that the theory of product differentiation, or imperfect competition, suggests an alternative line of development. If we modify our premises and assume that product differentiation is possible, we can no longer predict the emergence of single control in the industry. Instead, there may be established an equilibrium of many small firms, selling differentiated products. To determine which line of development will be actually followed, the assumptions of our theory would have to be enlarged to include specific data as to the cost of product differentiation, as well as its efficacy in protecting each firm's "particular market." Thus the concept of a particular

[7] *Ibid.*, p. 458; see also p. 849.

[8] E. H. Chamberlin, *Theory of Monopolistic Competition* (Cambridge, Mass., 1933); Joan Robinson, *Economics of Imperfect Competition* (London, 1933).

[9] F. W. Taussig, *Principles of Economics* (3d ed.; New York, 1924), II, 117; H. Clay, *Economics for the General Reader* (London, 1922), p. 134.

market supplies not only an explanation of the persistence of decreasing costs in an industry consisting of many "competing" firms but also an element in a theoretical analysis of the development of market situations. Economists have hitherto been so absorbed in the analysis of different market situations arising from differentiation of the product and so little interested in the construction of development theory that little or no attention has been given to the significance of product differentiation in the latter connection.

Discussions of the trend toward monopoly or competition are frequent enough in economic literature. Many writers have drawn attention to the effect of tariffs and the general background of commercial law, as well as the "technical advantages" of large-scale industry and the possibility of monopoly gains. On the other hand, attention has often been drawn to "the tendency of free enterprise to break down monopolitic positions."[10] All this falls within the theory of economic development, and it is suggested that the possibility of predicting the future development of various market situations would be increased if, in the analysis of each situation, attention were paid to the conditions which imply development into a new situation, as well as to the conditions necessary for equilibrium.

LOCATION OF INDUSTRY AND INTERNATIONAL TRADE

The theory of location of industry is essentially development theory, because it takes as its dependent variables the geographical distribution of persons and material agents, which serves in turn as a datum for ordinary equilibrium analysis. Moreover, the theory reveals certain tendencies toward cumulative change which are of particular interest. Among the conditions which determine the location of an industry are accessibility of the market and availability of an adequate supply of labor. Yet the establishment of an industry in a particular locality contributes its quota to both the market and the labor supply, by providing livelihoods for additional workers in that district and perhaps a demand for the products of subsidiary industries.[11]

Some of the most striking examples of development theory, however, are to be found in the modern theory of interregional and international trade, which, in Professor Ohlin's hands, becomes an extension of "localisation theory." The classical theory of international trade was based on the assumptions that labor and capital are mobile

---

[10] L. Robbins, *Economic Planning and International Order* (London, 1937), p. 157.

[11] Cf. E. A. G. Robinson, *The Structure of Competitive Industry* (London, 1931), chap. x.

as between different employments within a single country, but not as between different countries. Otherwise no special theory of international trade would be required. "The difference between a single country and many," wrote Ricardo, "is easily accounted for by considering the difficulty with which capital moves from one country to another to seek a more profitable employment, and the activity with which it invariably passes from one province to another in the same country."[12] Cairnes, who had established the existence of "non-competing groups" of workers within a country and observed the international mobility of capital, argued that the above distinction was one only of degree.[13] But the full significance of this qualification was not recognized until the effects of international mobility of the factors of production upon the course of commodity trade became the subject of systematic study.[14]

From Professor Ohlin's analysis there appear to be three economic processes by which international factor movements may be produced out of the original conditions which are necessary to initiate commodity trade. The first is indicated by the observation that commodity and factor movements may be alternative responses to a given set of data; the second arises through the effects of trade upon the relative earnings of the factors in different countries; and the third, already noticed in chapter vii, is the provision of transport facilities as a consequence of the establishment of commodity trade. These three processes may be considered in more detail, as elements in the theory of economic development.

The analysis is complicated by the fact that migration is not the only source of change in a country's factor endowment. The differences in earnings which stimulate migration involve absolute levels of earnings in each country. The growth of commodity trade cannot alter the relative earnings of the factors of production in different countries without altering the absolute levels in one or more countries, and this may cause a change in the natural increase of population and the accumulation of capital out of domestic savings. This type of reaction may have important effects upon the actual course of trade in the long run; and long-run predictions which did not take account of this factor in the development of the data would be correspondingly open

[12] Cf. D. Ricardo, *Works*, ed. McCulloch (2d ed.; London, 1852), p. 77.

[13] J. E. Cairnes, *Some Leading Principles of Political Economy* (London, 1874), p. 365.

[14] Cf. J. H. Williams, "The Theory of International Trade Reconsidered," *Economic Journal*, 1929, pp. 195–209.

to error. For short periods, however, it is the international migration of capital and labor that is most likely to throw predictions out, if allowance is not made for the economic processes in development.

First, we have to consider trade and migration as alternatives. Abstracting from consumers' preferences for products of a particular country, trade will be initiated by price differences. Two-way trade implies that each country has a price advantage in some goods and is at a price disadvantage in other goods. This in turn implies that there are differences in the ratios between the prices at which the goods would be produced in the respective countries in the absence of trade. "On one cardinal point, the Ricardian theory remains entirely unimpaired; the international exchange of goods must depend on differences in their comparative values in the countries concerned."[15] These differences in relative values depend, in large measure, upon differences in the relative values of the factors of production in the countries concerned; and in money terms there will be international differences in the absolute prices—or earnings—of the factors.[16] Apart from any obstacles to the movement of goods or of the factors of production, the fundamental conditions which tend to initiate trade, also tend to initiate migration of the factors of production from centers of low remuneration to centers of high remuneration. If we assume that factor mobility is impossible, the latter result is, of course, excluded from our theoretical analysis. But, if factor mobility is possible, the migration of capital and labor to centers of high remuneration will tend to equalize factor prices—or earnings—internationally and consequently alter the data in such a way as to reduce the incentive to commodity trade. Commodity and factor movements are, therefore, alternative modes of response to the same set of initial conditions; and the extent of each type of movement will depend, in the first instance, upon the relative obstacles to and costs of movement.[17] Thus the analysis provides a theory describing the conditions under which there will be economic development rather than adjustments of the "dependent variables" of market theory.

As trade develops, the prices of factors employed in the production

---

[15] B. Whale, *International Trade* (London, 1932), p. 113; see also E. R. Walker, "Comparative Costs in International Trade," *Economic Record*, June, 1937.

[16] The differences in factor prices cannot be deduced from the differences in commodity prices, because similar commodities are produced by different combinations of factors in different parts of the world.

[17] B. Ohlin, *Interregional and International Trade* (Cambridge, Mass., 1933), pp. 167–69.

of exports tend to rise relatively to the prices of factors employed in other industries, and especially in other industries which now meet the competition of imports. From the viewpoint of equilibrium theory, it is interesting that both trade and factor movements tend to equalize commodity and factor prices alike. But from the viewpoint of development theory the chief significance of changes in factor prices is that they affect the inducements to further factor movements and the future domestic supplies of various factors. "If we are interested in the short-run effects of certain variations, these reactions may be left out of account altogether. . . . . The further ahead we wish to look, the more attention we must give to factor supply reactions,"[18] for, unless the supply of a factor is completely rigid or negatively elastic, the effect of the changes in relative factor prices is gradually to increase the inequality of "factor endowment" as between different countries and thereby to modify the data to which the course of trade is adjusted through the market.[19] This means, that even though the initial conditions permit the growth of trade rather than immediate changes in the data, trade itself gives rise to economic development along the lines indicated by this analysis.

Finally, the growth of trade in response to the original conditions affects the facilities for factor movements. The relation of trade contacts and transport to migration of persons was noted in chapter vii. In the case of capital movements the relationship is even more intimate. Apart from gold shipments, capital can move internationally only in the form of goods or services. Conditions which imply the growth of trade also imply the establishment of a medium for capital movements.

These elements in the modern theory of trade owe their origin to the attempts to develop a more realistic analysis than that previously available. This necessitated enlarging its assumptions to permit certain endogenous data changes, thereby transforming parts of the theory into a partial analysis of economic development. It is suggested that the significance of this part of Professor Ohlin's work can be more easily grasped if it is considered as an extension of economic theory to take account of certain types of data changes, as well as adjustments to given data.

[18] *Ibid.*, p. 131.

[19] *Ibid.*, pp. 118 ff.; the thesis is subject to certain qualifications not considered above.

CONTROL OF THE DATA THROUGH THE MARKET

The examples we have been considering deal with processes of development arising out of the attempts of economic subjects to make the best out of existing conditions. The analysis involves no assumption of any ulterior motive. Yet much activity in the market is deliberately directed toward altering the market data, so that at some future time it will work more favorably for the persons concerned. The launching of a publicity campaign to change the public's attitude toward painting houses at different seasons of the year, the purchase of a patent to put it to sleep, corruption of officials to secure favorable treatment—these market adjustments may involve some immediate financial loss as compared with other possible adjustments. But, if they are successful, they promise better returns in the long run.

This type of behavior came up for consideration in chapter vi, where we had to consider borderline cases between market and extra-market operations. It was suggested that where the two are mixed a synthesis is necessary between market theory and the theory of extra-market operations. It now appears that market theory is more likely to contribute its quota to the synthesis if it is cultivated in the direction of the explanation of development, as well as the adjustment of the market to given conditions.

It must be recognized, however, that this class of market activity, designed to modify the conditions of the market, also includes many practices which are so common in the market that the possibility of any confusion with extra-market operations does not arise. Free delivery and other devices which establish "good-will" in the retail trade, are designed to change (or protect) the market situation; advertising is designed to change (or stabilize) consumers' tastes; expenditure on industrial welfare schemes is often intended to increase the efficiency of labor; and the maintenance of a research laboratory represents an attempt to add to the technology at the disposal of the firm. These are everyday features of our economic life, and economists have already wrestled with the problems they present for equilibrium analysis. But the purpose of these activities is to produce minor changes in the data of the market; and their investigation is fundamentally a problem for the theory of economic development.

From this point of view a distinction between market adjustments to given data and market operations designed to modify the data is useful, although a matter of degree. At the same time, the fact that this distinction is a matter of degree serves to emphasize the close relationship between economic development and economic behavior under given conditions and supports our claim for continuity between traditional economic theory and the theory of economic development. In order to advance our understanding of market operations designed to modify the data it is necessary to work along the lines adopted in our sketch of the theory of extra-market operations. The first problem is why people are dissatisfied with market conditions—a question on which market theory itself throws some light. The second problem is the possibility of modifying these conditions through market operations, as distinct from making the best of conditions as they are. Finally, there is the problem of the practical limits to such activities, imposed by the law, by moral codes, and by general attitudes toward different types of behavior. The last problem is not so prominent in the case of market operations designed to modify the data as in the case of extra-market operations, because the former involves less departure from the pattern of conventional market practices.

It would seem, therefore, that the methods suggested for the analysis of extra-market operations may assist the analysis of some of the processes of economic development, which work through the market. This, too, serves to illustrate the continuity between present-day economic theory and the extension proposed in this book.

DEVELOPMENT THROUGH EXTRA-MARKET OPERATIONS

To the explanation of economic processes which may involve the correction of predictions based on pure extrapolation we bring not merely market theory, developed and reorientated for this specific purpose, but also the theory of extra-market operations, which is designed primarily to guide the economist in the empirical investigation of some of the activities which, though common in industry, trade, and finance, escape from the categories of market theory. It may be remembered that, while these activities were represented as attempts to attain ends similar to those that are sought through the market, it was suggested that they involve the pursuit of certain *intermediate objectives*, which, if attained, open up the way to greater satisfaction than can be obtained through the market under existing conditions. Four intermediate objectives were distinguished, namely, (a) to circumvent the market altogether, (b) to alter the external data of the market, (c) to alter the principles of market behavior, and (*d*) to control the scope for extra-market operations by others.[20]

It was noted that the distinction between (*b*) and (*c*) is somewhat arbitrary, though useful in the theory of extra-market operations. For the purpose of the theory of economic development (*c*) falls under *the tastes and dispositions of the people*, in the list of data. Extra-market operations directed toward (*b*) and (*c*), therefore, must be regarded as economic processes in the development of the data; and the theory of extra-market operations, in so far as it analyzes activities under these heads, is a direct contribution to the theory of economic development, as well as an independent branch of the theory of economic behavior under given conditions.

Activities directed toward (*a*) may involve a change in the data for a subsequent period, because they may produce a redistribution of ownership of material agents. We have already seen that ordinary economic theory throws some light on changes in data under this heading; and the explanation of changes can be advanced a step further by the consideration of these extra-market operations.

Finally, activities directed toward (*d*) may produce changes in the conditions which determine the extent of market and extra-market operations, respectively; and the analysis of such activities may be regarded as being also a contribution to the theory of economic development.

This implies enlarging the scope of this theory to cover not only changes in the data to which market adjustments are made but also changes in the factors which serve as independent variables for the theory of extra-market operations. It might be possible to extrapolate the future development of dissatisfaction with the market and of the various techniques of extra-market operations that will be available and to correct these extrapolations according to such knowledge of the causes of change in these factors as can be gained from different sciences. It has already been suggested, in our analysis of dissatisfaction with the market, that economic theory throws some light on the causes at work and on the conditions determining the points at which dissatisfaction is likely to be acute. Possibly some sort of analysis of the causes of change in the technique of extra-market operations might be developed, though economic theory would contribute little or nothing.

While this further extension of the theory of economic development to embrace changes in the data of the theory of extra-market opera-

[20] See chap. vi, under the heading "Classification of Extra-market Operations."

tions would be logical enough and might prove useful in concrete problems, it would be premature to urge such an extension when the theory of extra-market operations and the theory of the development of market data are still in their infancy.

In conclusion we may draw attention to the wide range of the fragments of development theory which have come up for consideration in this and the preceding chapter. A change in the form of competition in a particular industry or in the number of people in a country is a small matter compared with Marx's views on the future of capitalism. From the viewpoint of practical policy, however, the economist is usually in greater need of light upon relatively small data changes than upon the long-period evolution of the economic system. And in seeking to establish development theory as a branch of economic theory, even small contributions are valuable, particularly when they point the way to more systematic investigations. In any case the fundamentals of method must be the same for those who foresee and would understand a coming social cataclysm and for those who desire to predict the detailed behavior of the present economic world.

CHAPTER X

THE ILLUSION OF NEUTRALITY

W E NOW take up the question raised at the beginning of the first chapter, namely, the extent to which the study of economics can assist the choice of objectives in economic policy. This is not quite the same question as that of how economists should behave when asked to advise on the desirability of various objectives. We have already seen, in chapter ii, that an economic adviser is sometimes expected to give his opinion as to *what ought to be done*. Nor can he hope for much attention to be given by those who seek his advice to any distinction he may wish to draw between scientific economics and nonscientific value judgments. There is such a large field for the exercise of opinion and judgment in deciding upon cause and effect in the economic world that the economist's insistence upon the personal nature of his views on *what ought to be* seems only in keeping with the recognition that opinions differ as to *what is*. The economist's scientific conscience may be satisfied by the presentation of his advice in words which involve no logical confusion between normative and positive statements, but in practice his advice amounts to the adoption of particular objectives, as well as the advocacy of particular methods of attaining these objectives.

"WHAT IS" AND "WHAT OUGHT TO BE"

In the textbooks of economics various attitudes toward objectives may be discerned. On the one hand, there are those expositions of economic practice and theory which set out to describe and analyze, without any attempt at valuation, criticism, or appreciation. Textbooks of this type are intended to depict economics as an objective science—an ideal typified by Pareto's motto: "Je ne propose rien, je n'oppose rien, j'expose." On the other hand, there are those works which are frankly concerned with some general objective of economic policy, such as the alleviation of poverty or the maximization of "economic welfare." The objective may be simply proposed as incontestable or may be made the subject of an introductory discussion, in which positive economic theory proper may or may not play some part. But it is still possible, once the goal has been adopted, to concentrate the main exposition upon the causal relationships between various conditions and the desired goal. These two viewpoints, though different, both involve the separation of normative and positive studies, either by excluding the former altogether from economics, as in the first case, or by treating them as a preliminary to the positive analysis, as in the second case. Both viewpoints may be contrasted with that found in a type of textbook, not yet extinct, which attempts to combine analysis and description with a running commentary on the "advantages" and "disadvantages" of various conditions and practices, the "desirability" of certain reforms and the "dangers" inherent in other proposals. The modern fashion is to deprecate this type of exposition, on the ground that it tends to promote confusion between two essentially different types of studies—the positive and the normative. The fact that most writers on positive economics still find it difficult to expunge from their vocabulary all the words that have normative associations is not regarded as a reason for abandoning the attempt to avoid a mixture of the two types of discussion.

Why this sharp distinction between what is and what ought to be? Professor Robbins rebuts Mr. Hawtrey's claim that "economics cannot be dissociated from ethics" by saying that "unfortunately it does not seem logically possible to associate the two studies in any form but mere juxtaposition. Economics deals with ascertainable facts; ethics with valuations and obligations. The two fields of enquiry are not on the same plane of discourse."[1] A somewhat similar point is made by Professor Florence, who claims that only propositions couched in the indicative mood have any place in science; accordingly, economic science should not include any propositions in the optative or imperative mood.[2] The basis of the distinction is the hope of building a scientific economics, coupled with the conviction that ethics cannot be scientific.

In the rough-and-tumble of political struggle, differences of opinion may arise either as a result of differences about ends or as a result of differences about the means of attaining ends. Now, as regards the first type of difference, neither Economics nor any other science can provide any solvent. If we disagree about ends it is a case of thy blood or mine—or live and let live, according to the importance of the difference, or the relative strength of our opponents. But if we disagree about means, then scientific analysis can often help us to resolve our differences. . . . . Surely, for the sake of securing what agreement we can in a world in which avoidable differences of opinion are all too common, it is worth while carefully delimiting those fields of enquiry where this

[1] L. Robbins, *Essay on the Nature and Significance of Economic Science* (2d ed.; London, 1937), p. 148.

[2] P. Sargant Florence, *Uplift in Economics* (London, 1929).

kind of settlement is possible from those where it is not to be hoped for—it is worth while delimiting the neutral area of science from that more disputable area of moral and political philosophy.[3]

This separation of the normative from the positive is not usually taken as implying that economics must not deal with objectives at all. We may "assume as postulates different judgments of value, and then on the assumption that these are valid, enquire what judgment is to be passed upon particular proposals for action."[4] For instance, if we assume that a fall in unemployment is desirable, we may recommend a particular measure as desirable because it will achieve this end. "Applied Economics consists of propositions of the form, 'If you want to do this, then you must do that,' "[5] but not of the form "You should want to do this." In other words, economic theory takes ends as given and does not choose among them.

The economist himself, however, is apparently not bound by the confines of his science. "Our methodological axioms involve no prohibition of outside interests." Professor Robbins disclaims the view that "economists should not deliver themselves on ethical questions."[6] nor has he hesitated to do so himself in his various popular writings. "Why should one be frightened of taking a stand on judgments which are not scientific, if they relate to matters outside the world of science?"[7] The only thing which the economist should *not* do is "to claim scientific sanction for judgments of questions not capable of scientific proof."

Although we have quoted mainly from Professor Robbins, it will be recognized that the methodological position outlined above is widely held by modern economists. The main division of opinion is as to the minimum normative element that is necessary for the formulation of a definite objective. Until recently many economists did not doubt that such notions as the maximization of satisfaction or the increase of economic welfare could be adopted as economic objectives without implying any further value judgment than that satisfactions are desirable. It is now widely recognized, however, that we cannot apply these notions to a group of individuals unless we are prepared to evaluate the

[3] Robbins, *op. cit.* pp. 150–51.

[4] *Ibid.*, p. 149.

[5] *Ibid.*

[6] *Ibid.*, pp. 149 and 150.

[7] L. Robbins, "Interpersonal Comparisons of Utility," *Economic Journal*, December, 1938, p. 638.

relative importance of the satisfactions enjoyed by each individual. "I do not believe," writes Professor Robbins, "that in fact men are necessarily equal or should always be judged as such. But I do believe that, in most cases, political calculations which do not treat them *as if* they were equal are *morally* revolting."[8] Only on some additional assumption such as this or one allocating different weights to different individuals can a precise meaning be attached to the notion of the total satisfaction gained by a group of people from their money incomes.[9]

This change in the attitude of many economists to the conventional objective of maximum satisfaction reflects the progressive nature of the movement toward a neutral economic theory, from which ethical precepts are excluded. When the movement began, the positive and normative elements in economic doctrine were thoroughly confused, and the first attempts to separate them were only partly successful. Some of the propositions which earlier economists accepted as positive statements are now seen to contain tacit value judgments and must therefore be transferred to the category of normative propositions. Assuming that different methods are appropriate to the positive study of things as they are and the choice of objectives, it would seem desirable to continue the scrutiny of all supposedly positive statements, with a view to weeding out any other unsuspected normative elements in economic theory. No one will deny Professor Robbins' observation that the sharp distinction between positive and normative studies helps to emphasize that independent study of objectives is needed, if the "neutral" findings of economic science are to be "applied to human improvement."[10]

As it stands today, however, the body of doctrine which is usually taught as economic theory is only superficially neutral. Upon examination it will be found to owe its own form largely to value judgments as to what is desirable; and many of its verbally positive analyses carry normative force in practice. It may also be argued that academic teaching of conventional theory, despite and to some extent because of its apparent "impartiality," helps to train the moral sensibility of pupils in a particular direction. Before addressing ourselves to the examination of various possible objectives of economic theory, it is necessary, therefore, to reconsider the supposed neutrality of economic theory.

[8] *Ibid.*, p. 635.

[9] This point is elaborated in chap. xii.   [10] *Ibid.*, p. 639.

BIAS IN ECONOMICS

When discussing the problems of normative economics it is often assumed that the desired ends are advantageous to the community as a whole or are, in some absolute sense, "good." Similarly, "ethics" is commonly supposed to deal with right and wrong, good and evil. But the objectives of an economic policy may be conceived in the interests of a smaller group, or even of a single individual, without any claim that they are desired by or good for the rest of the community. Economic theory itself is always studied under the impulse of an interest; it may be that of personal advantage as well as the desire to do good. At the beginning of all economic study, therefore, is a value judgment, namely, that the interest which impels the student is more important than other, weaker interests. Whatever the interest which leads him to economics, he will find a body of doctrine to hand, ready to be studied and mastered, if his interest is strong enough or if supplementary interests are aroused. But this body of doctrine was itself constructed under the impulse of the interests of its originators. Its present form reflects not only the intellectual powers of all who have added to the structure but also their various interests—their value judgments as to what is important.

We have already seen that the choice of assumptions and the direction in which chains of reasoning are developed have often been influenced by the desire to build a coherent and symmetrical theory. When this intellectual and aesthetic interest leads to constructions remote from reality, the result can be described as "theoretic blight."[11] This is, however, only a special case of a general tendency to select from the innumerable possible assumptions and inferences those that appear to be related to the investigator's own interests. This general tendency can best be described as "bias." Then theoretic blight is the result of a bias arising from the intellectual and aesthetic interests of the investigator. Our present concern, however, is with bias arising from other interests, such as the desire to preserve the status quo or the desire to achieve certain objectives. Where the emotional bias is strong, it may even lead to the construction of illogical theories, as Freud and Pareto have abundantly shown. But logical fallacies are more easily exposed than a biased choice of assumptions or direction of inferences, and it is in the latter regard that the interests of the investigator have left their strongest imprint upon economic theory.

[11] See above, chap. iv.

Many economists will object that the only bias in scientific economics, as they teach it, is toward the truth and that their dominant interest is to obtain a full picture of things *as they are*. This objection, however, implies a misunderstanding of the nature of economic theory, or
at least the complete rejection of the position adopted earlier in this
work. Economic theory is not a *full* description of reality in all its details, or even of all the economic aspects of the real world. A full description would be a mere replica, equally complex, and useless as a
guide to problems. Economic theory is a conceptual scheme, designed
to attract our attention to those facts which are significant for the
problems which we call "economic." Its method is to select certain
assumptions, corresponding to certain conditions in the real world,
which might be significant for the problem in hand and to draw out
from these assumptions all the implications which appear to bear on
that problem.[12] The resulting theory will owe its form as much to the
omission of certain assumptions as to the inclusion of others and as
much to the failure to explore certain implications of the chosen assumptions as to the elaboration of other chains of inference. For instance, the theory of the so-called distribution of income, in nineteenth-century economics, did not deal at all with personal inequality.
The classical writers were not interested in the objective of reducing inequality. It was for later writers, such as Cannan, to develop the theory by taking as assumptions the conditions that cause inequality and
by elaborating the implications of those conditions.[13]

Few economists have been interested in things purely as they are.
Adam Smith was interested in the then remote possibility of establishing free trade and developed his theory of the international division of
labor accordingly. Marx was interested in the overthrow of capitalism
and developed his theory of economic change. List was interested in
promoting the industrial strength of Germany and developed his theory of protection.

When a contrast is drawn between the positive study of "what is"
and the normative study of "what ought to be," it should be borne in
mind that in economics "what is" includes "what might be" if certain
conditions were different. Economic theory explores the implications
of selected assumptions. It attempts to forecast the effects of various
possible policies, as well as to predict the outcome of existing conditions in the real world. It cannot deal with the effect of *every* conceiv-

[12] See above, chap. iii.

[13] Cf. E. Cannan, *The Economic Outlook* (London, 1914).

able policy or indicate the means of achieving *every* conceivable objective. That would be a far greater task than the admittedly impossible one of preparing a *full* description of existing conditions and all their implications. Consequently, the student who approaches economics for the first time will find to hand a theory which reflects the earlier investigators' opinions as to which policies were worth examining and which objectives were worth pursuing. He may also find theories which show the evil effects of policies that these earlier writers disliked, as well as the methods of achieving objectives which they desired and any obstacles in the way of their achievement. But he will not find theories exposing the method by which one might achieve objectives that have never entered the heads of earlier investigators or which they have dismissed as not worthy of consideration.

LACK OF INTEREST MEANS LACK OF INVESTIGATION

The most striking example of this is the almost complete lack of any economic theory dealing with the distribution of working conditions and the adjustment of tasks to the interests of the worker. Economists have been so obsessed by the objective of increasing incomes and so little interested in the conceivable objective of increasing joy in work that almost the whole of economic theory is orientated toward the explanation of variations in productivity and the division of the product. The possibility that an increase in incomes may cause a net loss of satisfaction if it involves an undue increase in hours is verbally acknowledged by "welfare" economists;[14] and the inequality of working conditions has even been listed among the determinants of "material welfare."[15] But the main body of theory, even as developed by welfare economists, does not include discussion of the conditions under which leisure would be distributed more evenly or work assume a greater intrinsic interest. Similarly, the effects of inventions upon total production and upon the distribution of incomes are explored by economic theory, but not their effects upon the degree of boredom or the physical strain involved in production. At this stage we are not arguing that economics should include theories of this type; our first concern is to establish the fact that their absence is due largely to the predominant interest of economists in the objective of increased income and to the weakness of their interest in the objective of working just long enough and in such a way as to make work enjoyable. There is also

[14] E.g., A. C. Pigou, *Economics of Welfare* (3d ed.; London, 1929), p. 87.

[15] H. Dalton, "The Optimum Theory of Population," *Economica*, March, 1928, p. 31.

the consideration that, apart from working hours, these conditions of work, being less easily measured, do not lend themselves to the same quantitative treatment as prices and production. Thus the bias of intellectual interest reinforces the bias caused by the preference for the objective of increased income.

IS IMPARTIAL ECONOMICS IMPOSSIBLE?

In the light of the preceding discussion of the dependence of the form and content of economic theory upon the objectives which have aroused the sympathetic or adverse interest of earlier investigators, it is worth reconsidering the view, often advanced by socialist writers, that an impartial economic theory is impossible. It is argued that "in a class society" there can be only the economic theories which envisage the economic system in relation to the interests of particular classes. "Bourgeois" economics is contrasted with "proletarian" economics— the one depicting the alleged harmony of interests of different classes and the inevitability of the existing distribution of incomes, and the other revealing the fundamental contradictions which are tearing capitalist society apart. By others it has been argued that economic theory may reflect national interests, for instance, that the cosmopolitan economic theory of Adam Smith and his followers was designed to prevent the growth of manufactures in other countries than Britain.

This sort of criticism seems altogether unjustified to many modern economists, who may find in the received doctrines minor flaws of logic and some assumptions that seem out of step with present conditions but no gross distortion of reality in the interests of a particular class or nation. It is generally argued that positive economics does not, in fact, make many of the claims attributed to "bourgeois" or "cosmopolitan" economics and that the alternative "proletarian" or "national" economics, as usually expounded, is illogical as well as biased.

On general methodological lines the same position was adopted by Max Weber. While emphasizing that the direction of scientific interest is largely determined by its "value relevance" (*Wertbeziehung*), he insisted that the actual study of cause and effect within the selected field does not involve any value judgments.[16] It must be remembered, however, that the direction of scientific interest to particular details of the concrete world leads to the construction of a body of theory

[16] Cf. Talcott Parsons, *The Structure of Social Action* (New York, 1937), p. 594, where Weber's views are expounded and indorsed.

which inevitably gives an impressionistic picture of the world. If different objectives produce different orientations of scientific interest, so that different facts are singled out from complex reality as significant, somewhat different pictures of the world emerge from the resulting theories. Each body of theory, within its own frame of reference, may be internally consistent and its assumptions equally closely linked with certain characteristics of the real world. But, if each draws on a different set of characteristics of the real world for its assumptions, the theories must contain different series of inferences and different conclusions. If the abstract nature of the theories is borne in mind, these differences will cause no surprise, but, if the theories are taken as shorthand descriptions of the real world, they come into immediate conflict with one another.

The same point has been made by those who claim that "proletarian" economics is concerned with different problems from those studied by "bourgeois" economics. Different questions demand different answers. And even when two theories appear to give conflicting answers to the same question, the conflict is sometimes due to an unnoticed difference in the question that is asked in each case. For instance: "What is the largest average wage a particular country can afford to pay its workers?" A theory which always includes as a tacit assumption the maintenance of the existing system of free enterprise will give a different answer from a theory which makes no assumption of this kind. The form of the first theory is dominated by the objective of maintaining the present system; the second theory is not. A great deal of the difference between "proletarian" and "bourgeois" economics, even when dealing with problems common to both "systems," is due to the presence of different tacit premises of a normative nature. This constitutes a reason for the continual examination of all theories, with a view to detecting those tacit assumptions which give a class or other bias to a theory, even though it is apparently scientific throughout. Did not Marx claim to establish "scientific" socialism? The difficulty of achieving impartiality is increased by the fact that, when interest in a particular objective has once left its stamp on the form and content of a theory, the same aesthetic or intellectual interests which often produce theoretic blight may reinforce one's reluctance to drop certain premises of the theory, even though they are shown to be in the nature of value judgments. This, however, brings us closer to the cruder forms of bias, which lead men to deny the evidence before their eyes

and to maintain patent *non sequiturs*. Examples of this can be found in
the writings of both "bourgeois" and "proletarian" economists; they
represent human shortcomings, which are important obstacles to scientific objectivity in practice but are not so inherent in the nature of
economic theory as the other difficulties to which reference has been
made.

MUTUAL REACTIONS OF ANALYSIS AND VALUE JUDGMENTS

This question of the impartiality of economic theory becomes all the
more important when it is realized that even propositions couched in
the indicative mood can have imperative force. Who has not heard a
dispassionate lecturer on international trade policy, after carefully dis-
claiming any desire to advocate one policy or another, prove conclu-
sively that free trade promotes both peace and prosperity, while protection leads to war and imposes a barrier to economic progress? "If
recovery is to be maintained," wrote Professor Robbins in 1934, "and
further progress assured, there must be a more or less complete reversal of contemporary tendencies of governmental regulation of enterprise."[17] This is couched in the indicative mood, but the desirability of maintaining recovery was so evident in 1934 that this positive
statement had all the appearance, if not the results, of a clarion call to
action. Again, a perusal of the more popular writings of Cannan in
the period 1914–25 reveals few propositions in other than the indicative mood; yet nobody could have had any doubts as to what Cannan
was *for* and what *against*.[18] If further illustration is needed, we may
cite Mrs. Robinson's review of *Britain without Capitalists:*

> This book is propagandist in intention, but not in manner. Indeed no tricks of
> rhetoric are necessary in displaying the case against latter-day capitalism. A system
> which allows effective demand to fall off amongst a population which is overcrowded
> and underfed, which meets unemployment with schemes to restrict output and can
> offer no help to depressed areas except orders for armaments *needs only to be described.*[19]

It is sheer delusion to suppose that an appropriate choice of forms of
expression can relieve the economist of the responsibility which he assumes by the selection of his subject matter. He can prevent his analysis from having normative force only if he confines himself entirely to
the discussion of such abstract matters as the elasticity of substitution

[17] L. Robbins, *The Great Depression* (London, 1934), p. 193.

[18] See E. Cannan, *An Economist's Protest* (London, 1927), *passim.*

[19] *Economic Journal*, December, 1936, p. 704; my italics.

or the time structure of production. When he discusses concrete problems in terms of cause and effect, his audience is always ready to supply the normative premise which converts analysis into advocacy. If the analysis itself is influenced by the economist's own interest, the result of an irreproachably positive exposition may be to promote the adoption of his own favorite objectives.

Many writers have mentioned the "danger" of unconscious bias in economic studies, it being assumed that this is an obstacle to the discovery of the truth. When our purpose is positive analysis, such a view is undoubtedly correct. But its implications are wider than is usually recognized. The economist must be on his guard not only against the bias which impels him to the wrong conclusion from a given set of premises but also against the bias which impels him to work out certain analyses and to ignore others which do not bear on his own interests. Economic theory can become an instrument equally valuable to all, irrespective of the ends they have in view, only if economists are prepared to undertake a sympathetic study of those conceivable objectives which have not affected the development of economic theory in the past. It may be that some objectives, such as joy in work, are too dependent upon personal characteristics to fit neatly into any general theory similar to those that have been constructed to show sums of money as the conclusions implied in the appropriate premises. But this should be tested by experiment and not prejudged by the investigators' own preference for other objectives.

If it is intended to explore the conditions which would be necessary for the attainment of objectives not previously studied by economic theory, it appears to be necessary to determine as accurately as possible which particular objectives have in fact left their mark on economic theory. There is also the possibility that a clear formulation of these objectives will reveal varying degrees of influence upon the form and content of economic theory and point the way, not only to theories related to other objectives but also to theoretical developments which are necessary for a proper appreciation of the possibility of achieving these more traditional objectives. In the interest of the progress of positive economic science itself, therefore, we must qualify Professor Robbins' dictum that "economics is not concerned with ends as such."[20] At least, we must recognize that the discussion of various ends may stimulate the further growth of positive economics at many points.

At the same time, there is no escaping the fact that the discussion of

[20] *Nature and Significance of Economic Science*, p. 24.

various objectives is likely to cause some modification in the ends sought by anybody who follows the discussion. When economic theory takes ends, like other data, as "given," this often leaves the impression that they are the results of spontaneous self-generation. We all know, however, that the objectives of policy do not materialize out of thin air; they are influenced by debates about what ought to be, and even by our factual knowledge of what is. Although positive and normative studies may be on different planes, it must be recognized that their interaction is mutual. Not only are the form and content of positive analyses influenced by favored objectives, but value judgments are influenced by the results of positive analysis. If this is conceded, it would appear to follow that the purpose of objective analysis may include assisting the choice of objectives as well as the choice of methods. At least it is worth considering more closely the factors that are involved in the choice of objectives and to determine the role which positive knowledge of economics may play.

Up to the present the terms "objectives" and "ends" have been used interchangeably. Mr. MacFie has suggested that "economists should, perhaps, avoid the word 'end' because it is a philosophical term to which different philosophers have attached different meanings. The most widely used meaning is 'some experience which is at once self-contained and satisfies; an experience which is good in itself.' "[21] Obviously, many of the objectives of economic policy are not "ends" in this sense but means to other objectives. Similarly, the immediate "ends" of individual economic activity are usually the attainment of means to other ends—money to buy food with, food with which to keep up one's strength. The one thing that most people do not know is what they "really" want in life, what their ultimate goal is. But their choice of more immediate objectives is largely influenced by their beliefs regarding the relationship of these immediate objectives to more remote ones: whether they are instrumental or obstructive to the achievement of the latter. Positive science modifies our choice of immediate objectives whenever it changes our beliefs regarding their relationship to more remote ends. For instance, the spread of knowledge of nutritional science causes a change in consumers' wants for various foodstuffs.

In the fields of public policy an understanding of the implications or consequences of a particular objective, if it be attained, affects in advance our attitude toward this objective. If flexibility of wage rates

[21] A. MacFie, *An Essay on Economy and Value* (London, 1936), p. 19.

were believed to be a real cure for unemployment, flexibility would be a more popular objective of public policy. If the installation of a modern sewerage system promises to reduce the danger of typhoid epidemics, increased expenditure of public funds becomes a more desirable objective even in the eyes of the taxpayer. And if the private trade in armaments is proved to be an important cause of war, many citizens will support the objective of nationalization.

FACTORS IN CHOICE

In all value judgments, all acts of choice, there are two distinct elements. One is the *urge* toward a more or less clearly conceived future state or to a particular norm of conduct, and the other is the appraisal of the present issue in relation to that future state or that norm of conduct. Different individuals, and the same individual at different times, may judge the same issue differently, either because the fundamental urge is different or because the relationship between the immediate issue and the remoter goal appears to be different. The fundamental urge is the emotional, dynamic factor in choice; but there is also the more rational factor of comparison, classification, and appraisal.

On the dynamic side there is a mixture of interest and of the impulse to conformity. The interest may be centered on one's self, and it may be "other-regarding," as in the case of pure altruism arising out of the mysterious faculty of sympathy or affection. Again, the interest may be enlarged to include a group of people with whom one feels a sense of solidarity, of common interest. This is by no means the same thing as pure altruism, although it may promote similar reactions toward other members of the group. But group interests may be self-regarding, that is, restricted to the group, or, less frequently, other-regarding, as when a whole group is moved by sympathy with some members beyond its own membership. For most practical purposes, interest of these types can be distinguished from the impulse to conform to a moral standard: a sense of duty or righteousness, whether associated with religious experience or not. These conceptions, if not finally satisfying to psychological science, at least provide a scheme within which we can depict the role of positive economics in value judgments.

In the first place, positive economics may show a man where his interests lie. Reference has already been made to the persistent enthusiasm of farmers for further programs of land settlement. If farmers read and understood Professor Fisher's work on the economic consequences of technical progress,[22] they would choose a different objective. Positive economics may also classify the relationship between a man's several interests, for instance, his interest as consumer and his interest as wage-earner. But not merely self-interest is affected. Positive economics may change our attitude to certain objectives, such as the reduction of working hours, by throwing light upon its implications for other people and thereby playing upon our sympathies. Finally, positive economics may reveal an unsuspected community of interest among certain people, thereby establishing a sentiment of group solidarity. This has been the deliberate aim of Marxian economists. On the other hand, positive economics may reveal conflicts hitherto unrecognized and provoke the collapse of groups in which superficial solidarity previously reigned.

Turning to moral standards, which often overrule the more instinctive impulses, we find that the role of positive economics depends upon the comprehensiveness and the concrete detail of the moral code in question. The minute ethical precepts of the Old Testament stand in marked contrast to the broad principles of the New Testament in this regard. In the former many of the details of day-to-day conduct are set down in unambiguous language; in the latter, the Golden Rule and its variants ("the gospel of love," "the greatest commandment") are stated in general terms, and the few concrete illustrations apply to a rather different economic order than that in which modern value judgments must be made. Professor Knight has recorded his view that "love is no solvent of problems or reliable guide to conduct."[23] Even those who accept the Christian ethic as absolute give it varying practical application, and one cause of this variation is the differences in their understanding of the operation of the economic system. The moral legitimacy of various market practices and methods of investment must depend upon their consequences for other human beings and can be judged only in the light of one's knowledge of those consequences.

The same point may be made with regard to other moral standards, for instance, the "economic chivalry" which had so strong an appeal for Marshall, or simply "sportsmanship." Unless rules of conduct relate to specific acts, like codes of fair competition, their practical effect depends upon our view of the world of cause and effect. Accordingly, various economic objectives can be evaluated in terms of the more gen-

[22] Cf. A. G. B. Fisher, *The Clash of Progress and Security* (London, 1935), esp. p. 53.

[23] F. H. Knight, "Ethics and Economic Reform," *Economica*, November, 1939, p. 403.

eral moral standards only when the ethical norm is supplemented by positive knowledge.

It is obvious that economics has nothing to do with the dynamic factors that are basic to all value judgments; and this is the basis of the almost general recognition that normative and positive studies are on different planes of discourse. But the fact remains that positive science has an important role to play in the formulation of concrete objectives, as distinct from general moral standards or fundamental emotional dispositions. And it is better that this function be performed consciously, without claiming more for positive economics than is legitimate but without underestimating its influence upon the choice of objectives. In the next chapter, therefore, we shall review the principal objectives that have been explicitly or implicitly adopted by economists and discuss the contribution of economics and other sciences to the formulation of the element of belief about the facts, as distinct from the more dynamic elements.

An investigation of this type will probably influence attitudes toward the various objectives and may diminish differences of opinion about them. But it will not create unanimity, in so far as the ultimate moral standards of individuals or groups differ or in so far as common moral standards or altruistic sentiments are overbalanced by the self-regarding interests of individuals or groups. It is even conceivable that the result of such a study in some instances will be to create new conflicts or to sharpen existing ones.

This investigation will serve a further purpose, in throwing light upon certain aspects of economic development. Economics cannot explain the growth of the fundamental human interests or the evolution of moral standards; but the isolation and analysis of the beliefs which direct these dynamic factors toward the adoption of particular objectives should add to our understanding of the causes of change in the dominant objectives of policy and facilitate the prediction of future changes.

It is perhaps necessary to emphasize that the "positive economics" which is needed to guide us in this investigation cannot be confined to the tautologies of pure theory. The beliefs which influence value judgments are beliefs about the real world, not merely the logical relationships between hypothetical assumptions but the causal relations between various sets of concrete conditions. It is essential, therefore, that the theories to be used in the investigation of objectives should be free from theoretic blight; the assumptions should be realistic, and the theories should cover changes in the conditions of economic activity as well as adjustments to given conditions. A realistic study of extra-market operations is essential, too, because they are part of the complex reality which influences the choice of objectives. For instance, Marshall, in deciding his attitude toward protection in America, took into account not merely the market consequences but also "the political corruption which necessarily results from struggles about the tariff in a democratic country."[24] Again, the opposition to big business is grounded not only on the effects of its supremacy in the market but also on the political power which it enjoys and the intimidation of competitors which it sometimes uses in establishing its position. Beliefs about these extra-market operations influence the choice of objectives; and to this extent a theory which facilitates the study of extra-market operations can carry our investigation of objectives further than a theory which never goes beyond the market.

THE EDUCATIONAL FUNCTION OF THE STUDY OF OBJECTIVES

Our concern is primarily with the problems facing an economic adviser; but it is convenient at this stage to add a word regarding the place of normative studies in systematic economic education. Unintentionally, the effect of much academic teaching of economics is to set up an intellectual barrier between the study of facts and their evaluation. In attempting to make economics "scientific" many teachers are careful to avoid any comment on ethical or political issues, confining their exposition to description and analysis of various conditions. From the general educational point of view, this practice has grave disadvantages, for it trains the student in the art of turning a blind eye to the ethical problems of economic life. The world needs men and women who are sensitive to moral issues wherever they arise; and the faculty of moral judgment, like that of understanding, can be developed only by exercise. Taking a broad view of the purpose of education, the teacher of economics, as distinct from the scientific investigator, can, without assuming the role of a teacher of ethical principles, aid his students to recognize an ethical problem when it is present and can encourage them to exercise their own moral judgment on the material they encounter in their economic studies. This is altogether different from attempting to impose his own value judgments upon his students, either as desirable norms or under the dis-

---

[24] "Some Aspects of Competition," in A. C. Pigou (ed.), *Memorials of Alfred Marshall* (London, 1925), p. 263.

guise of scientific findings. The teacher's own stand on ethical questions need not be camouflaged. If it is stated, it can be studied as an illustration of the type of value judgment which may be made in the light of the facts of the case; and it can be contrasted with other judgments which might be made, on the same set of facts, if one's fundamental interests or moral standards were different, contrasted also with those that might be made, on the same interests and standards, if the facts of the case were somewhat different.

The teacher of economics, with his scientific aspirations, is inclined to leave all this to the "moralist," "social philosopher," or religious teacher. Professor Robbins remarks that at Oxford and London "the necessity for independent and systematic study of the ends" of policy "was recognised in the structure of the curriculum."[25] But specialization is carried further in some halls of learning (such as Cambridge). In others, which seek to provide education for business, the structure of the curriculum provides only that the positive amoral studies of economics shall be supplemented by the study of accountancy and administration. "To throw those who spend just one year in the subject on to society," writes MacFie, "with nothing but a smattering of demand curves and other implements of positive economics is at once harmful and unscholarly."[26] He would advise a "judicious mixture of the positive and the normative aspects" for this purpose. "In the second year of academic study, however, there is room," he says, "for three courses at least"—first, positive economics, second, a normative economics studying the most efficient methods of achieving an ideal society, and, third, social ethics. "The third is a glorious but neglected hybrid, which really ought to be worked out by social philosophers; but which can perhaps best progress in actual circumstances through both economists and social theorists reaching out towards it and striking its fire by rubbing against each other."[27]

The real trouble in these schools of commerce, which can find no time for the study of social philosophy, is that the curriculum itself is dominated by the ethics of the market place; economics, like accountancy and administration, is included because it is thought useful (with some doubts) to the businessman. But even in more enlightened places of learning, where the curriculum is designed to provide *inde-*

[25] L. Robbins, "Interpersonal Comparisons of Utility," *Economic Journal*, December, 1938, p. 638.

[26] *Op. cit.*, p. 85.

[27] *Ibid.*, p. 80.

pendent study of general social philosophy, it is doubtful whether the strict separation of positive and normative studies is desirable. In the first place, the social philosopher, unless he is an economist, does not possess sufficient insight into the implications of financial and industrial practices to perceive the ethical issues which lie beneath the surface. Meanwhile, the immature student is expected to make his own unaided synthesis of social philosophy and positive economics. A study of objectives along the lines suggested here would at least draw attention to the existence of ethical problems and indicate something of what is involved in various "solutions." Finally, it may be suggested that the surest way of emphasizing the distinction between positive and normative studies, as well as their mutual relations, is to place them in close juxtaposition to each other rather than to isolate them in logic-tight compartments.

CHAPTER XI

SOME OBJECTIVES OF POLICY

THE preceding chapter stated the case for the study of objectives by the economist, as distinct from methods of achieving given objectives. We now undertake an examination of various objectives proposed or adopted by economists. Our purpose is to consider what economists have had to say about such objectives and the extent to which economic science may be said to have contributed to their adoption, by forming those beliefs which guide the more dynamic elements in the choice of objectives. The discussion will not be exhaustive, and some vital issues of the present day will be left for a final chapter.

THE COMMON GOOD

Policy is the outcome of the interplay of influential groups within the community. The objectives of policy, so far as they can be inferred from actual practice, consist in varying degree of the interests of sectional groups and their respective conceptions of the general welfare of the community. The process by which definite objectives emerge as the controlling factors in policy involves the suppression of some sectional interests and the moderation of others. A basis for compromise between conflicting interests is sometimes found in the need for an ally to meet the opposition of other sectional groups and sometimes in the recognition that a degree of mutual tolerance is the only alternative to mutual destruction. But the compromise is more easily effected if sectional groups have some common aims, in addition to those that are in conflict; and the search for some overriding objectives which would command the loyalty of all sectional groups within the community has been the constant preoccupation of many thinkers.

Those economists who have advocated, or assumed, certain objectives for economic policy have, almost without exception, represented these objectives as contributing to the *general* welfare of the nation, or even of mankind and, therefore, as being preferable to the private objectives with which they might conflict. Even Marx, who taught that a conflict of interests was inevitable under capitalism, looked forward to the birth of a classless society, where the common interest would be supreme. And Ricardo's analysis of the opposed interests of different economic classes ran counter to the dominant social philosophy of his day. "During the eighteenth century," writes Professor Myrdal, "the philosophy of natural rights and utilitarianism dethroned the prince or the state, and replaced it with the people as the ultimate value in social and economic speculation. . . . . Hereafter all economic doctrines, before anything else, had to be based upon a consideration of what would be for the good of all."[1] Thus we find Wicksell defining political economy as "the theory of the manner of satisfying human needs which gives the greatest possible satisfaction to *society as a whole*." He considered it to be "the practical and social duty of political economy" to answer the question: "Which of two conflicting interests is to be preferred as contributing most to the general good?"[2] It would appear that this duty can be performed only by the adoption of an economic criterion of the general good.

There is much to be learned from a study of the evolution of economic thought on this matter, which might well form part of the instruction in normative economics and social ethics, proposed by Mr. MacFie as an adjunct to the study of positive economics.[3] Of particular interest is the attempt made by the utilitarians to build social objectives onto a basis of individualism[4]—a problem running through many subsequent attempts to establish an economic criterion. Nowadays the tendency is to seek allegiance to the ideal of the common good in the sentiment of social solidarity, particularly on the national scale (which is called "patriotism") or in the social sympathies—that element of *altruism* which is rarely completely absent from human character. We shall not, however, plunge into a consideration of the philosophical basis of the notion of the common good. Our concern is with its application to economic problems. We must consider which economic objectives are put forward as being for the common good and what evidence—from economics and other sciences—is offered in support of the claim that they are for the common good.

ECONOMIC AND NONECONOMIC OBJECTIVES

There is, however, one further preliminary point to be noted. The economist is not infrequently asked to advise on methods of achieving a given objective. The objective may be set before him, not for evalua-

---

[1] G. Myrdal, *Population: A Problem for Democracy* (Cambridge, Mass., 1940), p. 9.

[2] K. Wicksell, *Lectures on Political Economy* (1901), English trans. (London, 1934), p. 3.

[3] See above, chap. x at end.

[4] Cf. E. Halévy, *The Growth of Philosophical Radicalism* (London, 1928).

tion according to any criterion of "economic soundness" but for accomplishment, irrespective of whether it has been indorsed or condemned by economists or even never considered by them. This does not, however, relieve the economist of all interest in objectives. If he is asked to suggest the *best* method of achieving a *given* objective, as Mr. Harrod has pointed out,[5] there must be some criterion on which to judge the many possible methods which are available. The economist's criterion consists of some other objective, relating to the common good; he advocates or assumes the pursuit of this economic objective in so far as it is consistent with the overriding objective postulated by the person seeking the economist's advice.

Objectives, which are independently set for economic policy, irrespective of any criterion proposed by the economist, may fall on either side of the distinction commonly drawn between economic and noneconomic objectives. It sounds illogical to speak of noneconomic objectives of economic policy; but, in elementary discussions of applied economics, it is customary to warn the student that economic considerations do not necessarily exhaust a practical problem but may be overridden by noneconomic aims, such as military preparedness or the preservation of family life or the requirements of religion. These "noneconomic" objectives are contrasted with such "economic" objectives as an increase in production or a less unequal distribution of incomes, although the distinction is sometimes difficult to draw. In a wider sense, as Professor Robbins has argued, the choice between these various objectives may itself be regarded as a problem in economy.[6] But this does not render the conventional distinction superfluous. Instead, it reinforces the view that, when the effects of various policies on, say, the nations' income have been fully explored, the claims of other objectives may, nevertheless, impose measures which will cause a decline in national income. Economists have sometimes attempted to decide between an increase in national income and its more even distribution,[7] treating this choice as a problem of economy; but they have generally disclaimed any competence to choose between such "economic" objectives as these and "noneconomic" objectives of the type mentioned. "No reputable economist has ever maintained that ma-

[5] R. F. Harrod, "Scope and Method in Economics," *Economic Journal*, September, 1938, p. 391.

[6] L. Robbins, *Essay on the Nature and Significance of Economic Science* (2d ed.; London, 1937), p. 11.

[7] With what success is not our present concern.

terial progress was an end, good in itself, for the sake of which everything else had to be sacrificed."[8] The most that economists have felt capable of doing has been to expose the relationships which exist between particular "noneconomic" and "economic" objectives, often, but not always, with a view to showing that the achievement of the latter may contribute to the former.

INCREASE OF PRODUCTION AS THE COMMON GOOD

Adam Smith regarded "the annual produce of the land and labour of the society" as the main subject matter of economic theory; and the increase of production and consumption has usually been the most prominent of the objectives assumed or advocated by economists. With Bentham the emphasis shifted to maximum happiness; and the increase of production was considered to be for the common good, *because* the acquisition of goods and services was obviously a very important source of human pleasure. Since all sections of the community share in the annual produce, it is easily assumed that all sections gain when it is increased; and it is a commonplace that no redistribution of wealth at the beginning of the nineteenth century could have increased the quantity of goods and services available to the masses by anything like as much as they were increased as a result of the growth of total production in the following hundred years.

Today the most prominent economic objective is still undoubtedly that of increasing the *national real income*, by which is meant the total stream of goods and services acquired by a community over a given period of time (usually twelve months). This total is generally divided by the population, and income per head becomes the criterion of policy.[9]

Although the increase of the national income has generally been considered to promise a greater increase in human satisfaction than any alteration in the distribution of a static dividend, economists have always been interested in the factors which determine the "division of the product." The analysis of distribution between classes and between individuals reveals conflicts of interests, which may be pushed into the background by an all-around increase in income but are never completely solved. And in unstable periods, when relative market values of different types of labor and property are changing, these conflicts become particularly acute. On the whole, it seems true to say

[8] A. G. B. Fisher, *The Clash of Progress and Security* (London, 1935), p. 3.

[9] For further comment see chap. xii.

that this problem of conflicting interests in the distribution of income has been the chief ground on which the objective of increasing production has been felt to require qualification. The attainment of a less unequal distribution of incomes has come to be recognized as an economic objective with compelling claims. Its appeal rests far more on notions of elementary justice, on natural sympathy for the extremely poor, and on the fear that discontent among the poorer classes might lead to radical movements than upon the economists' "law" of diminishing marginal utility.

The position adopted by economists on the question of distribution has not been so definite as their support for the ideal of increasing the national income. On the one hand, the two objectives may be inconsistent; and economists have urged that too drastic an attack on inequality might check the incentive on which the growth of production rests. On the other hand, the notion that capacity for satisfaction from income is to some extent correlated with income received in the past has persisted as an argument against complete equality. Consequently, while economists have been ready to indorse the view that "a greater approach towards equality" would certainly increase the sum of human happiness, they have been rather vague as to how fast we should go in that direction.

Control over distribution has not been conceived in terms only of diminishing inequality *in general;* the protection of *particular* sections of the community against the hardships which economic conditions impose upon them has been increasingly admitted as a legitimate objective of economic policy. As in the case of a general reduction of inequality, such a policy is conceived as being for the common good and owes its appeal to the same notions of justice, social sympathies, and fear of social strife. It has been frequently argued that the state should step in and, in the public interest, settle the conflicts between particular interests in a fair manner. Economists have seen a great danger, however, in this type of policy, because they fear that the state will become the tool of sectional interests—a possibility that has received our attention in the theory of extra-market operations. But their protests and warnings have not been very effective. Even the term "state intervention" is becoming out of date, since state action is now so general that it tends to *dominate* rather than to *interfere* with the normal course of economic life.

As the scope of economic policy has developed, the liberal's conception of the dangers of protecting sectional groups has also expanded, until today liberalism makes its last stand, as it were, on the grounds that economic freedom and a less ambitious economic program for the state are essential factors in political freedom and peace. Professor von Hayek has argued persuasively that the objective of economic policy should be to establish a framework of general rules, within which the various conflicting interests of the economic world can work out their own compromise through the operations of the market. Hardships there will be under such a system, but they will appear as the result of impersonal market forces, which do not discriminate between individuals. "People will submit to misfortune which may hit anyone, but not so easily to suffering which is the result of arbitrary decision of authority."[10] Consequently, a government which sets out to put things right will be regarded as the source of hardships—either because its measures assist some people *at the expense of others* or because it fails to come to the help of everybody who is in difficulty. Control over public policy becomes an object of struggle, and intervention tends to spread until the whole economy is subject to regulation. To render this regulation effective, a "particularised code of values" must be imposed on the people, and all differences of opinion suppressed. "The economic dictator will soon find himself forced, even against his will, to assume dictatorship over the whole of the political and cultural life of the people."[11] Whereas economic freedom has often been advocated as the best way of securing the harmony of individual interests, Professor von Hayek argues that, in the absence of economic freedom, conflicting interests will destroy political and intellectual freedom. Even "the struggle for the survival of ideas will take the form of a war of ideologies between nations."[12] Thus the objective of aiding particular groups is rejected, because it menaces other, noneconomic objectives.

ECONOMIC FREEDOM

The economist cannot prove the superiority of political freedom over a more equitable distribution of incomes; nor can be appeal to economic science to test fundamentally the thesis that these two objectives are inconsistent. But there is a bias in favor of freedom, because in the past it has been advanced as a necessary condition for the fullest achievement of recognized *economic* objectives, such as the maximiza-

[10] F. A. von Hayek, *Freedom and the Economic System* (Chicago, 1939), p. 18.

[11] *Ibid.*, p. 29.

[12] *Ibid.*, p. 38; cf. also L. Robbins, *Economic Planning and International Order* (London, 1937).

tion of production. As Professor Knight has remarked, economic freedom has been approved on at least four different grounds, namely, (1)
as a source of efficiency; (2) as an end in itself, desired by men; (3) as
an absolute value—"men ought to be free, more or less whether they
want to be or not"; and (4) as a means of relieving the state of tasks
which would cripple it.[13] Of these, the third is a dogma which the
economist cannot prove or disprove and the fourth is Professor von
Hayek's argument noted above. Only the first two treat freedom as an
economic good: (1) as a means of increasing production and (2) as a
means of insuring the greatest satisfaction possible, within the range of
alternatives open to each individual. The prominence of economic
freedom as an objective of economic policy warrants a consideration
of what is meant by freedom in this context and why economic freedom is supposed to be for the common good.

In the abstract, freedom escapes all attempts at definition. Its meaning can be made clear only by thinking of *freedom from* some particular
restraint or *freedom to do* some particular thing. From the negative
point of view, economic freedom generally means the absence of coercion or state regulation of industry, trade, and expenditure, but not
necessarily freedom from want. The positive meaning of economic
freedom is the right to choose one's occupation, one's method of work,
and channels of expenditure, but not the right to enjoy any particular
standard of life. Hence the cynical reflection that the worker is free to
choose between the wages offered him and starvation. From either
point of view, economic freedom is never "absolute"; and in practice a
"reasonable" degree of economic freedom is considered a sufficient
objective.

On what economic grounds, then, is it considered likely that economic freedom will promote the common good? The first of these
grounds, distinguished by Professor Knight, applies more particularly
to the businessman. We may recall Marshall's observation that "the
advantages of economic freedom are never more strikingly manifest
than when a businessman endowed with genius is trying experiments,
at his own risk, to see whether some new method, or combination of
old methods, will be more efficient than the old."[14] But still more important is the argument that, if businessman are free to adapt their
production to the market indicators of prices and demand, consumers'
wants will be more fully satisfied than under a planned system. This

[13] F. H. Knight, "Ethics and Economic Reform," *Economica*, February, 1939, p. 11.

[14] A. Marshall, *Principles of Economics* (8th ed.; London, 1922), p. 406.

appeal to efficiency links economic freedom with the economic objectives of increasing production and directing it into the "right" channels.

Unfortunately, freedom also opens the gates to mistakes. A considerable proportion of the restrictions placed upon the freedom of
producers and businessmen has been justified by reference to the human propensity to direct production into the "wrong" channels. If we
may parody Marshall, "the disadvantages of economic freedom are
never more strikingly manifest than when a businessman, endowed
with supreme obstinacy, is carrying on the old methods, at the risk of
his employees and shareholders, and refuses to recognize that times
have changed." It may be admitted that restrictions are not always
well advised; but the fact remains that the association of freedom and
efficiency is not so self-apparent to the modern mind as it was to the
Victorians.

The second ground for indorsing freedom is that people are more
likely to be happy if they can choose for themselves. This applies particularly to the consumer and to the producer, considered as a consumer of his own time and energy. If the consumer is free to choose between different avenues of expenditure and the producer between different activities, according to their respective preferences, it is argued,
this tends to give the greatest possible satisfaction, under existing conditions, to all concerned. Mr. Harrod has suggested that this is *the* economic criterion. "If an individual prefers a commodity or service X
to Y, it is economically better that he should have it. Similarly, if the
individual prefers work X to Y, or dislikes it less, it is economically better that he should do it. The economic good is thus the preferred."[15]
This may be considered a matter of arbitrary definition of the term
"economic good"; but it is more usual to claim that greater satisfaction will ensue if people are free to follow their own preferences.

This claim is obviously subject to the qualification that freedom is
restricted by one's means and capacities. But there are two other
sources of doubt, namely, the possibility that people may choose
"wrongly," from the viewpoint of their own satisfaction, and the possibility that the necessity of having to choose may sometimes be distasteful.

Economists have generally disclaimed any ability to say whether an
individual would gain greater satisfaction by making a different
choice. Tastes differ; and any attempt to claim authority for the ob-

[15] *Op. cit.*, p. 389.

server's own standards of judgment is condemned as unscientific. It is therefore customary, "in economic analysis, to assume that human welfare can best be promoted by leaving each individual free to secure his own betterment in any way that he can, and to leave it to his instinct of self preservation to decide how he should spend the money available to him."[16] But the development of the science of nutrition is making it possible

to indicate the general direction in which the present dietaries of all countries of the world fall short of the minimum desirable for the maintenance of health and physiological well-being. . . . . While the other constituents of the real income of human beings cannot be treated in quite the same way as foodstuffs, they lend themselves to some form of quantitative measurement, and specialised knowledge can give approximate minimum standards of clothing, house space and equipment necessary under different conditions of climate and other factors, to secure the physiological well-being of the people.[17]

The deficiencies which are revealed by such studies are sometimes due, not to lack of means, but to ignorance; and few would deny that greater satisfaction can be obtained from a small income if the individual is fully informed regarding the minimum standards that are necessary for healthy living.

It would also appear that freedom of choice would be more likely to yield satisfaction if knowledge regarding various products and kinds of work were less imperfect. So far as consumers' freedom is concerned, its value is offset to a not inconsiderable extent by the combination of popular ignorance and misleading advertising. It might be argued that the provision of more knowledge, through consumers' advisory services and general education, while allowing choice to be better informed, really reduces its range. But this would not be regarded as a restriction on the buyer's freedom. In the choice of an occupation, too, freedom would yield greater satisfaction if young people (and their parents) knew more about the prospects of different trades and their own occupational aptitudes. The movement for vocational guidance may thus be considered as an attempt to make the most of the workers' freedom to choose his own work, within the limits imposed by geographical and economic circumstances. Without such assistance, freedom of choice often leads people into courses of action that they subsequently regret.

This brings us to the second doubt regarding the efficacy of free

---

[16] League of Nations, *Measures of a National or International Character for Raising the Standard of Living* (memorandum prepared by N. F. Hall) (Geneva, 1938), p. 14.

[17] *Ibid.*, p. 19.

choice as a source of satisfaction. Not everybody feels competent to choose or ready to take the trouble. Choice itself involves a cost in time and energy, "and we resort to various expedients to avoid or minimize it." Indeed, people often are prepared to pay others to choose for them when it is a question of alternative investments. A traveler prefers to dine table d'hôte rather than à la carte. And, if it were not for our own reluctance to admit our own ignorance, we should not make so much pretense of exercising our individual judgment in many matters.

These considerations explain in part the declining hold of economic freedom on the imagination of men. But still more important is the fact that people are discontented with the range of possibilities within which they are free to choose. The freedom they demand today is freedom from the conditions that press upon them, not freedom to choose between the limited opportunities that circumscribe their lives. "From now on," writes Dr. Mannheim, "men will find a higher form of freedom in allowing many aspects of their individual lives to be determined by the social order laid down by the group, provided that it is an order which they themselves have chosen."[18] Most workers would prefer a steady job to freedom to choose between two poorly paid temporary positions. Most businessmen would rather have a regular contract at a good price than freedom to choose between two unprofitable markets. The freedom to choose one's doctor has little value to the man who cannot afford a doctor; and many a consumer would abdicate from his sovereignty in exchange for more of the things which are at present beyond his reach. In some ways freedom from fear and insecurity is the most desired of all forms of freedom. When the question of security is raised, however, we reach a matter regarding which the economist has a good deal to say.

SECURITY VERSUS PROGRESS

We have already made some use of Professor Fisher's work on *The Clash of Progress and Security* in our discussion of theories of economic development and in our own essay in the theory of extra-market operations. It also serves to illustrate the possible conflict of objectives of economic policy. Professor Fisher writes:

Nearly all our economic problems to-day either find their origin in, or at least are made much more complicated by a widespread confusion of mind, which leaves us unable to decide how far material progress is to be made the sole or ultimate object

[18] K. Mannheim, *Man and Society* (London, 1940), p. 377.

of economic policy, or how far it should be sacrificed in the interests of individual security and stability. . . . . The modern world for the most part desires material progress, but with equal emphasis it also for the most part does not desire the changes without which material progress is impossible.[19]

Professor Fisher's chief concern is to clear up the intellectual confusion which prevents the issue between the objects of material progress and security from being clearly understood. In this connection he quotes Professor Robbins' observation that "the majority of the human race are still very poor, and if, in the interests of a supposed stability, a halt is to be called in the process of raising real incomes, it is an issue which should be squarely presented to those who are most affected by it."[20] The inequalities of the capitalist system, Professor Fisher argues, can be justified only if in this system "sufficient plasticity and flexibility are maintained to make possible a steady if irregular improvement in the standard of living."

Although Professor Fisher does not commit himself in so many words, it would appear from the tenor of his discussion that he regards the objective of material progress as superior to that of security. One factor in his attitude is the observation that the conflicts which arise out of the changes implied in progress are "to a large extent conflicts between the divergent interests of different sections of the community, or of different nations; or between the special interests of groups and the wider interests of the *whole* nation or of the whole world."[21] Progress is considered to be for the common good, while security is desired by sectional groups at the expense, if need be, of the rest of the community.

However, the prominence in recent times of measures designed to provide security of employment raises doubts as to whether the popularity of this objective can be attributed chiefly to intellectual confusion and the influence of sectional groups in the community. "In spite of all difficulties," writes Cannan, "it seems we may safely say that the tendency of modern civilisation is towards the better satisfying of the natural desire for security in the enjoyment of economic position."[22] Again, Professor MacGregor observes that "in a complex society, work itself is an object of search and desire; it may satisfy more

---

[19] Pp. 5–7.

[20] L. Robbins, *The Great Depression* (London, 1933), p. 142; quoted by Fisher, *op. cit.*, p. 5 n.

[21] *Op. cit.*, p. 7.

[22] E. Cannan, *A Review of Economic Theory* (London, 1929), p. 432.

urgent and important desires than some of its products do. Apart from the deprivation of the desire for work, the consciousness of a large degree of unemployment is a 'dissatisfaction' to the community. In other words, employment is itself one of the things that industry is 'for.' "[23] This emergence of security of employment as an objective of policy reflects, of course, the impression made on human minds by the mass unemployment of the period after 1920. For the unemployed man

the catastrophe lies not merely in the disappearance of external opportunities for work but also in the fact that his elaborate emotional system, intricately connected as it is with the smooth working of social institutions, now loses its object fixation. . . . . Even if the immediate needs of life are satisfied, by means of unemployment relief, the whole life-organisation and the family hopes and expectations are annihilated.[24]

As the number of the unemployed and the duration of unemployment assumed a hitherto unexperienced magnitude, the unemployed have grown from a few unfortunate individuals, to be pitied and assisted, into a symbol of the "partial dissolution of the social order." Nor has the absorption of the unemployed into armies and war production banished the specter from our minds. Social security, therefore, is likely to remain a dominant objective of economic policy, not because individual or sectional economic interests are to take precedence over the common good represented by increasing production, but because the provision of a reasonable measure of security will be a necessary condition for the stability of any political or social system. In other words, security is likely to be imposed on the economist as a "noneconomic" objective, which must be sought by economic policy, even if at some sacrifice of "economic" objectives.

This conclusion makes it all the more important that investigations, such as Professor Fisher's should be pursued. The cogency of the objective of security will depend on the magnitude of the sacrifice of other objectives which may be involved. "The world is . . . . a wretchedly poor place," writes Mr. Colin Clark, after reviewing estimates of national income for many countries.[25] And Professor Fisher claims to show that the provision of security for the individual may involve not merely the sacrifice of progress but, in certain circumstances, a decline in total production. "We must in fact choose between progress and retrogression; if we deliberately prefer stability to progress, we shall be-

---

[23] D. H. MacGregor, *Public Aspects of Finance* (Oxford, 1939), p. 103.

[24] Mannheim, *op. cit.*, p. 128.

[25] *The Conditions of Economic Progress* (London, 1940), p. 2.

fore long find that we have sacrificed both."[26] It will be important to know, in relation to specific instances, whether this thesis is applicable and, if so, to what extent.

At the same time, the whole problem of security will require study on a broader basis than economists have yet attempted. Three distinct problems may be distinguished under the head of insecurity. First, there is the loss of income, occupation, and social status; second, the frustration of social ambitions, including those of the dependent members of the family; and, finally, the change of activity or place of work or associates. The magnitude of these problems is affected by various aspects of social and economic policy; and the clash of progress and security in practice may be to some extent diminished by attacking these problems directly, instead of indirectly by preventing the changes associated with progress.

Professor Fisher finds the chief difficulty with the modern capitalist, who refuses to take the risks associated with new industrial developments, and he sees the initiative passing to public investment. He hints at a solution to the first of the three problems distinguished above: "The root of the labourer's objection to change lies not so much in his devotion to his customary work as in his devotion to his customary income. If he can be safeguarded against the risks associated with the transition from one kind of work to another, there will usually be very little objection to change as such."[27] This oversimplifies the problem, but it indicates the special importance of unemployment insurance or compensation in relation to progress. But most schemes of this type relate only to workers employed on wages, while the demand for security and the opposition to the changes implicit in progress come also from the small tradesman and shopkeeper. The scale of compensation, too, is often inadequate to prevent "the downward drag of unemployment,"[28] as far as the social status of the family is concerned. The second problem distinguished above, namely, the frustration of future hopes, recalls Bentham's use of the word "security" for the "disappointment-preventing principle."[29] It may be argued, however, that the prominence of social ambition is itself a function of the inequality of income and that the progressive diminu-

[26] *Op. cit.*, p. 91.

[27] *Ibid.*, p. 228.

[28] Cf. R. C. Davison, *The Unemployed: Old Policies and New* (London and New York, 1929).

[29] Cf. Halévy, *op. cit.*, p. 46.

tion of inequality through public policy would weaken this motive to resistance against change. The increasing socialization of education, health services, and housing also tend to diminish the significance of income grades as a measure of social status. Finally, the systematic cultivation of occupational mobility, through schooling and adult education, has not been seriously attempted in any country. "Education for insecurity" might therefore contribute something to the solution of the third problem. This leads us, however, into a field in which the economist has little to say.

But the conflict between progress and security, though it may be diminished by such measures, will not be completely solved. Though the economist may be able to help the statesman count the cost of social security, he cannot assume the right to settle the issue one way or the other. This conclusion should, however, cause no surprise. It implies a similar status for the objective of the security of individuals as is already accorded to that of the security of the whole nation—an objective which may be imposed on the economist by the circumstances of his time.

DEFENCE AND OPULENCE: THE OBJECTIVES OF WAR ECONOMICS

The problems of war economics reveal the clash of objectives in an unusually clear light. Adam Smith's famous dictum that "defence is of much more importance than opulence" constitutes an exception to the generalization that economists hesitate to pronounce on the relative desirability of "economic" and "noneconomic" objectives. The specific issue, which precipitated Smith's remark, was the desirability of "the act of navigation," which, although "not favourable to foreign commerce, or to the growth of that opulence which can arise from it," he considered to be "perhaps the wisest of all the commercial regulations of England" because "aimed at the diminution of the naval power of Holland."[30] But Smith's work covered much more, of course, than economics, as conceived by modern economists. When he comes, at a later stage, to discuss defense expenditure, he mixes war economics and military science indiscriminately and generalizes as readily about the relative military merits of the militia and the standing army as about the economic problems involved in maintaining an army in the field.

Modern discussions of war economics cover several related objec-

[30] *Wealth of Nations*, Book V, chap. ii.

tives. First, there is the objective of *economic mobilization;* or the industrial organization of the nation so as to produce the maximum war effort—in terms of trained and equipped fighting forces—from limited resources of man-power and other factors of production. Alternatively, if battle has not yet been joined, this objective may be stated as the maintenance of the *necessary* state of armed preparedness, with the minimum sacrifice of civilian living standards. Second, there is the objective of *economic warfare*, namely, to deprive the enemy of some of his productive resources and organization by armed attack, blockade, or forestalling in neutral markets. Third, there is the *economics of siege*, in which the objective is the adjustment of the economy to losses through economic warfare. Fourth, there is the objective of the *fair distribution of war costs* as between different sections of the community. The problem of compensation for losses, injuries, and damages is part of this larger question. Each of these problems has financial aspects, but it is often convenient to consider *war finance* as a single problem, namely, the choice of fiscal and monetary measures to facilitate the attainment of the four primary objectives of war economics. The problem of war finance is complicated by the fact that these four objectives are not always consistent with one another. In theory they might be regarded as subsidiary to the general objective of organization for *total* war; and any apparent conflicts might be considered as problems of war economy in the widest sense of the term.[31] But economists have not claimed any competence to settle such "economic" problems.

Moreover, complete subordination of *all* objectives to the war would involve pursuing the objectives of compensation and a fair distribution of war costs only as far as might be necessary to maintain morale and reduce resistance to other war measures; any further attention to these problems might be considered as an unnecessary diversion of energy from more important objectives. In practice, however, total war, in this absolute sense, is not readily imposed on any people; and independent objectives, including those of "security," an "equitable" distribution of the burden, and preparing for a rapid post-war reconstruction of civil life, exert some influence upon wartime economic policy.[32]

In so far as these independent objectives of war economics consist

[31] Cf. E. R. Walker, "War Economy: The Nature of the Problem," *Economic Record*, June, 1940.

[32] Cf. E. R. Walker, "Total War—with Reservations," *Economic Record*, December, 1941.

of purely *sectional* interests, they cannot be supported by appeal to conventional economic canons, for the latter are represented as arising only from the *common* good. It is only when the equitable distribution of the burden is considered to be in the best interests of the whole community that it is regarded as "economically sound." The other problems of war economics all owe their existence to the supremacy of the war effort over "normal" economic considerations; all involve some sacrifice of "economic" objectives. For instance, the maximization of war production, with the minimum reservation of men for industrial purposes, is very closely linked with the conventional economic objective of increasing the volume of production, the withdrawal of men for military service being regarded as equivalent to a reduction in the resources available to the economy. The withdrawal of these resources, however, may have to be stimulated by "economic" policy, such as investment control and restriction of civilian production; and in this case the normal economic objective of increasing total production gives way to the war objective. In so far as economic warfare involves economic policy, e.g., the purchase of "unwanted" export surpluses from neutrals, this too represents a sacrifice of real income in the interests of the war effort. So, too, the accumulation of reserve stocks of food and materials and the encouragement of "uneconomic" industries to replace imports run counter to "economic" objectives. The modern economist has no pretension to any capacity to decide whether these sacrifices of economic objectives are, in any particular case, likely to promote the good of all.

It is true that economists have sometimes argued that the defense argument for national self-sufficiency nullifies itself, when the economic cost (in terms of foregone production) is so great that the industrial foundations of military strength are undermined. But in this argument the economic criterion is definitely subordinate to the goal of national defense. The same applies to the argument that international trade builds up in the export industries an industrial reserve which can be diverted to war purposes in case of need[33] and to the suggestion that wartime economic controls, if carried too far, may sap the economic system of its enterprise and efficiency.

These observations suggest that "national defense" is usually accepted by the economist as a noneconomic objective to be pursued rather than evaluated, so far as he, as an economist, is concerned. If it

[33] *Weekly Report* of the German Institute for Business Research, January 26, 1939.

conflicts with an objective which economists have indorsed, the economist does not offer scientific authority for preferring one to the other; but, when defense considerations are paramount, the economic objectives serve to assist the choice as between otherwise equally attractive or unattractive measures.

There is also the possibility, however, of considering defensive or offensive war as itself an instrument, directed toward economic objectives. Professor Robbins has indorsed the view that "both in regard to trade and in regard to migration there may be very real national interests in the actual position of the boundaries";[34] and the economic gains to be had from success and the economic losses to be feared from defeat are part of the stock-in-trade of wartime propaganda. War may be conceived as a gigantic and costly extra-market operation, designed to alter the conditions to which normal national economic life must adjust itself. For the most part, however, economists have had a bias in favor of peace and have not elevated war to the status of an economic objective.

THE GROWTH OF POPULATION

The objective of national defense has sometimes involved the acceptance of an additional objective which economists have not previously indorsed on economic grounds, namely, the growth of population. Although it might be argued that the sum of human happiness is increased, if there are more humans to be happy, economists have been so impressed, since Malthus, with the dangers of "overpopulation" that they have concentrated on production or income *per head*. But, if defense requires more population, this may override any adverse reactions upon production.

In Australia, for instance, with densely populated countries as neighbors, it is commonly assumed that "the continent must be peopled if it is to be held." A committee of economists, which prepared a report on the Australian tariff in 1929, argued that "the maximum income per head for Australia would probably be obtained by reducing it to one large sheep-run with the necessary subsidiary and sheltered industries and a few rich mines—and a population of about 2 million people." But, "in view of the settled national policy," they took "as fundamental to the whole inquiry the necessity of maintaining at least our present population at the present standard of living. We might

[34] L. Robbins, *The Economic Causes of War* (London, 1939), p. 74.

bracket it," they said, "with the White Australia policy as a condition which must be satisfied by any form of alternative production to take the place of protected production," if the tariff were to be reduced.[35] They accordingly centered their investigation upon the question of whether population could have increased so rapidly, without any reduction in living standards, if a protectionist policy had not been followed.

Economists have generally not felt competent to question the view that a larger population might be desirable from the viewpoint of defense, even if at a lower level of income. They have contented themselves with indicating the extent of the economic difficulties which may be caused by a too rapid increase in population. In more recent years, however, with the prospect of declining populations, in Western countries at least, economists have found definite "economic advantages" in an increasing population: greater occupational mobility, a smaller proportion of elderly dependents, a stimulus to investment in housing and the staple industries, etc. The result is that the reversal of the present trend toward stationary or declining populations bids fair to be recognized as a prime "economic" objective, as well as a "political" one.

CONCLUSION

From this survey it is clear that a sharp distinction between economic and noneconomic objectives is difficult to maintain. The economist has been led to consider various objectives, but it has been the march of events and the development of public sentiment rather than the progress of economic science itself which have given particular objectives their place in economic literature. Our discussion also illustrates the suggestion made earlier that what the economist has to say about these objectives consists largely of analysis of their relationships to one another, revealing, on the one hand the conflicts between different objectives and, on the other, the role of some objectives as instrumental to other objectives. Economic science does not, unaided, establish the supremacy of any particular objectives; but it would be foolish to pretend that economists' discussions have been without influence.

[35] J. B. Brigden and Others, *The Australian Tariff* (Melbourne, 1929), p. 70.

CHAPTER XII

ECONOMIC WELFARE RECONSIDERED

WHILE the review of various objectives given in chapter xi throws some light on the contribution of economics to the formulation of objectives of policy, it by no means does justice to the strenuous efforts of economists to reconcile their desire to do good with their conviction that, as scientists, they cannot tell good from evil. The most systematic attempt to establish a set of definite objectives for economic policy is undoubtedly that of the "welfare" economists; and, though Professor Robbins appeared to have dealt welfare economics a mortal blow,[1] it was not long before it was resuscitated, even if somewhat diminished in stature and virility. It is proposed to review recent discussions of the possibility of a scientific welfare economics and its scope, as a preliminary to setting up certain economic objectives as being appropriate to the spirit of our times.

THE UNDERMINING OF WELFARE ECONOMICS

When one refers to "welfare economists," one has in mind particularly Professor A. C. Pigou and the late Edwin Cannan, though their pupils and followers have been legion. Despite the philosophical difficulties which their systems involve, they have proved an admirable framework for the presentation of economic theory. After a somewhat embarrassed discussion of the impossibility of clearly demarcating material or economic welfare from human welfare in general, the beginner is led readily to admit the importance, for material welfare, of national real income per head and the degree of inequality, perhaps also the stability of the national income over time and the conditions of work of those who produce it. Then, without any undue straining, the various analyses of economic theory fall into place, as conditions determining the size of the national income and its distribution and, a little less convincingly, fluctuations in income and the conditions of work. Following such an approach, the student completes his first year with a picture of the economic world and some idea of what is necessary to produce a further increase in material welfare.

What fault could be found with this adoption of material welfare as

---

[1] L. Robbins, *Essay on the Nature and Significance of Economic Science* (1st ed.; London, 1932).

the natural objective of economic policy? Although somewhat over-shadowed by Professor Robbins' work when it appeared two years later, the fullest criticism of material welfare is found in an article by Dr. Benham, published in 1930.[2] Three objections to "economic welfare" as the economic standard are advanced: it is a subjective concept, "which cannot be measured directly and about which statements are made which cannot be verified"; the concept forms part of the subject matter of psychology; and, most important, "economic welfare is a vague notion," and "all statements about it, whilst apparently scientific," really have a suppressed premise, embodying one's own personal opinion as to what economic welfare means; "thus the door is opened for personal opinions and prejudices to masquerade as science."[3] The third criticism is considered the most fundamental.

If an undefined term is used, the user need not make clear even to himself precisely what he means by it. Welfare economists "deduce" economic welfare from its objective *indicia* or counterparts (national income, etc.). But how many have clearly stated which *indicia* they choose? How many have considered what "weights" should be assigned to the different *indicia* for the purpose of combining them? How many have dealt with the "weighting" of the components of a composite *indicium* such as working conditions, which contains hours of work, temperature, risk of accident and sickness, ventilation, and other elements? How many have considered the question of measuring inequality of incomes and stating what mode of distribution of the national income (reactions on production apart) would tend to maximise economic welfare?[4]

Dr. Benham inclines to the view that the scientific combination of these indicia into a single standard of economic welfare is impossible and that economists would do better to adopt a number of objective standards, corresponding to the usual indicia of economic welfare.

The economic effects of different events or possibilities could be considered as the effects upon real income per head, upon the distribution of the group income, and so on, much as at present, but no "weighting" or "balancing" would be attempted. "Working conditions" would be resolved into its objective elements—hours of work, and so on—and effects upon each element considered separately. Any number of such "standards" could be considered. . . . . But economists, whilst prepared to study the effects of changes in one standard upon the others, could refrain from any attempt to combine their standards in a single whole.[5]

In practice, however, if all these aspects of policy are to be considered, they must be weighted and combined in a final judgment as to what ought to be done. It may be suggested that it is part of the function of the economist at least to pose the problem of synthesis, even if he cannot offer a scientific solution of it. Dr. Benham admits

[2] F. C. Benham, "Economic Welfare," *Economica*, June, 1930, p. 173.
[3] *Ibid.*, p. 174.   [4] *Ibid.*, pp. 181–82.   [5] *Ibid.*, p. 187.

as an alternative that any individual economist might select a personal scale and set it out plainly for others to inspect, without claiming any scientific authority for it. Discussion of a number of such personal scales might conceivably lead to a consensus as to which scale should be generally adopted. But at present no such conventional scale is recognized.

The difficulties of welfare economics are greatly increased, however, when it is realized that real income per head, which is commonly regarded as the principal standard or indicium of economic welfare, is itself a *composite* standard and can be measured at all only by adopting a conventional scale of values. "The idea of changes in the total value of production [of heterogeneous commodities] has no precise content."[6] Statisticians adopt money as a unit of measurement and add together the money values of the various goods and services produced. But these values represent only the ratios in which these commodities are exchanged for one another; "any given price, therefore, has significance only in relation to the other prices prevailing at that time. . . . . It follows that the addition of prices or individual incomes to form social aggregates is an operation with a very limited meaning"; the aggregate is "nothing but a stream of money payments."[7] To make it significant for welfare we have to assume that relative prices measure the relative importance of each commodity as a source of welfare or satisfaction to the community as a whole. Professor Robbins suggests that,

if we like to assume that preferences and distribution do not change rapidly within short periods, and that certain price changes may be regarded as particularly significant for the majority of economic subjects [i.e., individuals and firms] then no doubt we may assign to the movements of these aggregates a certain arbitrary meaning that is not without its uses. . . . . And this is all that is claimed for such estimates by the best statisticians.

This concession, however, understates the difficulties. It is not sufficient to assume that relative values do not change during the period under consideration or that any changes indicate agreement among the majority of individuals that the relative importance of commodities has varied accordingly. We must assume that the existing scale of prices at any particular time is a "correct" measure of the relative importance of commodities to the whole community; and this implies that any changes in relative prices measure changes in their relative

[6] Robbins, *op. cit.* (2d ed.; London, 1937), p. 66.

[7] *Ibid.*, pp. 55–57.

importance. When it is remembered that relative prices are affected by the distribution of incomes, this is equivalent to assuming that incomes are "correctly" distributed from the viewpoint of total satisfaction.

It may be argued that in estimating total production the commodities should be revalued according to some other scale of prices, for instance, that which would rule if incomes were more evenly distributed. The ideal measure of national income would be one in which goods and services were valued according to the prices which would rule if incomes were adjusted to capacity to obtain satisfaction from income.

This would imply, however, that there is some objective measure of this capacity for satisfaction, which enables us to say whether A's capacity for satisfaction is equal to B's and, if not, to determine the *proportion* of one to the other. Dr. Benham and Professor Robbins alike claim that no such measure exists. "*There is no means of testing the magnitude of A's satisfaction as compared with B's.* If we tested the state of their blood streams, that would be a test of blood, not of satisfaction. Introspection does not enable A to measure what is going on in B's mind, nor B to measure what is going on in A's. There is no way of comparing the satisfactions of different people."[8] This amounts to saying that there is no *scientific* foundation for the belief that the diminution of inequality will increase total satisfaction; and some of Professor Robbins' readers have considered the main import of his argument to be an attack on proposals for greater equality of distribution. He has therefore thought it necessary to state that, although he does not believe that "men are necessarily equal or should always be judged as such," nevertheless, he believes that "in most cases, political calculations which do not treat them as if they were equal are morally revolting." The difference between Professor Robbins' position and that of the welfare economists on this point is that "they think that propositions based upon the assumption of equality are essentially part of economic science," while he thinks that "the assumption of equality comes from outside, and that its justification is more ethical than scientific." In the realm of action, at any rate, the real difference of opinion is not between those who dispute concerning the exact area to be designated by the adjective scientific "but between those who hold

[8] *Ibid.*, pp. 139–40; cf. also Benham, *op. cit.*, p. 179; and, earlier, Pareto, *Manual d'économie politique* (Paris, 1927), p. 265.

that human beings should be treated as if they were equal and those who hold that they should not.[9]

The chief significance of Professor Robbins' submission, however, lies not in its implications for the distributions of incomes as a separate issue in economic policy but in its general application to the whole of economic policy. If it is impossible to observe one person's satisfaction and to compare it with that of another person, or of the same person at another time, it is impossible to determine the effects of any economic changes upon any individual's satisfaction, let alone the total satisfaction of the community. It is, however, customary to assume that an increase in each of the goods and services enjoyed by an individual brings him an increase in satisfaction, and a decline in all goods and services a decrease. This rests on the testimony of so many people regarding their own experience that we may regard it as almost universally true. On the same basis it may be assumed that if a particular measure confers more of everything upon everybody it adds to total satisfaction; and, conversely, if it robs everybody of a portion of everything previously enjoyed it diminishes total satisfaction. But every measure which requires one person to forego anything, whatever additional goods it provides for him or anybody else, "begs the great metaphysical question of the scientific comparability of different individual experiences."[10]

A NEW START FOR WELFARE ECONOMICS?

Mr. Harrod's conclusion on this point is that "if the incomparability of utility to different individuals is strictly pressed, not only are the prescriptions of the welfare school ruled out, but all prescriptions whatever. . . . . Some sort of postulate of equality has to be assumed, but it should be carefully formed and used with great caution, always subject to the proviso 'unless the contrary can be shown.' " For example, "in the case of the uneven distribution of income, there are many special characteristics of the rich as a class to which due consideration must be given."[11] Mr. Melville has suggested that the postulate of equality is not necessary, if we are considering policies which affect large groups of people.

[9] L. Robbins, "Interpersonal Comparisons of Utility," *Economic Journal*, December, 1938, pp. 635 and 641.

[10] Robbins, *Essay on the Nature and Significance of Economic Science* (2d ed.), p. 137.

[11] R. F. Harrod, "Scope and Method in Economics," *Economic Journal*, September, 1938, p. 397.

In a homogeneous population we know that measurable characteristics are distributed in much the same way in any two large groups. For example, if two large groups of equal numbers are selected at random we find about the same number in each group of any particular height or chest measurement. . . . . As far as we can measure mental characteristics by examinations or intelligence tests, the same kind of distribution is found. There is therefore good reason to expect that the same kind of distribution of *capacity to enjoy expenditure* would be found in any two groups selected at random.

Mr. Melville does not think that groups from different income levels differ sufficiently to invalidate this type of comparison:

We may imagine the two groups to be paired, and units of money transferred from individuals in the richer group to individuals of the same innate capacity to enjoy expenditure in the poorer. Each such transfer will bring a greater gain of utility to the member of the poorer group than the loss of utility suffered by the member of the richer group. Thus the whole transfer may be said to increase economic welfare.[12]

This statistical approach undoubtedly meets some of the difficulties of the purely individualistic approach of most writers on the subject; and it does not rule out of court any modifications of conclusions which might be required by a study of the "special characteristics of the rich as a class," referred to by Mr. Harrod.

Another suggestion for saving something from the wreck of welfare economics was made, simultaneously with the above, by Mr. Kaldor. Holding that "it is quite impossible to decide on economic grounds what particular pattern of income-distribution maximises social welfare," he argues that there is an economic case for all measures which make it possible both to improve the position of some persons and to compensate any others for whatever losses the measures may impose. Whether the compensation should, in fact, be given or not "is a political question on which the economist, *qua* economist, could hardly pronounce an opinion."[13] Mr. Kaldor indorses Professor Pigou's procedure of dividing "welfare economics" into two parts. "The first, and far the most important part, should include all those propositions for increasing social welfare which relate to the increase of aggregate production," since in all such cases there would be a net benefit if measures were also taken to prevent any individual losses. "In the second part, concerning distribution, the economist should not be concerned with 'prescriptions' at all, but with the relative advantages of different ways of carrying out certain political ends."[14] (Apparent-

[12] L. G. Melville, "Economic Welfare," *Economic Journal*, September, 1939, p. 553.

[13] N. Kaldor, "Welfare Propositions in Economics," *Economic Journal*, September, 1939, p. 550.

[14] *Ibid.*, p. 551.

ly, "the relative advantages" would be measured in terms of the effects on aggregate production.)

Professor Hicks has hailed Mr. Kaldor's suggestion as laying the foundation for a purely scientific welfare economics, as the study of measures "which will allow of compensation being paid and yet show a net advantage";[15] this, he claims, is "a perfectly objective test" of their social "efficiency."[16] By adopting this line of approach "it is possible to put welfare economics on a secure basis, and to render it immune from positivist criticism." There is also a practical advantage in that this line of approach "fixes attention upon the question of compensation."[17] Professor Hicks thinks there are many cases where measures making for efficiency would have a better chance of being adopted if the possibility of compensation were borne in mind. He suggests that we should

accustom ourselves, whenever we can, to thinking of every economic reform in close conjunction with some measure of compensation, designed to render it approximately innocuous from the distributive point of view. Since almost every conceivable kind of compensation [rearrangement of taxation] must itself be expected to have some influence on production, the task of the welfare economist is not completed until he has envisaged the total effects on both sides of the proposed reform. . . . . If, as will often happen, the best methods of compensation feasible involve some loss in productive efficiency, this loss will have to be taken into account.[18]

What Professor Hicks sets out to do is to demonstrate "the right of Welfare Economics [as redefined by himself] to be considered as an integral part of economic theory, capable of the same logical precision and the same significant elaboration as its twin brother, Positive Economics." This statement has just a faint odor of "theoretic blight" about it; and one's misgivings are strengthened by Professor Hicks's subsequent attempt to elaborate a portion of the new welfare economics in an essay ending with the words, "if economists are to play their part in shaping the canons of economic policy fit for a new age, they will have to build on the foundation of Consumers' Surplus."[19] On this line of approach it appears that the resuscitated welfare economics will be but a pale shadow of its former self.

[15] J. R. Hicks, "The Foundations of Welfare Economics," *Economic Journal*, December, 1939, p. 706.

[16] J. R. Hicks, "The Rehabilitation of Consumers' Surplus," *Review of Economic Studies*, February, 1941, p. 111.

[17] "The Foundations of Welfare Economics," p. 711.

[18] *Ibid.*, p. 712.

[19] "The Rehabilitation of Consumers' Surplus," p. 116.

This is not to suggest that it does not contain any positive contribution to the choice of objectives of policy. On the contrary, it provides a useful classification of possible measures, which may well influence statesmen's value judgments. The classification may be set out as follows: (1) measures which increase somebody's income without causing a decline in anybody else's (the extreme case under this heading is that of measures which increase everybody's income); (2) measures which decrease somebody's income without causing an increase in anybody else's; (3) measures which increase somebody's income so much that they can afford to compensate fully everybody whose income has been reduced by the policy in question; and (4) measures which increase somebody's income, but not sufficiently to enable them to compensate fully everybody whose income has been thereby reduced.

The classification of various measures under these heads may be regarded as a task for economic science. Under the first heading Mr. Kaldor would place the stimulation of employment; and it is likely that total war, carried to its logical conclusion, falls under the second heading. It might be thought that measures to stabilize business conditions, or at least to bring recovery from depression, also fall into the first class. "With negligible exceptions," writes Professor Knight, "the business cycle does not work to the advantage of any significant group or interest in capitalistic society. On the contrary, practically everyone suffers heavily from it, incurring serious economic loss, if not privation. Hence the problem of cycle analysis does not arise out of and does not involve conflict of interest."[20] In practice, however, measures are often recommended which do give rise to conflict. The Premiers' Plan of 1931 is still a source of bitterness in Australian politics. Nevertheless, the Keynesian type of policy, on the face of it, very nearly qualifies for inclusion in class 1.

The principal practical difficulty, when we come to measures excluded from classes 1 and 2, is that of determining what is meant by "full" compensation. The general principle would be for the individual to assess his own losses or gains, if we are to assume that interpersonal comparisons of utility are impossible. Where a definite financial loss can be attributed to a particular measure, however, and there is no obvious nonfinancial loss to be considered, the calculation of a compensation equal to the loss presents no difficulty.

[20] F. H. Knight, "The Business Cycle, Interest and Money," *Review of Economic Statistics*, May, 1941, p. 66.

It may be noted that Mr. Kaldor would place every increase in aggregate production under the third heading; and at first glance it appears unquestionable that if the total increases it will be possible to compensate for losses and leave a net gain for somebody. But, if we exclude interpersonal comparisons of utility and refuse to make any assumption about distribution, there is no significant method of measuring aggregate production. "As we have already seen, the idea of changes in the total value of production has no precise content."[21] Thus Mr. Kaldor excludes prescriptions regarding distribution but includes a concept which implies acceptance of the existing pattern of distribution, whatever that may be. Professor Hicks is more cautious when considering the general conditions which would bring a measure into the first class and makes a point of defining them in such a way that the definition of real income is not involved.[22] But, when he comes to consider the system of private enterprise, he finds that every simple reform "inflicts a loss of some sort on some people," and he is obliged to seek measures which "will allow of compensation being paid, and which will yet show a net advantage," i.e., falling in class 3. He then shows that, with perfect competition, an equilibrium tends to be established which leaves no further room for any reorganization of resources which would fall in class 3.[23] This really is the same argument as the one that aggregate production is maximized in perfect competition; and it involves the same assumption that the existing pattern of distribution, whatever that may be, supplies the correct set of prices by which to value various commodities.[24]

It would appear, therefore, that this attempt to restore welfare economics on a *wertfrei* basis is not altogether successful. Far more important, however, is the fact that, whatever economic theory deals with, economic policy must deal continually with questions of distribution and compensation. As a guide to practical policy, welfare economics has only limited value; and the problems which it ignores, as well as those which it pretends to solve, require either the adoption of the postulate of equality (although, as Mr. Melville has pointed out, equality of groups rather than of individuals is a necessary postulate) or a systematic investigation, along some other lines, into the relation of equality to welfare.

[21] Robbins, *Essay on the Nature and Significance of Economic Science*, p. 66.

[22] "The Foundations of Welfare Economics," p. 704, n. 1.

[23] Various qualifications are noted (*ibid.*, pp. 707–8).

[24] Cf. K. Wicksell, *Lectures on Political Economy* (London, 1934), I, 77.

MINIMUM STANDARDS OF WELFARE AS OBJECTIVES

Admittedly, either course takes us outside the competence of analytical economic theory; and the most promising approach to the problem of the relation of inequality to welfare has its origin in studies by other sciences than economics, especially the sciences associated with public health. Medical science, with the aid of biochemistry and physiology, has determined the optimum diet from the viewpoint of physical health, taking into account such variable factors as age, type of work, and climate and the special needs of pregnancy and the nursing of infants. Similarly, minimum housing standards have been widely indorsed, since it can be shown that overcrowding, lack of air and sunlight, and inadequate toilet facilities are inimical to good health. Although less systematically studied in the past, minimum standards of clothing can be determined for various climates and types of work. One need only think of scientific polar exploration, the equipment of military forces for arctic and tropical service, respectively, the prevalence of hookworm in barefooted communities, and the amount of bronchitis and pneumonia in cold parts of India, where cotton clothes predominate, to recognize that there is a field for scientific study of clothing needs. Finally, there are medical and dental services, which a person of moderate means takes as a matter of course but the inadequacy of which is a factor in the unsatisfactory health of the poorer classes.

The first considerable impact of such studies on economic theory was Mr. Penrose's modification of the optimum theory of population, in which he proposed as a standard not maximum income per head but "consumption of the composite commodity that, in the light of existing scientific knowledge, makes a greater contribution to welfare than, in the existing state of the arts, can be made by any alternative composite commodity."[25] To establish such a standard, "what is required is a consensus among those who have special qualifications for judging the effect on welfare of the consumption of this or that commodity in this or that quantity." Admittedly, such a consensus has not yet been completed and for certain commodities will never be established. But it is in sight, as far as the goods and services that are essential to healthy living are concerned.

[25] E. F. Penrose, *Population Theories and Their Application* (Stanford, 1934), p. 84. The concept of an objective composite standard was noted earlier, but not elaborated, by Professor Pigou in his discussion of "A National Minimum Standard of Real Income," in *Economics of Welfare* (3d ed.; London, 1929), Book IV.

Much the same procedure has been advocated by Mrs. Wootton, in order "to form rough ideas as to the limits within which the market can be trusted in the interpretation of social ends." She would "round up a miscellaneous body of experts, and collect from them all they have to say about the nature, and the relative urgency, of various human needs, as these appear to each from his own standpoint." Subsequently, she thinks, "some sort of balance has to be struck between what the expert thinks we ought to want, and what we ourselves think that we do want."[26]

If, however, we do not attempt to cover the whole range of commodities but confine ourselves to the question of what is necessary for physical health, the conflict between what we think we want and what is good for us sinks into the background. It is true that a family which can afford to purchase only the bare minimum required on such a standard will almost universally prefer to spend some of its income on going to the movies or other purposes not covered by the standard, even if this involves accepting an inferior standard of health. This tendency, though often condemned by moralists, may be welcomed as evidence of the unconquerable spirit of man. But it is not suggested that everybody should be forced to adopt this "health" standard as the objective of their economic activity. The important point is that the vast majority of the human race cannot enjoy such a standard under present conditions, even if each family hands over its choice of expenditure to the experts on nutrition, housing, and the rest. Even in the most prosperous countries in the world, malnutrition, inferior housing, and other factors in inferior health are widespread. As Mr. Lewis Mumford has remarked, there is a striking contrast between the stress which economists lay on the insatiability of human wants and the failure of modern economic society to provide for the most elementary wants.

Had it not been for the outbreak of war in 1939, this problem would have been thrust increasingly upon our attention, and it will loom large in discussions of post-war reconstruction. The League of Nations and the International Labour Office have both published the results of comprehensive surveys of nutritional problems in relation to income and various aspects of current economic policy; and in 1937 they had initiated similar investigations into other factors in living standards and their mutual relationships.[27] Material already avail-

---

[26] B. Wootton, *Lament for Economics* (London, 1938), pp. 283–88.

[27] Cf. League of Nations, *Final Report of the Mixed Committee on the Relation of Nutrition to Health, Agriculture and Economic Policy* (Geneva, 1937); also *Preliminary Investigation into Meas-*

able indicates such vast needs for the increased production and distribution to the poorer classes of certain goods and services fundamental to healthy living, if present deficiencies are to be remedied, that the theoretical debate over the possibility of making "interpersonal comparisons of utility" dwindles into the utmost insignificance. The popularization of this knowledge cannot but affect the public's attitude toward the question of income distribution and the desirability of planning production, even if this involves some diminution of "economic freedom."

To know what is necessary for the mere survival of the many should make it intolerable for the few with a relatively high standard of living to contemplate a state of affairs in which this minimum is not attained. In the absence of any higher motives, the mere instinct of self-preservation should oblige them to strive to make good contemporary deficiencies. . . . . It appears not untrue to say that the maintenance of the economic and political security of prosperous nations and of wealthy individuals has come to depend to a very substantial degree on the prosecution of measures designed to give at least a minimum standard of physiological living to the masses of the people. . . . . We can take it as axiomatic that the attainment by the peoples of the different countries of the world of that level of consumption which is necessary to secure for them a tolerable degree of physiological well-being is a *conditio sine qua non* of progress in all other directions. Man may not live by bread alone; but, without the necessary minimum of "bread," the ordinary individual can scarcely be said to "live" at all.[28]

It is perhaps necessary to stress the fact that the adoption of the objective of supplying everybody with at least the bare minimum for healthy living does not imply that we "regard our fellow creatures as though they were cattle or slaves, whose health or fitness is of the greatest importance to their masters, but who are without any voice in their own destiny"; the objective is to give everybody a chance to be something more.[29] Nor does it imply that future policy should be dominated by a static ideal of a physiological minimum. The standard essential for healthy living must seem to people of moderate circumstances a rather dull and uninspiring one. When "ideal" workers' diets have been published in Australia, they have raised a storm of protest from skilled, organized workers (or their self-appointed spokesmen); for it seems inhuman to "condemn" the worker to such a miser-

---

ures of a National or International Character for Raising the Standard of Living (Geneva, 1938, and *Urban and Rural Housing* (Geneva, 1939); International Labour Office, *Workers' Nutrition and Social Policy* (Geneva, 1936), and *The Workers' Standard of Living* (Geneva, 1938); J. B. Orr, *Food, Health, and Income* (London, 1936); F. L. McDougall, *Food and Welfare* (Geneva, 1938).

[28] *Preliminary Investigation into Measures of a National or International Character for Raising the Standard of Living*, pp. 12–13.

[29] Wootton, *op. cit.*, p. 283.

able way of life. The minimum must be a dynamic ideal; and there are social forces which will tend to promote its expansion and development in the course of time.

Where does the economist come into all this, if at all? Dr. Benham has argued that the conventional indicia of economic welfare "are chosen, or accepted, for discussion by economists because the spirit of the time has singled them out as having special significance."[30] It is the spirit of the time and the progress of other human sciences that are pressing this new objective upon the notice of statesmen and economists alike. But the definition of the problem requires the co-operation of economic science. This is equally confirmed by a study of the League of Nations' *Final Report on Nutrition*, in the preparation of which economists played an important part, and of the Australian government's inquiry into nutrition, which was left in the hands of medical scientists. If a broader standard than nutrition alone is adopted, the economic interrelations of the production of the various goods and services makes a special call on the economist; and, indeed, the same problem arises in connection with different foodstuffs. Economic science is certainly relevant to the formulation of immediate objectives, since it should be able to indicate what is possible in the way of raising existing standards of consumption in those countries where the desirable minimum is still far from being attained—which means almost every country.

THE PROBLEM OF INEQUALITY

The revelation of the "fact that the present consumption of the great mass of the people is inadequate, both in character and in quantity, to secure that basic physiological satisfaction, the attainment of which should mark the first stage in human progress,"[31] places the problem of inequality in a rather different light. Although economic science may produce evidence to qualify the common belief that redistribution would be an important method of raising the standards of the poor, the satisfaction to be had out of a comfortable income is greatly diminished, for sensitive persons, by the knowledge that others are denied the bare means of healthy living. From this point of view social stratification may be regarded as a device to protect the comfortable classes from that contact with the actual living conditions of poor people, which might work on the formers' social sympathies and even pro-

---

[30] *Op. cit.*, p. 186.

[31] League of Nations, *Preliminary Investigation* . . . . , p. 13.

mote a sense of guilt. If greater equality were presented as an integral part of a plan to raise everybody to the minimum necessary for healthy living, a certain proportion of comfortably off people would accept it cheerfully; and the proportion would be larger according to the extent to which they were familiar with the conditions of life of those on very small incomes.

As between income grades well above the "bread line," the case for diminishing inequality must be argued on other grounds. Mr. Kaldor has argued that "the prospect of improving one's income by one's own efforts" is a source of direct satisfaction, and this prospect rests on the existence of inequality.[32] Professor Pigou suggests that a considerable proportion of the satisfaction yielded by the incomes of rich people comes from the fact that they are richer than other people. He finds in this a justification of transfers from the rich to the poor, because, if the incomes of all the rich are diminished together, differences between them will remain and will continue to yield some satisfaction at least.[33] The same argument might be used in support of the maintenance of inequality, once everybody received at least the minimum standard.

It will be noted that the problem is essentially a psychological one and that the economist can test Mr. Kaldor's thesis, or Professor Pigou's, only by amateur psychologizing. The problem might well be investigated by specialists in psychology, but it must be posed and brought to their attention by the economist. Meanwhile, it may be recalled that in chapter vi, in discussing reasons why a decline in income causes such dissatisfaction, we drew attention to the fact that much economic activity is devoted to reaching for the next higher rung of the social ladder. When this is achieved, it yields satisfaction for a time; but this satisfaction sinks into the background of consciousness as the new social status comes to be taken for granted and attention shifts to the next rung of the ladder, which, though still out of reach, has now come into the realm of possibility. With every increase in income, a certain part of the increment is spent on objects which serve to mark one's new social status and which yield correspondingly less satisfaction as one grows accustomed to them. In other words, a society of unequal incomes, with its stress on pecuniary emulation, encourages much ostentatious expenditure,[34] which yields only temporary satis-

[32] *Op. cit.*, p. 551.

[33] Pigou, *op. cit.*, p. 92.

[34] Cf. T. Veblen, *The Theory of the Leisure Class* (New York, 1899).

faction and, indeed, becomes an obligation to be met rather than a satisfaction to be enjoyed. This consideration must be set against the points already mentioned, which seem to support inequality as a source of satisfaction.

On such matters as these, however, it is better to reserve judgment, in the hope that psychologists, stimulated by economists, may sooner or later provide us with more definite information about the degree of satisfaction to be had from the fact of inequality about us, assuming that nobody is so poor as to fall short of the minimum standard which is agreed to be necessary. The strongest impulse toward the reduction of inequality, on the latter assumption, is probably based on ethical and political considerations rather than on views as to the amount of satisfaction individuals get from their various incomes. Inequality of incomes tends to produce a frame of mind which values people according to their financial position and encourages expenditures which many moralists condemn as frivolous. It also leads to inequality of political power and breeds class conflict. These are considerations outside the normal scope of economics. But, in relation to any attempt to correct these faults, economics comes into the picture with an analysis of the roles which inequality plays as an incentive in economic life. The free play of the market implies some degree of inequality of income, and there are limits to the extent to which inequality can be reduced without altering the very basis of the economic system. This consideration, too, is relevant to the choice of objectives of policy.

A BROADER CONCEPT OF WELFARE

It is suggested, in view of the preceding discussion, that the welfare economics of the immediate future may well take as its principal subject matter the various methods (in the fields of both production and distribution) by which minimum standards of welfare, scientifically determined, can be provided for all members of the community. This may come to be regarded as the primary economic objective of economic policy for the time being and the principal economic criterion to apply to the search for the best method of attaining some other objective—perhaps a noneconomic one—which is set before the economist as the goal toward which policy must be directed. It has already been suggested in several quarters that the only limitation on the economic war effort should be the provision of a national minimum standard of this type. In peacetime it might constitute the limitation upon the range to be allowed for economic freedom and the receipt of large incomes. For some time to come our attitude toward inequality of incomes may well be determined by its relationship to this more fundamental objective.

These opinions are not advanced as the findings of economic science. They clearly involve value judgments. But they indicate a field for welfare economics which can be cultivated by scientific methods, even if the collaboration of other scientists is necessary in the formulation of its standards.[35] And this welfare economics is a more worthy successor to that of Cannan and Pigou[36] than that suggested by Professor Hicks.

But our objectives, as so far defined, may be criticized, as was the older welfare economics, as involving too narrow a concept of welfare or too arbitrary a distinction between material and other elements in welfare. In practice the economist's study of welfare has always been chiefly in terms of monetary transactions and, although economists themselves have often been conscious of the inadequacy of such an approach from the viewpoint of "a human valuation of industry" it may be claimed that their practice has tended to encourage the neglect of other aspects by those who formulate public policy. This was the basis of Ruskin's protest that "there is no wealth but life." He conceived it to be the task of political economy "to determine what are in reality useful or life giving things," irrespective of pecuniary standards, and consequently had next to no influence upon the development of economic science. Building on Ruskin's premises, J. A. Hobson attempted a "human valuation of industry," substituting "for the monetary standard of wealth a standard of human well-being";[37] but his incidental attack on the "marginalism," which figures so prominently in economic analysis, diverted even the welfare economists' attention from Hobson's contribution to the broader problem of the selection of objectives for economic policy.

Now it is evident that in a value judgment of this sort economic science contributes no ground for attaching greater importance to the standard of consumption than to the conditions under which people work and the extent to which they find joy in work or merely drudgery. Lewis Mumford writes:

[35] As we have seen, it is equally necessary in the prediction of data changes (chaps. vii and ix).

[36] Indeed, as we have noted, Professor Pigou considered the establishment of a national minimum standard, though he did not elevate it to be the supreme objective of economic policy (cf. *Economics of Welfare*, Book IV, chap. xiii).

[37] *Work and Wealth: A Human Valuation* (New York, 1931), p. 9.

Our disregard for the quality of work itself, for work as a vital and educational process, is so habitual that it scarcely ever enters into our social demands. Yet it is plain that in the decision as to whether to build a bridge or a tunnel there is a human question that should outweigh the question of cheapness or human feasibility: namely, the number of lives that will be lost in the actual building or the advisability of condemning a certain number of men to spend their entire working days underground supervising tunnel traffic. . . . . Similarly the social choice between silk and rayon is not one that can be made simply on the different costs of production, or the difference in quality between the fibres themselves: there also remains to be integrated in the decision, the question as to differences in working pleasure between tending silk worms and assisting in rayon production. What the product contributes to the labourer is just as important as what the worker contributes to the product.[38]

Here, again, we are entering the realm of opinion. But the way in which economists have handled this issue may have contributed somewhat to the development of opinion. We have already noted that the economist's comparative neglect of the less easily measured elements in human welfare has affected the general picture of the world which tends to be gained from the study of present-day economic theory. There has also been a tendency to assume that the worker himself, in balancing the real advantages as well as the financial advantages, of different occupations, maximizes his own net satisfaction. It is argued, for instance, that a worker who prefers good conditions and interesting work to extra income can choose his occupation accordingly. But the range of employment opportunities is always limited by the directions into which capital and enterprise flow. The main reason why joy in work and good conditions have not figured more prominently in the objectives of economic policy is that the initiative for the establishment of industries and the promotion of public works rarely rests with the people who are most closely affected by conditions of work. The recognition of conditions of work as a factor in welfare raises, as definitely as any proposals for the redistribution of income, the problem of balancing conflicting interests.

This problem cannot be solved without a value judgment. But it is desirable that this value judgment be based on the fullest knowledge of the particular interests involved. This knowledge can be supplied only in part by economic science. The factors in joy in work and the relationship of conditions to the welfare of the worker can be systematically studied, but this is obviously a task for the psychologist and industrial medicine. Economic science can undertake the exploration of the economic consequences, for all concerned, of a policy which treats interesting work and good conditions as more important than

[38] *Technics and Civilization* (New York, 1934), p. 411.

productive efficiency. If this task is undertaken, economists will at least be acquitted of the charge of passive resistance to the formulation of still broader objectives for economic policy. The evidence already available is admittedly fragmentary; but the author's own feelings impel him to indorse the view that the improvement of conditions is an objective comparable in value with the provision of a physiological optimum standard of consumption and that it should, like the latter objective, impose limits upon the permitted range of inequality of income and economic freedom. Such working conditions as can be measured can be investigated with a view to determining scientifically the optimum standards of conditions from the viewpoint of health; but the more subjective aspects of working conditions, such as joy in work, will escape such treatment. There seems to be a strong case, however, for extending the application of the principle, already admitted in the case of extremely noxious occupations, of prohibiting or restricting work which is judged intrinsically deleterious to human welfare. Moreover, just as certain kinds of production must be increased by special measures if minimum standards of consumption are to be established, so, too, definite measures must be taken to provide more agreeable work and better conditions in the industries which are not inherently degrading to labor.

At what point these two objectives—a minimum standard of consumption and the improvement of working conditions—may come into conflict with each other cannot be determined at this stage. The point of conflict would be reached more quickly if the existing pattern of inequality and of economic freedom were to be protected at all costs. If these latter objectives are placed lower in our scale of values—as seems almost inescapable—some progress toward both the other objectives can be made before they clash. The value judgments which must be made if and when this conflict emerges will present difficulty. It is all the more important, therefore, that the relevant facts be thoroughly explored in advance.

INDEX OF AUTHORS CITED

INDEX OF SUBJECTS

[NOTE.—In the subject index, reference to persons does not indicate direct citation from their writings]

PRINTED
IN U·S·A